Ancient Israel and Ancient Greece

Ancient Israel and Ancient Greece
Religion, Politics, and Culture

John Pairman Brown

FORTRESS PRESS
Minneapolis

ANCIENT ISRAEL AND ANCIENT GREECE
Religion, Politics, and Culture

These essays are drawn from three volumes by John Pairman Brown, titled *Israel and Hellas,* Beihefte zur Zeitschrift für die alttestamentliche Wissenschaft 231, 276, 299 (copyright © Walter de Gruyter, 1995, 2000, 2001). This volume appears under license from Walter de Gruyter GmbH & Co. and with the kind permission of the series editor, Prof. Otto Kaiser.

Cover art © Photodisc, Inc.
Cover design: Brad Norr Design
Interior design: Beth Wright

Library of Congress Cataloging-in-Publication Data

Brown, John Pairman.
  Ancient Israel and ancient Greece : religion, politics, and culture /
John Pairman Brown.
     p. cm.
Includes bibliographical references (p.) and index.
  ISBN 0-8006-3591-4
  1. Judaism—Relations—Greek. 2. Greece—Religion—History—To 1500.
3. Judaism—History—Post-exilic period, 586 B.C.-210 A.D.
4. Jews—Civilization—Greek influences. 5. Jews—History—586 B.C.-70 A.D.
6. Jews—Palestine—Civilization. 7. Jews—History—586 B.C.-70 A.D.
8. Greece—Civilization. 9. Hellenism. I. Title.
  BM536.G7B76 2003
  933—dc21
                            2003004820

Manufactured in the U.S.A.
07   06   05   04   03   1   2   3   4   5   6   7   8   9   10

Contents

≋≋≋≋≋

Preface

The research recorded here was born one warm summer evening of 1960 at Ras Beirut, with the Sputnik passing overhead and the lighthouse beam from the Manara circling. The banana seller with his pushcart calling *mawz* had left some hours before; we would sit out front and add our quota to the gentle rain of pistachio nut shells falling from all the balconies. In those days I was a great reader of dictionaries covering the polyglot speech on the Beirut streets, both in recent and in older times. Suddenly it came over me: "Greek and Hebrew have the same word for 'gold' except for one vowel, *chrysos* and *ḥarûṣ*. (Later I learned that Lebanese Phoenicians reduced the first vowel, which made the correspondence perfect.) Then they must have corresponding phrases for a gold brick, a gold shekel, a golden bowl. Perhaps somebody has collected them." After some search I discovered that nobody had. And likewise with the words for "frankincense and myrrh," "tunic," "jasper and emerald," the "horned bull," a "jar of wine." Etymologists had made the connections, but no cultural historian had followed them up. So what I found lacking in the literature I wrote down myself. It appeared that Phoenician seatrade, and donkey caravans in Asia Minor (modern Turkey), had carried the things named, their names, and their associated symbolism back and forth between the societies.

One thought led to another. How did it happen that for two millennia Europe had Hebrew and Greek grammarians to copy their books and read them aloud, but no grammarians from the much older and wealthier civilizations of Egypt and Mesopotamia? Those cultures indeed had books, but written in the difficult and nonphonetic scripts of hieroglyphic and cuneiform—scripts held as a monopoly by the scribes of a businessman, a priest, a king—and so when trade, religion, monarchy fell, the tradition died. But in Israel and Greece the simple alphabetic scripts were the valued possession of a whole society of free men, and some women too; and even under colonization or in exile they copied the books and taught schoolchildren how to read them out loud.

And yet a final thought: How had Israel and Greece alone in the ancient world, before Rome came on the scene as the heiress of both, produced free peoples willing and able to criticize businesses, priesthoods, rulers, and set their own thoughts down in texts unimproved from that day to this? And I answered: "Because they built their own freedom in citadels defended by iron weapons, and surrounded with rain-watered fields. The High God who sent the rain delivered them from subjection to functionaries opening and shutting sluicegates to water the fields, as in arid Egypt and Mesopotamia. And the books taught them to value and support the freedom that originally had made the books possible." And so, I concluded, when the citadels were finally conquered by new empires, a whole literate people in dispersion or subjugation preserved the books whose message now maintained itself by its own right.

Little by little in the decades that followed, in time stolen from seeming unrelated pursuits, I began to write up those results, at first in academic periodicals mostly German, but glad to accept studies written in English. As the years went on, I moved from essays based on the keywords of trade, "gold and frankincense and myrrh," and on to deeper structural analysis of those two original free societies. When sometimes all avenues seemed closed, I could never fail for support from a long-term friend and colleague, Saul Levin at the State University of New York in Binghamton. Finally, after thirty years an amazing patron arose, Professor Otto Kaiser at Marburg, whom then I had not met personally but who proposed a selection of articles for the series Beihefte zur Zeitschrift für die alttestamentliche Wissenschaft. I redid a first set of studies, adding Greek and Hebrew fonts wherever I had left them out before. At some expense, and through several sets of proofs, Walter de Gruyter set them in type off my untidy hand; that first volume came out in 1995. It was followed by two successors in 2000 and 2001, listed elsewhere in this book.

My first essays revolved around special features of the Hebrew and Greek languages and could hardly have been understood without them. As I moved ahead, more and more my results could be supported by texts in translation. Still, I should like to encourage students of the human past (and present and future too) to acquire the rudiments of Hebrew and Greek: a beginning is quickly made; the benefits accrue throughout a lifetime—far more enjoyably than with what are called computer languages. However, for those through no fault of their own lacking knowledge of the old tongues, and unable to afford the big Berlin volumes, Walter de Gruyter and Fortress Press have generously collaborated to make available here a selection of chapters, unchanged from the original except for deletion of the foreign fonts and a few other features that went along with them. So finally this work is conveyed back from the Continent to the States that gave the author birth.

Of the six chapters gathered here, the first and last cover, respectively, the differences and similarities between classical Israel and Greece. In particular, the differences are not in ultimate value or relevance to ourselves. Both students of the Hebrew Bible and traditional classicists will find that their specialty is, if anything, placed on a higher pedestal than before—but with another alongside it. The New Testament is in a more absolute manner than usual seen as the inheritor of both.

The four intermediate chapters discuss some principal institutions of Israel and Greece—or of any culture: government, religion, social and gender classes, and the environment. Trade and warfare—the principal enterprises bringing peoples together—are not treated separately as such, but the results of omitted chapters are very fully summarized in chapter 6.

Chapter 2, "Divine Kingship, Civic Institutions, and Imperial Rule," considers both the constant obstacles that the maintenance of freedom had to overcome and the assemblies that at their best maintained that freedom.

Chapter 3, "The Mediterranean Seer and the Shaman," discusses unofficial forms of religious cult, with special connections to the boreal shamanism still extant. Their official counterpart appears in volume 1, chapter 6, "The Sacrificial Cult and Its Critique."

Chapter 4, "The Shifting Roles of Women," treats the special conditions of half the human race, during the centuries when male-dominated societies discovered and built freedoms, only today grudgingly being handed on to their consorts.

Chapter 5, "Paradise and the Forest of Lebanon," is the one I personally insisted on appearing, based on a little fieldwork in the Lebanon and a historical study of mine published elsewhere. Along with volume 1, chapter 4 ("The Mediterranean Vocabulary of the Vine") and volume 3, chapter 19 ("Blessedness in Better Lands"), it treats some symbols of ecstasy and transcendence.

Everybody likes to feel that their lifetime has not been wasted. So here I express my glad appreciation of the two who have made this selection of my work more generally accessible, in form, scope, and cost: Claus-Jürgen Thornton at Walter de Gruyter and K. C. Hanson at Fortress Press. Thank you both!

In decades when the human race faces unprecedented dangers—political, military, environmental—I propose that one necessary feature of our response is to study how we got where we are. From the civilizations of the Nile and Tigris-Euphrates we can learn most of all not to repeat their false starts; from Iran (volume 3, chapter 20, "Iranian Imperialism and the Rebel Victim") the dangers of imperialism. Rome, heir of both Israel and Greece, as well as of Iran and the Hellenistic empires, is here seen as the bridge to the ambiguities and dilemmas of *our* world. In the end, then, this work is a plea for better and deeper understanding of the societies that lie behind us *in our best moments*. Try for a fresh look at Greek sculpture; read Homer, tragedy, history, philosophy, ideally with a quick glance at the Greek original, but anyway read them; listen to the Hebrew Bible—ask somebody to read the original to you; above all read the New Testament—what an Old Testament professor (Cuthbert A. Simpson) called "the Greek postscript to the Hebrew Bible"! Those are the springs from which first flowed the wisdom we cannot do without—along with our very selves.

A note on format: K. C. Hanson has kindly compiled a supplementary bibliography and conformed usage to American style. Transcriptions of Greek and Hebrew are much simplified. Undocumented statements (especially in chapter 6) may be verified by reference to the original volumes of *Israel and Hellas*. Beth Wright magically transformed my messy markings on the galleys into intelligible English.

Abbreviations and Short Titles

AJ	*Antiquitates judaicae*
AJA	*American Journal of Archaeology*
AJP	*American Journal of Philology*
*ANEP*²	*The Ancient Near East in Pictures Relating to the Old Testament,* 2d ed., ed. J. A. Pritchard (Princeton: Princeton Univ. Press, 1969)
*ANET*³	*Ancient Near Eastern Texts Relating to the Old Testament,* 3d ed., ed. J. A. Pritchard (Princeton: Princeton Univ. Press, 1969)
ANRW	*Aufstieg und Niedergang der römischen Welt,* ed. H. Temporini and W. Haase (Berlin: de Gruyter, 1972–)
b.	Babylonian Talmud (*Babli*)
BAH	Bibliothèque Archéologique et Historique
BCH	*Bulletin de correspondance hellénique*
BJ	*Bellum judaicum*
BZ	*Biblische Zeitschrift*
CAH	Cambridge Ancient History
CIL	*Corpus inscriptionum latinarum*
CIS	*Corpus inscriptionum semiticarum*
CCSL	Corpus Christianorum: Series latina (Turnhout: Brepols, 1953–)
CPG	*Corpus Paroemiographorum Graecorum,* ed. E. Leutsch and F. G. Schneidewin, 2 vols. (Göttingen: Vandenhoek & Ruprecht, 1839–51)
CPSS	Cambridge Philological Society Supplement
CQ	*Classical Quarterly*
CSCO	Corpus scriptorum christianorum orientalium

DCPP	Edouard Lipiński, ed., *Dictionnaire de la civilisation phénicienne et punique* (Paris: Brepols, 1992)
DJD	Discoveries in the Judaean Desert
EFH	M. L. West, *The East Face of Helicon: West Asiatic Elements in Greek Poetry and Myth* (Oxford: Clarendon, 1997)
EPROER	Études préliminaires aux religions orientales dans l'empire romain
FGH	*Die Fragmente der griechischen Historiker,* ed. F. Jacoby (Leiden: Brill, 1957–)
FHG	*Fragmenta historicorum graecorum,* ed. C. Müller, 5 vols. (Paris: Didot, 1841–70)
FRLANT	Forschungen zur Religion und Literatur des Alten und Neuen Testaments
FVS⁸	H. Diels and W. Kranz, *Die Fragmente der Vorsokratiker,* 3 vols., 8th ed. (Berlin: Weidmann, 1956)
Gabba	Emilio Gabba, *Iscrizioni greche e latine per lo studio della Bibbia,* Sintesi dell'oriente e della Bibbia, Monografie 3 (Torino: Marietti, 1958)
Hist. Plant.	*Historia plantarum*
HUCA	*Hebrew Union College Annual*
IDB	*The Interpreter's Dictionary of the Bible,* ed. G. A. Buttrick, 4 vols. (Nashville: Abingdon, 1962)
IDBS	*The Interpreter's Dictionary of the Bible, Supplementary Volume,* ed. K. Crim (Nashville: Abingdon, 1976)
IG	*Inscriptiones graecae,* editio minor (de Gruyter, 1924–)
IGLS	Inscriptions Grecques et Latines de la Syrie, in the series BAH
IGRR	R. Cagnat and G. Lafaye, *Inscriptiones Graecae ad res romanas pertinentes* (Paris: Leroux, 1906–27)
ILS	H. Dessau, *Inscriptiones Latinae Selectae,* 5 vols., 3d ed. (Berlin: Weidmann, 1962)
JAOS	*Journal of the American Oriental Society*
JBL	*Journal of Biblical Literature*
j.	Jerusalem Talmud (*Yerushalmi*)
JHS	*Journal of Hellenic Studies*
JNES	*Journal of Near Eastern Studies*
JSOT	*Journal for the Study of the Old Testament*
JSOTSup	Journal for the Study of the Old Testament: Supplement Series

KAI	H. Donner and W. Röllig, *Kanaanäische und aramäische Inschriften,* 3 vols. (Wiesbaden: Harrassowitz, 1962–64)
Kent	R. G. Kent, *Old Persian: Grammar, Texts, Lexicon,* 2d ed. (American Oriental Series 33; New Haven: American Oriental Society, 1953)
KJV	King James Version of the English Bible
Kock, *Fragmenta*	T. Kock, *Comicorum Atticorum Fragmenta,* 3 vols. (Leipzig: Teubner, 1880–88), being replaced by R. Kassel and C. Austin, *Poetae Comici Graeci*
KTU	*The Cuneiform Alphabetic Texts from Ugarit, Ras Ibn Hani and Other Places,* M. Dietrich et al. (KTU: second, enlarged edition), Abhandlungen zur Literatur Alt-Syrien-Palästinas und Mesopotamiens, vol. 8 (Münster: Ugarit-Verlag, 1995), replaces idem, *Die Keilalphabetischen Texte aus Ugarit,* vol. 1, Alter Orient und Altes Testament 24 (Neukirchen-Vluyn: Neukirchener, 1976)
LACUS	Linguistic Association of Canada and the United States
LCL	Loeb Classical Library
LIMC	*Lexicon Iconographicum Mythologiae Classicae,* 6 vols. (Zurich: Artemis, 1981–94)
LSJ	Liddell, H. G., R. Scott, H. S. Jones, *A Greek-English Lexicon,* 9th ed. Oxford, 1996
LXX	Septuagint
m.	Mishna
Metam.	*Metamorphoses*
NovT	*Novum Testamentum*
NYT	*New York Times*
OCD	*Oxford Classical Dictionary.* Edited by S. Hornblower and A. Spawforth. 3d ed. Oxford, 1996
OGIS	*Orientis graeci inscriptiones selectae,* ed. W. Dittenberger. 2 vols. (Leipzig: Hirzel, 1903–5)
OTP	*Old Testament Pseudepigrapha,* 2 vols., ed. J. A. Charlesworth (Garden City, N.Y.: Doubleday, 1983–85)
PAT	*Palmyrene Aramaic Texts,* ed. Delbert R. Hillers and Eleonora Cussini (Baltimore: Johns Hopkins Univ. Press, 1996)
PG	Patrologia graeca, ed. J.-P. Migne, 162 vols. (Paris: Garnier, 1857–86)

PLF	*Poetarum Lesbiorum Fragmenta,* ed. E. Lobel and D. L. Page, 2d ed. (Oxford: Clarendon, 1963)
PMG	*Poetae Melici Graeci,* ed. D. L. Page (Oxford: Clarendon, 1962)
PW	*Paulys Real-encyclopädie der klassischen Altertumswissenschaft,* ed. G. Wissowa. 1894–
RSV	Revised Standard Version
SGDI	Sammlung der griechischen Dialekt-Inschriften (Göttingen: Vandenhoeck & Ruprecht, 1884–1915)
SHA	Scriptores Historiae Augustae
SIE	Saul Levin, *Semitic and Indo-European: The Principal Etymologies, with Observations on Afro-Asiatic,* Amsterdam Studies in the Theory and History of Linguistic Science, Series 4, vol. 129 (Amsterdam: John Benjamins, 1995)
SJLA	Studies in Judaism in Late Antiquity
Strack-Billerbeck, *Kommentar*	H. L. Strack and P. Billerbeck, *Kommentar zum NT aus Talmud und Midrasch,* 6 vols. (Munich: Beck, 1922–61)
SVMB	*The History of the Jewish People in the Age of Jesus Christ (175 B.C.—A.D. 135)* by Emil Schürer, rev. by Geza Vermes, Fergus Millar, and Matthew Black, 3 vols. (Edinburgh: T. & T. Clark, 1973–87)
t.	Tosefta
TDNT	*Theological Dictionary of the New Testament,* ed. G. Kittel and G. Friedrich, trans. G. W. Bromiley, 10 vols. (Grand Rapids: Eerdmans, 1964–76)
TLE	Massimo Pallottino, *Testimonia Linguae Etruscae,* 2d ed. (Biblioteca di Studi Superiori 24; Florence: La Nuova Italia, 1968)
TWNT	*Theologisches Wörterbuch zum Neuen Testament,* ed. G. Kittel and G. Friedrich (Stuttgart: Kohlhammer, 1932–79)
UNP	Simon B. Parker, ed., *Ugaritic Narrative Poetry* (Society of Biblical Literature Writings from the Ancient World 9; Atlanta: Society of Biblical Literature, 1997)
UT	C. H. Gordon, *Ugaritic Textbook,* 3 vols. (Analecta Orientalia 38; Rome: Pontifical Biblical Institute, 1965)
Vg	Vulgate
VT	*Vetus Testamentum*
ZAW	*Zeitschrift für die alttestamentliche Wissenschaft*

CHAPTER 1

The Complementarity
of Ancient Israel and Ancient Greece

It is not easy to keep in mind simultaneously a pair of correlative truths: (I) Two things contrasted must be comparable; (II) Two things compared can always be contrasted. For (I) things can be contrasted only with respect to some attribute, which constitutes a ground of comparison between them. And (II) when things are compared in their possession of some attribute, they must possess it in different and contrasted ways; otherwise they would be identical. The authors who contrast Israel and Hellas—Arnold, Boman, Havelock, Auerbach—lose sight of truth I, following Tertullian (*Prescription against Heretics* 7.9). For, when he asked, "What do Athens and Jerusalem have to do with each other?" he failed to answer his own question by noting that each city was the center of a free society generating a novel literature.

Children in a family create environmental niches, each claiming vacant territory: one is tidy, one messy; one loud, one quiet; one industrious, one lazy. The classical Hebrew and Greek worlds are a little more distant than that, cousins rather than siblings, in touch only at one or more removes, through trade by land and sea; wars of their allies; common subjection to imperialism; foreign princesses and mercenaries, colonists, artisans, exiles. But the principle of differentiation still holds. In their joint breakout from ancient Near Eastern absolutism, each develops its own version of newly emergent freedom. They fit neatly into each other, supplementing each other's strengths, remedying each other's defects, just as the bright masculine positive sun-principle or Yang fits into the dark feminine negative moon-principle or Yin.[1] Partially

---

1. The Greek and Latin names of the luminaries follow the Chinese gender: *hēlios* with *selēnē*, *sol* with *luna*. But both feminine moon-words are adjectives by etymology, not nouns. The genders of the various Semitic names are fluctuating.

in the Septuagint, and fully in the New Testament, the cousins are married and produce a novel offspring, in some ways more vigorous than either, while each maintaining its individuality. We may then describe the reciprocal relationship of Israel and Hellas as one of *complementarity*.

Every comparison we make in these chapters can be seen from the other side as a contrast. Here we lift out the most coherent from among all those contrasts. In some places we rework themes of our predecessors. At the end we revert to the conventional wisdom—not all that incorrect—which sees Israel as the fountainhead of religion, Hellas of science. Perhaps the novel framework we set around those timeworn materials will put them in a fresher light.

The initial obvious difference we find between the two societies is *style of dialogue:* in Israel between man (or an occasional woman) and God, in Hellas between man and man. It is explained by differences both in time and in space. In time: Israel as an *old* society, Hellas as a *young* one. And in space: Israel as a society *just inside* the ancient Near East locked into landtrade, Hellas as one *just outside* enjoying a cosmopolitan seatrade.

Each of those three contrasts has a further extension. The contrasted dialogues generate different imaging of the *divine:* in Israel concrete symbols are never fully adequate pointers to God; Hellas is content with them. As the two societies look behind them in time to varying distances, Israel goes back so deeply as to gain a vision of historical *survival*; Hellas can only see so far as to identify the situations that create *tragedy*. Looking out in space from their center, the two societies adopt different standards of *membership:* Israel sharply within its speech-community accepts only those reputed to have the same *lineage*; Hellas accepts as its own all those who speak the same *language*.

Where the two societies merge in the *New Testament,* the same three contrasts regarding divinity, time, and space determine the nature of the confluence and the respective roles of the two parents in the merger. There follow two sections regarding the character of the *written texts* that the two societies (and now also the early church) hand down to us. Partly due to intrinsic features of the two languages, partly to technical features of their scripts (arising from their respective insider and outsider status), their *literary canons* markedly differ: small and fixed in both Testaments, large and open in Hellas. Closely related is their degree of *translatability:* high in Hebrew texts, due to their concrete character and relative lack of internal elegances; variable in Greek, where the New Testament in the end moves back toward the simplicity of Hebrew.

In the period of the Greek New Testament and rabbinic exegesis, each society takes on *attributes of the other.* But the contemporary perception of Israel as the source of *religious faith,* Hellas of *reason and logic,* has its own legitimacy. In the end we revert to the geographical contrast of the two societies. Modern nations in their claims on the individual approach the absolutist character of the ancient Near Eastern empires as mediated to us via Rome. The places where the two traditions are transmitted to us—the congregation and the classroom—speak to us from the same place as their forerunners did: Hebrew-Christian religious faith offers guidance and critique of our world from the *inside,* Greek scientific reason as from the *outside.*

Complementarity in Style of Dialogue

We may approach the common features of Israel and Hellas through their architectural deposits in our cities: a university where Greek texts are widely read in translation, and, among a smaller circle, in the original; around it, churches where the Hebrew Bible (along with the Greek New Testament) is publicly read in translation, and a synagogue or seminary where it is studied in the original. Buildings where people read books!—often silently, but sometimes, in the old style, out loud. For what purposes? For the light that those books, the earliest records that lie behind us, studied somewhere in every generation, throw on our own institutions, which they more than anything else created. And therefore for help in forming our own thought and character within those institutions.

The Greek enterprise most directly formative for us is philosophy, which trains us to think clearly about our world and ourselves. We may take Plato's *Dialogues* as the books, and the classroom as the normal site, where Greek reason is most accessible. The Hebrew enterprise most directly formative for us is a proclamation about the source of justice, by which we are empowered to search out the places where justice is needed, and to strive for it. We may take prophetic works like Jeremiah as the books, and the place of worship as the normal site, where that proclamation is most accessible.

How do Plato's Socrates and Jeremiah most clearly differ? Socrates is constantly in dialogue with other human beings (always, in fact, men) of different viewpoints, from which ideally a resolution on a higher level is achieved; whereas Jeremiah is in dialogue only with God. (In this context, by "God" we mean the seemingly external source of novel thoughts that one finds in one's heart, challenging or confirming one's "own" thoughts.) Perhaps none of

Plato's *Dialogues* records an actual conversation, but they may have been acted out in the Academy. Jeremiah 36 describes how the prophet spoke out or dictated his message for others to pass on. His first chapter records dialogue between himself and God, in which God puts words in the prophet's mouth. (The same experience is attested by Greek poets who find a message not their own put on their tongue.)

For any particular Israelite, there is only one preexisting point of view on a topic. Any other is the prompting of God; we may, if we wish, attribute it to the unconscious side of the speaker, but for him it is the word of Another, with whom he enters into confrontation. Adam and Job hear unexpected responses from their God. For the Greek, things come in contrasted pairs, both of which are affirmed: the very structure of the language encourages sentences to come with "on the one hand" *(men),* "on the other" *(de).*[2] (Only the context tells us whether Hebrew *wa-* is better heard as "and" or "but.") A Greek's neighbor can be counted on to provide an opposite to his thought; there is no need to wait for a suggestion from the gods.

Israel as an Old Society, Hellas as a Young One

How to explain the contrast: dialogue of man and man in Hellas, of man and God in Israel? Hellas is an experimental society with no fixed view how a city-state should be governed, about the nature of the gods, what duties a man has to his neighbor. Israelites at each epoch feel that such questions are settled by a known relationship between themselves and their God, although we, looking back, perceive big changes. We can understand the contrast in two ways: here by a contrast in *time.* All falls into place when we see Hellas, in spite of its seeming old legendary memory, as a *young society* where the historical period is disconnected from the heroic age; and Israel, in spite of its innovations over against the Near Eastern empires, as an *old society* with a long, continuous memory (of course, holding legendary elements) spanning many setbacks and recoveries. A couple of features show this contrast.

Literacy
Genesis is the history of a people without writing. But writing is there in the background, and the Hebrews show no interest in its origins; they were

2. Saul Levin, "The Connective 'Particles' of Classical Greek Discourse," *CUNY Forum* nos. 5–6 (1979) 52–58, proposes in fact that behind *men* is a word for "hand"; cf. Latin *manus.*

surely aware of both cuneiform and hieroglyphic before they began using the local alphabet. Pharaoh's signet ring (Exod 41:42) can have had no other function than to authenticate documents produced by Joseph. In Exodus, writing appears abruptly in the command to Moses: "Write this as a memorial in a book" (Exod 17:14). At Exod 24:4 Moses writes the words of Yahweh, and reads the book of the covenant to the people (Exod 24:7). We are to assume that the two tables of stone, "written with the finger of God" (Exod 31:18), had been written previously. The rabbis further take it for granted that both Moses and his God wrote in Hebrew.

The Homeric poems presuppose writing only where Proetus gives Bellerophon a baneful message (*Iliad* 6.168–69); no language is suggested, if indeed the "scratchings" are not pure ideograms. Herodotus (5.58–59), recognizing a novelty, has great interest in the introduction of "Phoenician" or "Cadmeian scratchings." Nowhere do classical Greeks betray any knowledge that an earlier form of their own language (and apparently others) was written in the Mycenaean palaces and in Minoan Crete.

Genealogy

Hebrew writers take it for granted that in principle the descent of every Israelite back to the beginning of humanity was known, even though parts of the tradition might be conflicting or unrecorded. The backbone of the historical books is genealogy. And so in the New Testament. Matthew records the descent of Jesus from Abraham in 3 x 14 = 42 generations; Luke records 56 (perhaps = 4 x 14) generations back to Abraham and 20 more back to Adam. Two Punic inscriptions of the third century B.C.E., one from Sardinia (*KAI* 68) and one from Carthage (*KAI* 78), each gives a man 16 generations of ancestors, taking the ancestry back to the seventh century.

In classical Hellas, few genealogies go back before one's grandfather. Within the legendary heroic past a man could boast of knowing five generations back; Aeolus father of Sisyphus of Glaucus of Bellerophon of Hippolochus of another Glaucus (*Iliad* 6.145–211). The seven generations of Tiresias can be counted. Thomas documents the few claimed genealogies.[3] An isolated stone of Chios records the ancestors of one Heropythos to fourteen generations.[4] When historic Greeks draw their genealogy back to the heroic

---

3. Rosalind Thomas, *Oral Tradition and Written Record in Classical Athens* (Cambridge Studies in Oral and Literate Culture 18; Cambridge: Cambridge Univ. Press, 1985).
4. SGDI 5656.

age, the intervening generations are normally not listed. According to Phere-cydes,[5] Hippocrates the physician traced his ancestry back (along different lines) to Heracles in twenty generations and to Asclepius in nineteen. Hecataeus told Egyptian priests that his family went back to a god in the six-teenth generation (Herodotus 2.143). The missing generations are unrecorded from Euagoras of Cyprus back to Teucer,[6] Andocides to Odysseus,[7] Alcibiades to Eurysaces (and therefore Zeus).[8] The exception is that of Miltiades to a son of Ajax, where the generations are in fact given;[9] but Thomas (161–63) finds even the historical part contradicted by external evidence. She sees these genealogies less as deposits of oral tradition than as artificial constructions by professionals. Only in Sparta was a genealogy of kings recorded: Leonidas (I) king 490–480 B.C.E. was the descendant of Heracles through twenty genera-tions (Herodotus 7.204); Leotychidas likewise was the son of Heracles through twenty generations (the last few not kings, Herodotus 8.131). In the second passage, Herodotus notes in contrast that the Athenian commander was just "Xanthippus son of Ariphron."

Thus, apart from the genealogies of Sparta, there is a break in Greek leg-endary memory between the fall of Troy and the earliest historical records of the mainland city-states. It was honorific to claim a heroic ancestor; superflu-ous to search out the generations in between. That selective memory corre-sponds to the break in literacy between the end of Linear B and the first alphabetic inscriptions. As Greeks contrasted their rainfall with Egyptian irrigation, and their alphabet with hieroglyphics, so their recent appearance: the Egyptian priest tells Solon (Plato *Tim.* 22 B), "you Hellenes are only chil-dren." The partly legendary Israelite record for the period of Joshua and the Judges is still a unique witness behind the scenes to the disruptive societies that ended the palace cultures of the eastern Mediterranean. As a result, the Hebrews felt that they had a continuous unbroken record extending indefi-nitely far back into prehistory.

Insiders and Outsiders of the Ancient Near East

Four conditions were necessary (but not sufficient) for the emergence of a new freedom over against the ancient Near East: (1) *geographical*—a defensible

5. *FGH* 3 frag. 59.
6. Isocrates, *Euagoras* 12–19.
7. Plutarch, *Alcib.* 21.1 = Hellanicus *FGH* 323a frag. 24.
8. Plato, *Alcib. I* 121A.
9. Marcellinus, *Vita Thuc.* 2–4 = Pherecydes *FGH* 3 frag. 2.

citadel surrounded by rain-watered fields; (2) *technological*—iron for weapons and tools, lime for waterproofing cisterns in the dry summer; (3) *social*—elements of democracy; and (4) *scribal*—a phonetic alphabetic script. Here the geographical is key. For five thousand years autonomous local societies have never appeared in Egypt or Iraq, because of central bureaucratic control over the only source of water, the river. The Hittite empire, in rain-watered territory, did not generate free cities either: here other explanations come into play—the lack of a phonetic alphabet, the lack of access to the sea. For precisely the Hittite successor states closest to the Greek are on the sea like Lycia, which eventually borrowed a phonetic script from Hellas.

Earlier I presupposed, but should have added, one more condition: (5) *proximity* to the Near Eastern empires, which developed technology, city life, commerce, central administration, standing armies, literacy (mostly non-phonetic), organized cult—even though all under absolutist regimes. Those conditions delimit in both time and space the places where (in Lincoln's words) a "new birth of freedom" was possible. Neither during the rise of the Near Eastern empires nor during their decay: *early in the Iron Age,* then. Neither at the heart of the ancient Near East, nor beyond the sphere of its trade and influence: therefore either *just inside* the ancient Near East, or *just outside*. As it turned out, the decisive evolution took place in *only one society* "just inside," namely Israel; and in *only one society* "just outside," namely, Hellas. Greeks described irrigation in Egypt as outside visitors, Hebrews from a memory of having lived there; Herodotus describes brickmaking in Babylon as of his own day, Hebrews as at its first building. It might seem that Latins and Etruscans were nearly as ready as Hellas to take the decisive step forward to a free society; but, except by language, they were in the Greek sphere of influence from the beginning, and it is speculative to ask how they might have developed without it. The position of Israel inside the ancient Near East explains why it could not see itself otherwise than as an old society; the position of Hellas outside meant that it could only be a new society.

Their respective situations also gave Israelites and Greeks contrasted relationships to their neighbors. Israel was in effect a landlocked country, and her foreign trade was carried by caravans, which further did not normally take Hebrews far from home; it is an Ishmaelite spice caravan (Gen 37:25) that carries Joseph to Egypt. Greeks, living in a land of drowned mountain-ranges, naturally traveled and traded by sea; more extensively even than the Phoenicians, they engaged in colonization. Only for the time of Solomon do Hebrews remember a time of seatrade, perhaps inflated in memory.

What resources did young Israel and Hellas have? Originally the Hebrews had few cultural institutions not available to their neighbors—the maritime and colonizing Phoenicians, the even more landlocked Ammonites and Moabites. Their language was at most a distinct dialect of Canaanite, but fully comprehensible to their neighbors; the earliest Yahwism reconstructible hardly differs from the cult of Chemosh attested in the inscription of King Mesha of Moab; their sacrificial cult, mostly monopolized by a hereditary priesthood, in early texts shows no special originality.

The peoples of Canaan sat where armies of the great empires, Egyptian, Mesopotamian, and Hittite,[10] passed back and forth. It is unclear whether the memory of an Egyptian captivity is truly part of the earliest Israelite tradition; and, even if so, how it distinguished them from their neighbors—for the Philistines likewise remembered their arrival from "Caphtor" (Crete?) and the Aramaeans from unknown "Kir" (Amos 9:7). With the advantage of hindsight we can see the first shoots of independence in the unconquerable hillvillages of Israel. But they had little independent cultural heritage. Their originality, then, had to rest on the decision—which their defensible geographical position made possible—to *accept or reject* inherited Near Eastern elements. But the historian cannot get so close as to say why the decision was made there rather than in Phoenicia, Moab, or Damascus.

Hellenic culture in large part grew up in cities formerly of the Minoan-Mycenaean world with their palaces, scribal literacy, luxury goods, commerce reaching Cyprus, Phoenicia, Ugarit, Egypt. But its *remembered* beginnings are later and further away, on both sides of the upper Aegean, where the Homeric epics record an indigenous culture, with tenuous recollections of the Hittites. M. L. West has shown how Akkadian phrases made their way into the epic; we shall see how shared Mediterranean enterprises contributed vocabulary to both Hellas and Israel, as well (surely) as to lost literatures. Early on, Hellas is aware of the Near Eastern empires out there as representing a higher level of material culture; unlike Israel, it was not frightened off by them. Its inherited Indo-European language and institutions were so strong, and its character so robust and curious, that it saw the empires rather as societies to be learned from. Hence, in Hellas we find a series of borrowings from the Near East, some (by comparison with Israel) progressive, others retrograde.

Thus we may enlarge our former contrast to a geographical-cultural one:

Israel is an old inland society just inside the ancient Near East, the terminus of traderoutes by land, struggling to escape, which, however, it can do only in the most critical areas.

10. Hittites at the battle of Kadesh on the Orontes, 1274 B.C.E.; Trevor Bryce, *The Kingdom of the Hittites* (Oxford: Clarendon, 1998), 256–63.

Hellas is a new seaboard society just outside the ancient Near East, to which the Mediterranean is open for trade and colonization, enjoying indigenous cultural resources, on which the Near East exercises an ongoing fascination.

Now Hellas, now Israel is the cultural innovator.

Hellas as the Cultural Innovator

Israel and Hellas share over against the Near East a *sacrificial cult* with special vocabulary and practices. Although in the beginnings of Israel any man can be his own priest (Gideon at Ophrah, Judg 6:25), in the centralized kingdom sacrifice becomes the monopoly of a hereditary priesthood, down to the Maccabean priest-kings and the high priests of the Herodian temple. From the time when "every man did what was right in his own eyes" (Judg 21:25), a steady retrograde movement leads back to the ancient Near Eastern pattern. While both cult and priests are criticized, there is no suggestion of carrying it out without them. By contrast, in Hellas from the beginning every man can sacrifice for himself.

Again in the realm of *kingship*. The emergence of Israel as a true state coincides with the taking up of Near Eastern patterns of kingship. Israel hardly existed as such until the elders came to Samuel and said (1 Sam 8:5), "Give us a king to judge over us like all the *goyim* [foreigners]." When the state split into two at Solomon's death it is taken for granted that both parts will be under kingship; the independent state re-created by the Maccabees was under rulers who called themselves king or high priest. There is always some current of thought in Israel for which kingship contradicts its true nature—but none that has any substitute for it. The Minoan and Mycenaean palaces were surely the residence of kings. But from the time of Homer on, Greek kingship everywhere except in Macedon (perhaps not Greek-speaking) undergoes a progressive reduction. Other patterns of Indo-European social structure win out, take over the city of Rome, influence Carthage, and perhaps by reflex Phoenicia also. The invention of the polis in its Greek form weakened any residual Indo-European kingship and blocked any takeover of the absolutist functions of Near Eastern kingship, which Greeks (correctly) saw as an alien tyranny.

So with *literacy*. From somewhere in Canaan, Hebrews inherited a phonetic consonantal alphabet, for we find one such four centuries before them at Ugarit, though still in cuneiform script. Its inadequacy is sufficiently marked that every Hebrew written text required an accompanying tradition of recitation. By inspired reinterpretation of the Phoenician alphabet, Greeks made it into a nearly adequate record of their language, from which oral recitation was possible. The results for the production and preservation of texts were profound.

And finally in the realm of *science*. Through unclear modes of contact, Greeks learned from Babylonians the art of astronomy (which they partly disengaged from astrology), and, mostly as an independent development, the logic of mathematics, in particular geometry. There is no such takeover in Israel.

Israel as the Cultural Innovator

At the earliest point where we can see both societies, Israel is on its way to a full *monotheism,* while Hellenes (in spite of Zeus's role as king of the gods) have an extended *pantheon*[11] as in Babylon, Ugarit, Egypt, Phoenicia. Far from feeling threatened by Near Eastern pantheons, Greeks either adopted their members outright or identified them with local divinities. Indo-European antiquity also had such a pantheon, but of the divine names only Zeus the father is inherited by Hellas. For some Greek divinities we can find a home here or there around the Aegean; others remain mysterious; but the Near Eastern pantheons were the pattern. The *Iliad* is prematurely rationalistic in that immortal gods serve as comic relief against the all-too-mortal heroes; Aeschylus and Pindar recover the gods' reality. The religious development in Israel is a progressive deepening in the concept of the single God whom in principle it professes from the beginning. The development in Hellas is a philosophical movement toward affirmation of a single deity—at the cost of losing such functions as the Hesiodic understanding of Zeus to be the guarantor of justice.

With the monotheism of Israel goes rejection of *divination*. The Urim and Thummim no doubt represent a purified form of divination; but there are almost no relics of divination by the flight of birds, thunder, or the appearance of portents; the sacrificial regulations to prevent divination by the form of the liver show that it was known and rejected. Joseph (Gen 44:5) has a silver cup with which he supposedly divines;[12] but it plays no essential role as such in the tale. Hellenes, feeling that divided rule in the pantheon left much undecided, saw nothing to be lost by assessing the whims of Moira or Tyche through divination. In this respect Etruscans and Romans are more Greek

---

11. For the pantheon, see EFH 107–13.

12. The Versions interpret the Hebrew by the role of "augury" through bird flight in their own societies. But the supposed divination may be one more of Joseph's false clues.

than the Greeks; here as elsewhere they must have had a direct conduit to the Near East that bypassed the Greek mainland.

Above all, the *failure* of Israel to develop a slave economy comparable to that of Athens is a progressive feature. The exceptional level of democracy in Athens is precisely correlated with its slave economy, in which slaves were likely a third of the free population. Homer never brings on a male slave designated *doulos,* although he is aware of the "day of slavery" (*Iliad* 6.463, etc.). While in Israel both foreigners and Hebrews could become slaves, a bad conscience about the institution led to provisions at least theoretical for their emancipation. The slaves in Jesus' parables (translated "servants" in the RSV) represent a partial Hellenization of the social structure. But Exod 21:21 does say "for the slave is his silver"; so Aristotle calls a slave a "living tool" (*Ethica nichomachea* 8.13 = 1161b4); as in the Roman Empire with its vast expansion of slavery equivalently *instrumentum uocale,* "a speaking tool" (Varro, *De re rustica* 1.17.1).

The role of Yahweh as creator gives the *natural order* a numinous character lacking in Hellas. Psalm 104 affectionately surveys the Lebanese coastline from the high springs on the mountains down through the forest to the sea, along with the birds and beasts on each level, as well as the human habitation. While Theophrastus admires the Lebanese forest, the Hebrews see it as an integral part of the divine order. Already the environments best known to the Greeks were much degraded, and none of the gods claimed the forest as a special province.

And, while we hear much about lawgivers and laws in the Greek tradition, and find much miscellaneous ethical advice in both prose and poetry, there is nothing like the Hebrew Ten Commandments representing a *fixed traditional moral code.* The body of Delphic sayings attributed also to the Seven Sages could be expanded or contracted at will. Familiarity has dulled the novelty we ought to feel in the notion of a unique High God sufficiently in touch with his people to deliver in person an easily remembered set of principles for life in community.

Transcendence or Immanence of the Divine World

The most obvious difference between the two societies is Hebrew monotheism over against the Greek pantheon. "Monotheism" deserves two qualifications, which, however, do not seriously affect its difference from the Greek pattern: (1) *The divine names.* Strata of the Hebrew Bible employ different divine names, which have been interpreted as the usage of different tribal groupings: "Yahweh" (with unknown vowels) as revealed to Moses, though in the narrative used since Gen 2:4; "Shadday" as archaic usage by the Patriarchs and in the book of Job; "El" also archaic but less clearly located. *Adonay* "Lord" from a title becomes the pronunciation of *Yhwh*. (Perhaps "Elohim" with its anomalous grammar was seen as a neutral term to cover all the others.) But it is precarious to ascribe different characters to the three or four names; and any differences that existed were (it appears) successfully bridged over. (2) *Gods of neighbors*. At one point Yahweh is seen (like Zeus!) as "a great king above all gods" (Ps 95:3); but "all the gods of the peoples are idols" (Ps 96:5). There is a tension, not fully resolved until late, between seeing foreign cults by analogy with Israelite as to a definable high being, and seeing them as merely empty; but that tension does not seriously undercut the Hebrews' understanding of their own cult.

Since for Hebrews the primary dialogue is between man and God, it is a key matter how that God is understood. Since there is ultimately no other true god in Israel from whom Yahweh its God needs to be distinguished, a visual representation of Yahweh is at the least superfluous; and in fact was absolutely rejected. Nowhere are the relations of the two societies to the ancient Near East more opposite than in the realm of the plastic arts. Archaic Greeks took the image of the standing youth or *kouros* (human or divine) from Egypt, while bringing it to life; composite animals, Gorgons and griffins, from the Hittite world. The language used about the God of Israel attributes to him, as to a mountain and to the Greek gods, the features of a man's body: arms and legs, hands and feet; a face, eyes and ears, nostrils (to express his anger). You would think him "anthropomorphic," as Strabo noted that Egyptian temples had "no statue, or at least none of human form, but of one of the irrational beasts" (17.1.28). But here Israel differs most strongly from its neighbors, where Melqarth, identified in an Aramaic inscription, appears in a stele of Aleppo carrying an axe.[13] Millar[14] discusses the theory of Bickerman[15] that the cult set up in the Temple of Jerusalem by Antiochus IV Epiphanes in 167 B.C.E. was not Hellenizing at all, but an adaptation of Syrian aniconic practice whereby the altar itself became the cult object. Still, the old Hebrew practice is a better testimony to aniconic worship. Here is a realm where the fascination exercised on the Greek imagination by the Near East outside Israel is patent and long-continuing, however much Greeks

13. *ANEP*² 499; *KAI* 201.

14. Fergus Millar, *The Roman Near East, 31 B.C.—A.D. 337* (Cambridge: Harvard Univ. Press, 1993), 12–13.

15. Elias Bickerman, *The God of the Maccabees*, trans. H. R. Moehring (SJLA 32; Leiden: Brill, 1979), 70.

improved on their models; and where correspondingly the stubbornness of Israel in breaking with the Near East is stiffest. Both strategies, the ways of affirmation and of rejection of images, represent complementary aspects of how humanity views the divine. Neither warrants one of the labels "progressive" or "retrograde."

The *linguistic* "anthropomorphism" of both Hebrew and Greek occasionally results in parallel expressions. Thus Exod 13:9: "For with a strong hand Yahweh has brought you out of Egypt." *Iliad* 15.694–95: "and Zeus pushed [Hector] forward with his most long hand." Similarly, the eye of the High God is spoken of. But in poetic comparisons, a small but significant difference makes the Greek divine realm immanent, and the Hebrew one transcendent. In Hellas, natural objects are seen as an adequate symbol of the divine; in Israel, inadequate. The difference is especially noteworthy where the vocabulary as such is shared.

Gold and jewels. For Pindar (frag. 209) "gold is the child of Zeus"; again (*Olymp.* 1.1–2):

> Water is preeminent and gold, like a fire
> burning in the night, outshines
> all possessions that magnify men's pride.[16]

What could be better than gold? Hebrew finds something (Wisdom speaking): "Take my instruction rather than silver, and knowledge rather than refined gold; for wisdom is better than jewels" (Prov 8:10-11), and similarly Prov 3:13-14; 8:19. Proverbs here is in the Phoenician orbit, using the foreign name of gold that went into Greek, rather than native *zahav.*[17]

Sand and stars. Again, in Israel, Hellas, and Rome the sand on the seashore and the stars stand for what is uncountable, even though certain ones are given credit for having counted them: Archimedes and Archytas (Horace *Carm.* 1.28.1-2) the sand, Yahweh the stars (Ps 147:4). But once something is *more than* the sand (Ps 139:17-18): "How precious to me are thy thoughts, O El! . . . if I count them, they are *more* than the sand."

Time and eternity. Time, says Plato (*Timaeus* 38B), and the heavens came into being together, so that, if necessary, they should be dissolved together; but earlier (37D), when he calls time "a certain moving image of eternity," he

16. *Pindar's Victory Songs,* trans. F. J. Nisetich (Baltimore: Johns Hopkins Univ. Press, 1980).

17. But where the actual names of jewels appear, jasper and emeralds, both Greek and Hebrew use them as adequate symbols of a better world.

describes it as an "eternal image." Heraclitus says that "this cosmos, the same for all beings, was made by no gods or men, but always was and is and shall be ever-living fire, kindled by measure and extinguished by measure."[18] Both authors, in spite of subtleties, appear to be saying that time and the universe partake of eternity; conversely, then, eternity can be grasped through the objects of the universe. In clear contrast, Ps 102:27 (see the whole context) says of heavens and earth, "They will perish, but you endure; they will all wear out like a garment."

Tragedy and Survival

A further difference between the societies emerges from the centrality of the tragic vision in Hellas and its absence in Israel. Tragedy, says Aristotle (*Poetics* 13.5), is the story of one who falls into misfortune through some flaw. The story of the *Iliad* is the anger or grudge of Achilles responsible for the death of his best friend Patroclus. The story of Oedipus is the hot temper of one who in a crossroads encounter kills another old enough to be his father. The story told by Thucydides is the disaster of the Sicilian expedition arising from the Athenians' inflated estimate of their own abilities, documented in Pericles' Funeral Oration—much admired, not always for the right reasons. Perhaps it will be agreed that a pattern here runs through earlier Greek literature. Is it to be found in Hebrew?[19] David suffers reverses seen as caused by his own failings, like the death of his first child by Bathsheba, but his life goes on as life does—the story seems more based on real life than Greek tragedy. The story from Genesis to Kings is the continuity of a people in spite of all setbacks. The exile is seen as retribution for the faults of Judah, but only Lamentations makes it a total disaster. Second Kings ends with Jehoiachin eating at the king's table. In spite of harsh words against Babylon, Jeremiah says in God's name to the actual exiles there (29:7) "But seek the peace of the city where I have sent you into exile."

18. Heraclitus frag. 30 FVS[8] from Plutarch.

19. Here I disagree with Flemming A. J. Nielsen, *The Tragedy in History: Herodotus and the Deuteronomistic History* (JSOTSup 251; Sheffield: JSOT Press, 1997). Nielsen finds, to his own satisfaction, a tragic theme running through the Hebrew Bible. Like some others of an American-Danish school, he dates the final redaction of the biblical history (including its "tragic" elements) so late that it could reflect Herodotus. His last sentence (p. 164): "Thus it becomes probable that [the Deuteronomistic history] was written at a time and in a milieu where the Hellenistic influence was important in the Israelite or more correctly, the Jewish tradition." But this bold claim is not buttressed by any proposed linguistic borrowing from Herodotus or Greek generally, such as we find in Qoheleth or Daniel.

Hebrews looking beyond their own traditions, to Egypt or Babylonia, were in touch with societies that traced their history hundreds and thousands of years into the remote past; and, even while struggling to escape, they learned from those empires to record and cherish their own distant history. For a supremely practical purpose. Levin on *Elohim* in the Hebrew Bible says:

> The conviction of the Bible authors [about the nature of the Hebrew God] came (I think) from observing which patterns of human associa-tion are viable in the long run, and which ones end in failure. Their wis-dom was a kind of pre-scientific sociology, far-sighted and practical at the same time; modern research is more methodical but not more acute or penetrating. They fastened upon the relation of father to son, as the basis of society and of all wholesome growth and development.[20]

Thus the distinction between clean and unclean beasts is a traditional hygiene; the development of the (seemingly) instinctive abhorrence of incest is an observational eugenics; the sabbatical rest of the land is a heuristic agronomy. All such principles in the books of Moses required data over numerous generations in order to be verified. In contrast, the moral and social principles in Hesiod's *Works and Days,* while often persuasive and in agree-ment with Moses, rest mostly on one man's observations, even though (no doubt) drawing to some degree on traditional experience.

The Hellenes at no period had a long enough history behind them, leg-endary or historical, to say for certain which patterns of life in the human family (particular or universal) were sustainable in the long run. But they had a long enough history to say that certain patterns of life were self-destructive and doomed to failure even in a short run. The formative events of Israelite history made it the primary depository in the ancient world of both levels of wisdom. Moderns with our individualism, like the Greeks, need to identify and ward off social patterns that will implode upon ourselves in our own life-times. But with the flux of technological innovation and changing family structures we are giving up even the prospect of founding a dynasty; we expect in advance that our grandchildren will strike out in different ways. The uniqueness of the Kennedy clan is just the fact of its existence with a seeming unchangeable Catholicism. For ourselves we can hardly imagine any proposal (in the nature of things never fully demonstrative) that certain social patterns over an indefinite period of time actually *work.*

20. Saul Levin, *Guide to the Bible,* 5th ed., laser-printed (Binghamton: SUNY Press, 1996), 12.

Criteria of Membership: Lineage versus Language

Israelites, once they undertook to define themselves over against other peoples, precisely because they differed so slightly in material culture from other Canaanites, adopted a rigid definition of the difference between themselves and their neighbors. Thus they answered the question, "What makes us different from other peoples?" much otherwise than the Greeks. The noun *Israel* is masculine (except when seen as an army) while *Hellas* is feminine.[21] Israel/Jacob is the father of *twelve* tribes. Hellen is the father of three in Hesiod: "And from Hellen the war-loving king came Doros, Xouthos and Aiolos the chariot-fighter."[22] Xouthos was the father of Achaios, and of Ion the ancestor of the Ionians (Apollodorus 1.7.3) with their *twelve* cities in Achaea and in Ionia (Herodotus 1.145). But Hellenes came to name themselves not after the man but the region Hellas, whose original referent is variously reported, but that already Hesiod *Opera* 651–53 uses for the whole Achaean host: "Aulis, where once the Achaeans, after waiting out a storm, gathered a great host from sacred Hellas to Troy the land of fair women."

Herodotus also uses "Hellas" as a feminine adjective to denote the Greek *language*. At 6.98.3 he explains the names of the Persian kings "in Greek"; at 9.16.2 he represents a Persian as "speaking in Greek" to a Theban. Later *hellēnisti* is the only way of saying "in Greek." Plato (*Tim.* 21E) says that the "founding divinity" (feminine!) of Egyptian Sais "is named in Egyptian Neith, in Greek . . . Athena." At Xenophon *Anab.* 7.6.8 Seuthes the Thracian "had an interpreter, although he himself understood most of what was said in Greek." At Acts 21:37 the tribune Claudius Lysias (23:26), taking Paul for a different agitator, is surprised that he can understand Greek. Thus the primary connotation of "Hellas" comes to be *the land and society of all those who speak Greek.*

When an earlier Alexander of Macedon urged the Athenians to submit to Xerxes, and the Spartans urged them to stand fast, the Athenians said No to Alexander, and to the Spartans defined the features of their commonality that blocked any thought of becoming traitors (Herodotus 8.144.2):

> The Hellenic [nation], being of one blood and one language, along with the common shrines and sacrifices of the gods, as also the customs arising from a shared upbringing. . . .

21. But we should resist the temptation to see the polar opposites Israel/Hellas as masculine/feminine, much less with the other attributes of Chinese Yang/Yin.

22. Hesiod frag. 9, Merkelbach-West.

Here four things are seen as constituting the Hellenes: common descent, language, temples, and customs. But Isocrates (*Panegyricus* 49–50) sets a priority among them:

> But so far has our city [Athens] left behind other men in regards to thought and speech, that her pupils have become teachers of the others, and have brought it about that the name of the Hellenes no longer is felt to refer to a race but a mental disposition, and that those are called Hellenes who share our education rather than a common descent.

Earlier Isocrates had said that the best sign of "our [Athenian] education" was "things said" by those who "use speech well." While like other men he puts his own profession in first place, his claim that the use of language is the surest sign of Hellenism is supported by Herodotus's usage.

Israelites have no specific name for their language. "The lip of Canaan" (Isa 19:18) defines the common language of Canaan, including Hebrew, Phoenician, Moabite, Ammonite—and perhaps even Philistine, so far as its speakers had taken over Canaanite as with king Achish of Ekron. At 2 Kgs 18:26 the contrast between "Judaean" and "Aramaic" refers to the peoples who spoke those tongues rather than to any clear concept of the languages themselves. In John's Gospel, *hebraisti* is attached to proper names that can only be Aramaic, Bethzatha (5:2), Gabbatha (19:13), Golgotha (19:17); it then likewise refers to the language spoken by people who called themselves "Hebrews," rather than to any clear distinction between what we know as Hebrew and Aramaic. In the Hellenistic period, most must have thought the Aramaic they spoke simply a vernacular form of the Hebrew they heard in the synagogue without full understanding; only an occasional rabbi and Jerome understood the true situation.

The fact that all Hebrews speak the same language is taken for granted but not emphasized. Ezekiel (3:5) is told, "You are not sent to a people hard of lip and heavy of tongue, [but] to the house of Israel," even though his message will be more acceptable to foreigners than to Israel. One dialectal difference in the sibilants is noted, between Gileadite "ear of wheat" and Ephraimite (Judg 12:6); modern scholars find others. Moabite and Phoenician inscriptions prove that those languages, along with Hebrew, were closely related dialects of Canaanite and mutually comprehensible. We find little difference between the material cultures of Israel and Phoenicia, so that Phoenicians could transport to Hellas many objects, institutions, and words today only attested from Israel. But the Israelites found a world of difference in cult and manners. (It is unknown how the much broader cults at Elephantine were regarded in Jerusalem.) Commonality of language hardly appears as a definition of what constitutes Israel. When Hebrew was replaced by Aramaic (which had previously supplanted Akkadian in Babylon) at the Exile, with Phoenician succumbing somewhat later, the self-image of the Israelites was, if anything, intensified. For many centuries *no* Jew grew up speaking either Hebrew or Aramaic as his mother tongue. But there never came a time when a speaker of Greek would call a nonspeaker a Hellene.

Thus "Israel" refers to a markedly smaller group than those who spoke the same language: namely, those who in the categories of Herodotus had the same shrine of the same God, with the same sacrifices and customs—all codified in the books of the Law. The name "Israel" reflects the conviction that those commonalities were restricted to clans or families tracing their ancestry (physically or conventionally) to the twelve sons of Jacob/Israel. Herodotus vaguely takes it for granted that the community of those who speak Greek is coterminous with those of common descent; Isocrates sharply defines it that language correctly used *rather than lineage* is what defines a Hellene.

The same contrast defines how the two peoples thought of *outsiders*. While Cretans (themselves mostly Greeks, but marginalized) are distrusted by other Greeks generally as liars, and Cilicians suspected as bloodthirsty, Carians are looked down on as speaking strangely, "Carians speaking barbarously" (*Iliad* 2.867), and therefore a suitable *corpus uile* ("worthless tool") for taking risks with (Cicero, *pro Flacco* 65). Sanskrit *barbara* "non-Aryan" is conventionally taken as the source of *barbaros* with the onomatopoetic connotation "stammering"; but Levin finds it poorly attested and proposes that in fact it is derived *from* the Greek. Hellenes never hold it against "barbarians" that they worship the wrong gods. On the contrary, the gods of foreigners are just the gods of the Hellenes under different names: Babylonian Belos is Zeus (Herodotus 3.158.2), Egyptian Neith is Athena; Aphrodite has different names among Assyrians, Arabs, and Persians (Herodotus 1.131.3). For Hebrews, the error of the goyim is to worship the wrong god in the wrong way. David says to his God (2 Sam 7:23): "And what one nation on earth is like your people, like Israel, whose God[s?] went[23] to redeem them to himself as a people?" Initially Israel and Hellas, through their presumed superiority, respectively, in worship and in language, see themselves as set apart

---

23. The plural verb suggests that the reference is to the gods of another nation: none such went out to create a people. First Chronicles 17:21 simplifies, reading the singular: "a people [Israel] whom God went out to redeem to himself as a people."

from other nations. (But precisely through that superiority they later come to see themselves as having a universal mission with something of infinite value to offer to all.)

Israel as defined by its lineage is much smaller than Hellas as defined by its language. The area of all peoples who spoke dialects of Canaanite (including then Punic of Carthage) is larger than Israel, and more nearly comparable with the area of all who spoke Greek. But there was no common history or cult holding Canaanite speakers together: Egypt and Babylon put down attempted coalitions; there is no record that Carthage brought texts from the homeland. In the Near East, far from imposing their language on neighbors, Canaanites in the north and east kept losing adherents to speakers of Aramaic—which really *was* a missionary language, although likewise without common history or cult. At the earliest point where we can see the spread of Greek speakers, they are held together by the Homeric poems—doubtless earlier by predecessors of those poems, heroic lays about the siege of Troy. And so with cult. Greeks fought with each other as often as neighbors anywhere in the ancient world; but they held the same pantheon of gods, and the festivals of those gods in peacetime were a bond of union. In Canaan, as elsewhere in the Near East (and more conventionally in Homer), the enmities of peoples were symbolized and reinforced by the presumed enmities of their gods.

To determine who their true associates were, Israelites looked back in time, to the genealogy theoretically known through tradition or writing; Greeks looked out in space, to see whom they could understand by virtue of their speaking the same language. Seatrade further naturally gave Greeks a spacious outlook and a familiarity, at least superficial, with foreigners—Carians, Cilicians, Lydians, Libyans, Lycians, as well as Cretans, half-foreigners; Israel knew those as mercenaries serving in their midst, and their land-neighbors mostly as potential rivals in war. Through that trade the Anatolians learned Greek and after Alexander joined the Greek world. Through their relations with Mesopotamia and Egypt, Hebrews felt themselves surrounded by monuments of a distant antiquity, and in their tradition maintained connections (however adversarial) with those remote eras. When Greeks came to see those same monuments, they could only interpret them as *somebody else's* antiquity. The legendary migration of Danaus and his daughters from Egypt, or of Cadmus from Phoenicia, is not thought of as bringing any knowledge of foreign social institutions.

Confluence in the New Testament

The worlds of Israel and Hellas come into full contact with the conquest of the Near East by Alexander when speakers of Aramaic (including now Jews) took on simplified Greek as a second language. Already before Alexander Phoenician Tripolis had its Greek name, and Greek loanwords, *glyphō* ("carve") and *statēr* ("stater"), had infiltrated the Aramaic of Egypt. The Book of Jeremiah (42–44) shows that a substantial Jewish population had made its way into Egypt; along with other nationalities they came to the new city of Alexandria and prospered, and there the Hebrew Bible was translated into Greek, according to the legend of Aristeas by seventy(-two) scholars. A Greek-speaking school of Jewish philosophy grew up, attested by the *Wisdom* ascribed to Solomon, and later by Philo. Perhaps more from Alexandria than Jerusalem, Greek-speaking synagogues grew up around the Mediterranean, wherever Jewish traders or artisans took up residence.

The Book of Acts (however schematic its history), along with the letters of Paul, shows that Christianity spread out from those Hellenistic synagogues before forming its own congregations. An Aramaic-speaking Jewish-Christian church in Palestine maintained a shadowy existence for many decades, but left little record. All the preserved literature of the earliest church is in Greek. Only in Edessa of Syria did Aramaic-speaking Christians form their own church and translate the Greek New Testament into their dialect, Syriac. Not until after Constantine did Aramaic-speaking Christians in Palestine itself produce a translation in *their* dialect, the so-called Palestinian Syriac, now extant except for fragments only in the Gospels. With both, at most some lingering traditions remained of the Aramaic originals of Jesus' sayings. (But the Syriac versions are precious reconstructions of the original, for they were made by men whose native language was Aramaic, living under conditions not all that different from Galilee.)

Hellenistic Judaism died out except so far as its Greek Bible was preserved in the new Christian church; the Greek-speaking synagogues were the seedbed of the church, which, however, became so threatening that they reverted to Hebrew or eventually went out of business. Some texts will document the continuance of Hellenistic synagogues. An inscribed pillar in Greek from Aphrodisias of Asia Minor of the third century C.E.[24] lists a large number of

---

24. Joyce Reynolds and Robert Tannenbaum, *Jews and God-Fearers at Aphrodisias: Greek Inscriptions with Commentary* (CPSS; Cambridge: Cambridge Univ. Press, 1987). Discussion by Louis H. Feldman, *Jew and Gentile in the Ancient World: Attitudes and Interactions from Alexander to Justinian* (Princeton: Princeton Univ. Press, 1993), 362–69.

men with Jewish names and a not much smaller list of men with pagan names introduced by "and all those who were Godfearers." The first nine of the *theosebeis* Godfearers are noted as *boul(eutēs)*—that is, members of the city Senate or of a synagogue organization? We have here the same two categories as those attested at Antioch of Pisidia in varying formulas: "Men of Israel and you who fear God" (Acts 13:16); and "Judeans and devout proselytes" (13:43). So at Athens (17:17) Paul converses in the synagogue with "Judeans and devout ones." An individual is called "one who worships God" (Acts 16:14; 18:7). *Theosebēs* (John 9:31) may reflect the Hellenistic category. Evidently at Aphrodisias a category of *theosebeis* (partial or full converts?) joined Jews in the synagogue, and surely the bulk of the service must have been in Greek with readings from the Greek Bible.[25]

On February 8, 553 C.E., Justinian issued an edict at Constantinople on languages in the synagogue worship and some other topics.[26] The Greek text is the original, the ancient Latin translation is faulty. He has received petitions from one or both parties of those who wish to use Hebrew or Greek in the service. He permits both, and Latin too; he prefers the Septuagint on the grounds that prophecies to the coming Christ appear more clearly in it, but grudgingly permits that of Aquila also. He absolutely forbids use of the *deuterōsis,* which must surely be the Mishnah. Reading between the lines, we may conjecture that Hebrew liturgy along with the Mishnah was winning the day, but that advocates of the Septuagint remained, whom the Emperor supports as far as he can.

We think of the New Testament as the Greek account of a Jewish spiritual movement. But that omits an important factor, by leaving the character of the Greek account undefined. Back to Alexander: How did the Macedonian conceive the idea of a campaign against the Near East? It was already united in the Persian empire: with a few exceptions like Phoenician Tyre, there would be no independent centers of resistance. We said that Hellas (to which we may now add Macedon) was a society just outside the ancient Near East,

25. An inscription of uncertain imperial date from the theater at Miletus (Gabba 33) has "Place of the Jews known as *theosebeis*"—i.e., semi-converts? See Emilio Gabba, *Iscrizioni greche e latine per lo studio della Bibbia* (Sintesi dell'oriente e della Bibbia 3; Turin: Brepol, 1958), 33.

26. *Corpus Juris Civilis, III, Novellae {of Justinian},* ed. R. Schoell and W. Kroll (Berlin: Weidmann, 1895), no. 146, 714–18. Greek text, translation, and discussion in Amnon Linder, *The Jews in Roman Imperial Legislation* (Detroit: Wayne State Univ. Press, 1987), 402–11. See also James Parkes, *The Conflict of the Church and the Synagogue: A Study in the Origins of Antisemitism* (Cleveland: Meridian; Philadelphia: Jewish Publication Society of America, 1961), 251–53.

with its own resources, but on which the Near Eastern empires exercised an ongoing fascination. One of the items in that fascination, it now turns out, was precisely the lure of empire! Athens for a time under Pericles maintained an empire with taxation—but over *poleis* that remained independent. Alexander has been called the last of the Achaemenids; from them he learned the very concept of a world empire. After Alexander's victories and death, Palestine shifted between Ptolemaic and Seleucid control; then, after a brief, heady independence under the Maccabees, it fell under Rome, whether or not it was ruled by nominally autonomous client kings, a Herod or Agrippa in Jerusalem, an Antipas in Galilee. And the Romans in turn had learned how to conduct an empire from their competitors, the Semitic Carthaginians and the Hellenistic kingdoms. Rome also was the student of ancient Near Eastern imperialism, at one more remove.

The courts of the Palestinian client kings, in particular the Herods, intermarrying with other Near Eastern dynastic houses, must have been largely Greek-speaking. Roman administration in the East operated almost exclusively in Greek. Thus Greek was not merely the language of trade and of an upper-class culture in Palestine; above all, it was the language of *imperial control*. The three languages of the lingua franca are mirrored in the three facets of the New Testament: its narrative and spiritual theme is Israelite; its linguistic form and social institutions are Greek; but the political reality it faces is Roman. We may then redefine the confluence of Israel and Hellas in the New Testament. Its founding events exist just inside the ancient Near East, at the heart of old Israel; they are shaped and narrated by the language and spirit of Hellas—but a Hellas that had learned from its stance just outside the Near East what it meant to speak for an empire. In those special senses, its matter is Israelite and its form Hellenic.

We may now look at some features of Christianity in relation to its parents, in the same sequence as above.

Language about God in the New Testament
One thing that sets the New Testament apart from Greek literature—classical, contemporary to it, or subsequent—is its unargued presupposition of a single God. How did the New Testament as a Greek book achieve that certainty? The obvious answer is, From the Greek Bible, the Septuagint. While we can detect several translators at work, each with some peculiarities, their differences do not at all coincide with the great variety of styles in the Hebrew Bible. Hebrew *Esther,* which nowhere mentions the God of Israel or his name, has additions in the Greek that abundantly make up for that defect.

It is in the Septuagint that the conviction of a single God enters the stream of Greek literature.

A belated and partial record of the innovation brought by the Septuagint appears in philosophical writers of the second century C.E. Epictetus (in Arrian 1.3.1–3) found no inconsistency in saying *"God* is the father of men and of *gods,"* and then in going on to assume that one knows himself to be "the son of *Zeus."* For Marcus Aurelius it is the same thing to say "you are arguing with *God,"* and "we were debating with the *gods"* (12.5). Plutarch, in his beautiful essay "On Those Whose Vengeance by *the Divine* Is Delayed" (*Mor.* 548A), can speak (551C) of "the gentleness and magnanimity that *God* displays." I suggest that the alternative of expressing their thought in the "theistic" mode is due to the subterranean influence of Hellenistic Judaism. Epictetus knows that Jews have specific dietary regulations (Arrian 1.11.12–13, 1.22.4); Marcus at least knows of the Jews and finds them unruly (Ammianus 22.5.5); Plutarch (*Quaest. Conviv.* 6.1–2 = *Mor.* 671–72) has a speaker to his own satisfaction prove that the god of the Jews is identical with Dionysus.

Thus the New Testament uses and much extends a language about God already implanted in Greek by the Septuagint, and being adopted by Greek writers of the second century C.E. But it goes beyond both Hebrew austerity and Greek tentativeness in its language about God as Father, concerned for every sparrow and hair, ravens and lilies; it sees a specific new series of events as the work of God in history; in its universality it breaks down all remnants of both Hebrew and Greek ethnocentrism. One factor of its success in the Greco-Roman world was its reinforcement of the optional theism already current there.

Why Is the New Testament Not a Tragedy?
Like the Hebrew Bible, and deriving from it, the New Testament looks back to the remotest origins of humanity. We said that the lack of tragedy in the Israelite world was due to the conviction that the pattern of life chronicled in the Hebrew Bible, and deposited in the Law, was a guarantee for continuance of the family and people that led it. But not continuance of the individual. What would happen if external events blocked the continuance of family and people? Such immortality as the classical Hebrew man knows is derived from the conviction that his sons and their sons have a promised future existence. Any individual life after death was at best ambiguously hinted at in the Psalms. Ezekiel's vision of the valley of dry bones coming to life (37:1-14) is explicitly a symbol of the reviving of the exiled collective people, not of individuals. The conviction of a future continuance was not shaken by the Babylonian exile; it *was*

shaken by the Maccabean martyrs, and at that time a doctrine of the "resurrection" of the dead explicitly appears (Dan 12:2; 2 Macc 12:43-45).

The narrative of the Gospels up until the end reads for all the world like a tragedy. The coming destruction of Jerusalem, which colors all the New Testament through prophetic expectation, perhaps in places through prophecies after the fact, even more than the exile raised doubts about any future continuance of the Jewish people. All along, Greek heroes and ordinary people found only partial comfort in the continuance of their descendants after their own death. The Homeric heroes were more interested in perpetual fame. The prospect of going down to Hades monopolized Greek attention more strongly than Sheol for the Hebrews. And so the lively imagination of the Greeks more strongly than with the Hebrews constructed hopes of blessedness in better lands, first for military heroes, then for the morally virtuous. Perhaps the Hellenization of the Near East then assisted the rabbis in constructing the doctrine of the "raising of the dead" out of the ambiguous hints in the Psalms.

But no historical antecedent explains Paul's confident hope in the reality of Christ's resurrection as a pledge of his own; nor the multiform Gospel narratives of Jesus' resurrection appearances. That conviction was one of two or three features of the new faith that commended it to the masses of the Hellenistic-Roman world, oppressed by the fear of death. What is marginal in Judaism becomes absolutely central in Christianity, based on narratives with no correspondents in Israel.

The last of the thirteen principles of faith of Maimonides, inserted in our prayer books in Hebrew, is that "there will be a raising of the dead at the time when it shall please the Creator." In the formation of American Reform Judaism it was explicitly dropped. The "Pittsburgh Platform" of 1885, the basic statement of Reform from 1889 to 1937, says:

> We reassert the doctrine of Judaism, that the soul of man is immortal, grounding this belief on the divine nature of the human spirit. . . . We reject as ideas not rooted in Judaism the beliefs both in bodily resurrection and in Gehenna and Eden (Hell and Paradise) as abodes for everlasting punishment or reward.[27]

And that high-water mark of liberalism has not been fully reversed.

---

27. *Encyclopaedia Judaica* (Jerusalem: Macmillan, 1971), 13:570–71. Neil Gilman considers that Maimonides in fact found the doctrine of resurrection problematical, and "care[d] desperately that Jews understand the afterlife in terms of spiritual immortality" (*The Death of*

The Nazi Holocaust, the greatest trauma to Israel in all of history, was named *Shoah* after Zeph 1:15: " A day of wrath is that day . . . a day of ruin [*shoah*] and devastation." It drove occasional Jewish thinkers like Richard Rubenstein toward something like atheism:

> When I say we live in the time of the death of God, I mean that the thread uniting God and man, heaven and earth, has been broken. We stand in a cold, silent, unfeeling cosmos, unaided by any purposeful power beyond our own resources. After Auschwitz, what else can a Jew say about God?[28]

But Zephaniah (1:14) still called it "the great day *of Yahweh.*" Rubenstein finds that unacceptable:

> Traditional Jewish theology . . . has interpreted every major catastrophe in Jewish history as God's punishment of a sinful Israel. I fail to see how this position can be maintained without regarding Hitler and the SS as instruments of God's will. . . . The idea is simply too obscene for me to accept.

And still, contemplation of the *Shoah,* which has created overwhelming political support for the state of Israel among Jews both in America and elsewhere, has not created an overwhelming agreed conviction of the resurrection among them. Perhaps this "Sadducean" tendency (Mark 12:18) comes from a feeling that Christianity has preempted the doctrine.

Thus, without intending it, modern Hebrew has found the name of what English calls the "Holocaust" (itself a word with endless overtones) in the text that above all for the Christian West evokes the death of the individual and of the creation. The sequence *Dies Irae (Wrath of God)* is anonymous; its popular attribution to Thomas of Celano rests on no specific evidence. It first appears in manuscripts of 1255, and was adopted in the Tridentine Missal for a requiem mass. The haunting melody, uniquely for Gregorian, infiltrates modern compositions since the *Symphonie Fantastique* of Berlioz. The author

---

Death: Resurrection and Immortality in Jewish Thought [Woodstock, Vt.: Jewish Lights, 1997], 154). Gilman further chronicles the substantial replacement of resurrection by immortality in both the Reform and Conservative wings of American Judaism.

28. Richard L. Rubenstein, *After Auschwitz: Radical Theology and Contemporary Judaism* (Indianapolis: Bobbs-Merrill, 1966), 152–53. This is the original edition; later ones somewhat soften the thought.

appears to be using Augustine *de civ. Dei (City of God)* 18.23 or some such source for the Sibylline verses:

> Dies irae dies illa
> Soluet saeclum in fauilla
> Teste Dauid cum Sibylla.

Membership: Why Did Christianity Succeed?

Why did Christianity catch on so widely in the Roman world—and beyond—when the Greek language and the Jewish synagogue as such did not? (Below we discuss how one component of Hellenism, reason and logic, has seemingly caught on universally, outdoing all competitors.) Its success can in large part be laid simply to the fact that it does not need to recognize the existence of any outsiders. In both Hellas and Israel, the old rejection of the foreigner, barbarians or goyim, was replaced by a new conviction that one's own culture contained a precious novelty that deserved to be made available to all peoples. But Hellas and Israel were never able to make that gift unconditional: the Greeks could not separate it from their language, the Hebrews from their ancestry. In the New Testament with its new universal appeal, both blockages were overcome.

The simplicity of New Testament Greek gave it a special translatability, so that the new community was not restricted to any *language*; the abandonment of circumcision removed the restriction to any *lineage*. Christianity can be seen as the creation of a new family, in principle universal: "Behold my mother and my brothers!" (Mark 3:34). A conscious decision to join (risky in the first centuries) must be made; but the act of entrance by baptism was non-threatening, the door was kept open for all. The preexisting harmony between Hellenic and Hebraic cultures analyzed here explains in part why the new church found footing throughout the Greco-Roman world—and to its Bible added superstructures of Greek philosophy and Roman law.

Literary Canons, Closed and Open

Primarily we know the two peoples through their texts—Hellas secondarily through its art and architecture. During the long centuries when the texts were preserved by rabbinic and Byzantine scribes, their status differed somewhat: among Jews the canon is seen as the charter of an ongoing community; in the Greek world, the texts are studied for their own sake, in tension with the new Christian books. In both worlds, the texts become the subject of a large exegetical literature. Elsewhere I have compared Hebrew and Greek texts in several characteristics: their continuity of preservation, their phonetic script, their origin from a whole people, their theism and humanism, their exemplary character and originality. Those mark the common status of the texts as recording, and constituting, a new emergent of self-knowledge and freedom in sister societies. But the two bodies of texts have obvious differences also.

Hebrew literature is a sharply defined canon of twenty-four books (five of law, four each of Former and Latter Prophets, eleven of writings). One can read it through in translation in a few weeks—though not exhaust it in a lifetime. Greek literature is a much larger body of verse and prose, which only the brazen-gutted can work through; Egyptian papyri (many literary) and inscriptions put it beyond any individual's scope. What accounts for the difference? In part the small size of Israel over against Hellas, due to its more rigid self-definition, in part technical features of Hebrew composition and deficiencies of its script. But these also can be attributed to its being inside the ancient Near East, and to the restricted realms in which it was able to manage a clean breakout.

Scattered evidence suggests that Hebrew literature was once somewhat more extensive than now. The compilers of the history in a few places quote from a collection of verse. From the "Book of the Upright" comes David's lament over Saul and Jonathan (2 Sam 1:19-27); Joshua's couplet on the arrest of sun and moon (Josh 10:12-13, where, however, the LXX omits the attribution); and the verse of Solomon on the completion of the Temple (1 Kgs 8:12-13, attributed at 8:53a LXX to some book).[29] From "the Book of the Wars of Yahweh" comes the geographical note at Num 21:14. Kings and Chronicles (with Neh 12:23) often cite other chronicles variously titled.[30] Still, the rabbis who discussed the status of the twenty-four books found no competitors; rather, they raised doubts about some of the writings. At most, the canonical books existed in variant forms, as witnessed by the changed order of materials in the LXX of 2 Kings, Jeremiah, and Proverbs. (But the Qumran manuscript of Jeremiah 4Q72 seems to follow the Masoretic order.)

29. The LXX attributes it to "The Book of the Song."

30. But the "Book of the Chronicles of the Kings of Media and Persia" at Esther 10:2 may be a mere invention. For after the Daiva inscription of Xerxes, the cuneiform record of later kings markedly deteriorates. We have no evidence that specifically Aramaic chronicles existed, and it is not easy to imagine how the author of Esther would have gotten hold of such.

The classical passage is *m. Yadayim* 3.5, "All the sacred Writings render the hands unclean." The only doubts were whether the Song of Songs and Qoheleth were sacred writings. Rabbi 'Aqiba summed up what became the ruling, "All the writings are holy, but the Song of Songs is the Holy of Holies." Rab Judah said in the name of Samuel, "[The scroll of] Esther does not render the hands unclean" (*b. Megillah* 7a); paraphrasing, the editor asks incredulously whether Samuel truly believed that Esther "was not spoken through the Holy Spirit." In the end all preserved books ended up on nearly the same level.

The manuscripts from Qumran provide fragments of Aramaic Tobit; Aramaic *Enoch*; Hebrew *Jubilees*; and perhaps the *Testaments of the Twelve Patriarchs*. The Manual of Discipline, War Scroll, and Psalms from Qumran are compositions of the sect itself. All these materials are in a wholly other—I will say *inferior*—realm beside the Hebrew Bible. The Book of Sirach occupies a middle ground. The endless rabbinic literature—even including its crown jewel, the tractate *Avoth* of the Mishnah—purports to be commentary rather than supplement to the Hebrew Bible, although the careful reader finds important advances, as in the doctrine of the "raising of the dead."

The Greek books best attested in manuscripts either imposed themselves on the whole people or were chosen out by *grammatikoi* for preservation as models of their kind. These are more than what we mean by "grammarians": they did declamations themselves (Polybius 32.2.5); they were previously called *kritikoi* (Dio Chrysostom 53.1). Aristophanes "the grammarian" arranged the dialogues of Plato in trilogies (Diogenes Laertius 3.61); Aristarchus, the great Homeric critic, is called *grammatikōtatos* (Athenaeus 15.672A). Other books came through dark ages in a few manuscripts or a single one; fragments of many others are preserved in the sands of Egypt. While the library at Alexandria contained far more works than we possess, popular taste and the grammarians certainly retained a selection well above the average. All evidence indicates that the lost epics stood on a far lower level than the *Iliad* and *Odyssey*. Already Solon, it was said (Diogenes Laertius 1.57), decreed that the Homeric poems should be recited in some fixed order.

The criterion for choosing the dramas to be preserved is uncertain: literary excellence? suitability for teaching beginners? grammatical interest? Probably not suitability for performance; the Hellenistic and Roman periods mostly put on their own plays. The entire corpus of tragedy made its way safely to Alexandria. Lycurgus sponsored a law that the tragedies of Aeschylus, Sophocles, and Euripides "should be written out and preserved in a public place," and that the "city scribe" should rehearse the actors from those copies.[31] Ptolemy II Philadelphus of Egypt put down a deposit of fifteen talents of silver to borrow the originals from Athens for copying; but when he got them, he sent copies back to Athens and kept the originals, forfeiting the fifteen talents.[32] The time and place are unknown at which were made the selections from the corpus that have come down to us.

The grammarians had some historical interest, for they preserved a sequence of historians: Herodotus, Thucydides, Xenophon, Arrian, Polybius. In that respect they were like the makers of the Hebrew Bible, who forcibly shaped available materials into a single narrative from the beginning to the exile—and then abbreviated it from a new point of view in Chronicles, with a later appendix in Ezra and Nehemiah. The Greek historians lent themselves to that treatment, in that Thucydides consciously sets himself up as a successor to Herodotus, and Xenophon to Thucydides. Either grammarians or philosophers determined that Plato and Aristotle needed to be read; we admire their choice, much as we would like to have more writings of the Presocratics and Stoics. But because several different criteria were operative, many minor works came through also.

The whole enterprise of classical studies would be different if the holdings of the library of Alexandria had been preserved entire or in part.[33] It would be more like the study of medieval or modern literature, where nobody can read everything, and both casual readers and scholars must rely initially on other people's judgment. Perhaps Greek literature would be *less* influential than now, since even its best works would seem more optional. But that imaginary contrast mirrors the actual relation of our present "canon" of Greek literature to the Hebrew Bible. For Jews, Christians, and ordinary readers alike, the limitations of the Hebrew Bible make each book precious in a special way, over against the chaotic spread of even the Greek literature we do possess. If instead of our thirty-two Greek tragedies we had just the *Oedipus Rex* and thirty-two Hebrew works like Job (if indeed such ever existed), the *Oedipus* would take on an even more absolute character, and we would find limitations in Job now invisible. The Hebrew Bible (and after it the New Testament) is

31. *Lives of the Orators,* preserved in the appendix to Plutarch, *Moralia* 841E.

32. Surprisingly recorded by Galen in his commentary on the *Epidemics* of Hippocrates, Kühn xvii.1.607.

33. It is unclear how long any particular collections of the library were preserved. Already in Caesar's siege of Alexandria in 48 B.C.E. some of the library at least was burned (Plutarch, *Caesar* 49.3; Dio Cassius 42.38.2); under Aurelian, 272 C.E., the library of the Bruchion was in large part destroyed (Ammianus 22.16.13–15).

comparatively so short and imposing that, even outside the communities where it is heard in a special sense as Revelation, it is taken in utmost seriousness as an object with no obvious parallel.

But this does not yet explain why the Greek canon was so much bigger than the Hebrew one in the first place. In part it is because the community of those who spoke Greek—from Massilia to Cyprus, from the Black Sea to Libya—was much bigger than the twelve tribes of Israel, or even than all those (including Carthaginians) who spoke a dialect of Canaanite. But it also has to do with differences between the Greek and Hebrew languages, and between the alphabetic scripts in which they were respectively expressed.

Memorizability of Languages

Greek verse is much more memorizable than Hebrew. Elsewhere I have insisted that equally in Israel and Hellas all "literary" compositions existed primarily as oral performances. But long Greek compositions were easier to get by heart. Ion the rhapsode had *Iliad* and *Odyssey* by heart (Plato *Ion* 530B); in a few months a bright American twelve-year-old learned to recite *Iliad* 1.1–52 with good conventional pronunciation and moderate understanding. The reason is that Greek is fully syllabic, and in hexameter (as in iambic) it has a form of verse where varying syllabic patterns are controlled by an overall fixed structure. Unlike the Sapphic stanza, paralleled in Sanskrit, dactylic hexameter has no Indo-European parallels. But the obscure words in hexameter, besides metrical anomalies only explained by an older form of the language, show that it had a long previous history in Greek and in the Aegean.

In contrast, the Hebrew short indistinct vowel *(shewa)* prevents any syllabic analysis. (Syriac verse, which had the same problem, is supposed to have a syllabic pattern, but it is surely on a Greek model.) Hebrew verse is thought accentual, with patterns such as 3:3, 2:2, and (in the *qinah* or lament) 3:2; but poetical books vary greatly in the accuracy of the accentual count, with Psalms among the most irregular. A rare syllabic approximation to the Greek pattern will point up the differences. "He who sheds the blood of man, by man shall his blood be shed" (Gen 9:6):

šofek dam ha'adam || ba'adam damô yiššafek

has an elegant ABC:CBA pattern with B and C rhyming, and (by chance or intention?) all full vowels. Its 6:8 pattern of syllables is occasionally found in hexameter: see Hesiod *Opera* 348: "Not even an ox would die, if it were not for a bad neighbor."[34] The Hebrew line is easily memorizable, but isolated. It has no distinction of long and short syllables; and no vowel harmony, for of its fourteen vowels, eight are identical, the *qames*. The Greek line is not especially musical, but of its fourteen vowels, there are seven different, and the commonest, *a* and *ei,* only occur three times each. The metrical pattern is commoner in Latin.

> Happy was he who could learn the causes of things.
> *fē´līx | quī´ potu-|ít || rē-|rúm cog-|nóscere | caúsās* (Vergil *Georgica* 2.490)

where further each of the six vowels under the ictus is different.

Hebrew texts, both prose and verse, were undoubtedly recited orally each in its appropriate context. But in contrast to Greek, both prose and verse are broken up into short sections, memorizable by diligence rather than by internal cues. In the narrative of Jeremiah 36, for a longer recitation, particularly with a mixture of prose and verse, a scroll was essential as *aide-mémoire,* an aid to memory. Alma-Tadema's notorious *A Recitation from Homer,*[35] besides other anachronisms (square Roman columns, doubled roses, public affection to a young *lady*), has the reciter use a scroll, which would have mortified Ion.

Superiority of Greek Script

Likewise differences in alphabetic scripts blocked large-scale composition in Hebrew but encouraged it in Greek. The deciding element is the appearance of the vowels in Greek script, derived in part from the vocalic offglides in Semitic script (that is, diphthongs in -*y* and -*w*) but entered with full consistency. Several features of the Hebrew language as the Masoretes heard it made any simple marking of its vowels impractical. Classical Arabic (and in part Ugaritic) marks only three vowels *aiu,* with a further notation in Arabic for long vowels. The vowel system of Phoenician is unknown. But Hebrew has seven vowel qualities (further modified by offglides), of which three also come short, in addition to the vocalic *shewa*. In the inflection of nouns and verbs, the vowels shift in complex patterns; the numerous variants show that oral usage fluctuated. It might have happened that the original writing system included vowels by imposing an artificial unity. It did not. From

---

34. West explains, "Friendly neighbors would often be able to prevent the loss of the animal by their own intervention or by timely warning."

35. Lawrence Alma-Tadema, *A Recitation from Homer* (Philadelphia: Philadelphia Museum of Art, 1885).

Phoenician or some predecessor Canaanite dialect, Hebrew, like Aramaic, adopted the twenty-two-letter alphabet of consonants only, which, unlike the vowels, were extremely stable. The frication of single stops after a vowel, although surely an old feature of the Hebrew dialect, did not block recognition of the stop and the fricative as to be represented by the same letter. In Israel pressure for innovation had to be selective. Where the society could get by with what it found around it, it kept things unchanged; as with kingship and the sacrificing priesthood, so with the alphabet.

As a result, only simple Hebrew texts could be read aloud from a previously unseen document.[36] Our Phoenician inscriptions, which modern scholars believe we mostly understand, were perhaps intended as simple texts. But Ugaritic verse, comparable to Hebrew, must conceal many subtleties forever lost for its want of vowels. If the Book of Job had been transmitted without vowels, nobody could understand it even so far as we do today, nor read it out aloud. As a result, as Levin has shown, each book of the Hebrew Bible required for its preservation—that is, for its ongoing oral recitation—a *double tradition:* the written text that reminded the reciter of the unpredictable materials coming next; and an oral tradition of the pronunciation, above all of the vowels.

Hebrew society was a small one, with limited specialization of function. Each division of our Hebrew Bible was the property of one group in society: the books of the Law, probably of the priests; the Former Prophets, perhaps of court historians; the three major prophets, each of a group of disciples like Jeremiah's Baruch; Proverbs (I have suggested) of a banker class; Psalms of some Temple functionaries. But most of the groups were not full-time scribes or grammarians. Each had the double task of safeguarding the written text of their book, and of teaching young men to pronounce it exactly according to the received tradition. The total of twenty-four books must then represent about the maximum that Israelite society could find custodians for. When a new composition like the Book of Job came on the scene, it must either be rejected or completely assimilated.

The contrast with Greek compositions is then clear. The very earliest Greek scrolls, it is true, were not all that easy to read from either. The lines may have been "as an ox plows a field" *(boustrophēdon),* the first beginning at the right, the second at the left, and so on; there were no word divisions, the lines of verse were probably unmarked. West in his *Works and Days* (p. 60)

36. See the English version of Saul Levin's fundamental article, "The 'Qeri' as the Primary Text of the Hebrew Bible," *General Linguistics* 35 (1997) 181–223, ed. J. P. Brown (Levin Festschrift).

creates a sample of what its first text may have looked like.[37] But the indispensable phonetic feature of the vowels was present. A reciter, faced with such a scroll even of an unfamiliar text, had two sets of data previously internalized: the patterns of the hexameter, and the two or three possible accentuations of a word with known letters. After having heard the *Works and Days* or a book of Homer a few times, he would have the sounds recalled to his mind by the written text, since most of its phonetic features were represented there somehow. The most important function of the written text was as a corrective of creative or unintentional oral changes. The prose of Herodotus or Thucydides would seem a tougher nut to crack. But long prose texts, written later, must have been set out more clearly; and their transmission by itself shows that their script was lucid enough for the reader—people read aloud even to themselves—to proceed through the text at normal speed, and provide it with the proper word divisions and accents. The particles marked the pauses—they were put into the original oral text for precisely that purpose.

Thus the character of the Hebrew canon was the product of several factors all working in the same direction. Its mandatory character was in part the result of its small size. Its small size was due to (1) the small size of the community that preserved it; (2) the resistance of Hebrew texts to memorization; (3) the defects of the writing system, which required a separate dual tradition of each preserved work. Likewise in reverse for the Greek "canon." Its more nearly optional character was in part the result of its large size. Its large size was due to (1) the widespread geographical spread of its writers and custodians; (2) the memorizability of Greek verse; (3) the merit of the writing system, which did not require prior hearing to the comprehension of a written verse or prose text.

The Canon of the New Testament

The New Testament, although written in Greek, looks more like a compact Hebrew compilation than an expansive Greek one. But soon enough, in the Greek, Latin, and Syriac churches, a very copious literature sprang up, larger than the preserved body of pagan Greek and Latin literature, perhaps also than the rabbinic. In the judgment of its own authors, as in the judgment of their contemporaries and of moderns, this enterprise is commentary on an original that infinitely surpasses them. Augustine's *Confessions* stands by itself for many centuries as a book running parallel to the New Testament with a narrative of experience. Although the defects of the Hebrew writing system

---

37. But Levin thinks the early poetic scrolls were already easier to read than this.

no longer blocked the production of the earliest Christian literature, the mere fact of the limited Hebrew canon seemingly operated to keep the New Testament down to size. Further, it came from a small community with not many natural writers in a very few generations.

The formation of the New Testament canon generated what today we *mean* by a "book": the codex. Perhaps at first each book of the New Testament was written on a scroll—smaller than the scrolls of the twenty-four books of the Hebrew Bible, as befitted a community on the road. But the first witnesses to the New Testament text, the papyri from Egypt, are written in a new format, the codex—the form of our printed books today—which then spread to all Greek and Latin books, and eventually most Jewish ones also.[38] From Christians or Muslims the Masoretes took the idea of a non-sacred codex to record their pronunciation of the text, while scrolls of the Torah went on containing just the sacred consonants. Levin explains the advantages of the codex in the new situation:

> For many generations the leading Christians were chiefly adult converts from pagan worship. That circumstance disposed them all the more to a book form that made the entire text quickly accessible. . . . In exegetical works above all, where they were commenting on a given holy book, they needed other relevant passages to prove or confirm their point.[39]

Roberts and Skeat, while doubting this argument, provide additional support for it (p. 50): "One thinks of Augustine in the famous 'Tolle, lege' episode [*Conf.* 8.(12).28], when he kept a finger in the codex of the Pauline Epistles to mark the place of the providential passage he had found." And so Augustine (*Conf.* 4.[3.]5): "When by chance one consults the *pages* of a certain poet." For any church use—the gospel locally received, Paul's letters—there was pressure to have a single codex.

In two respects, then, the New Testament *reflects* its Palestinian setting: in spite of all appearances it turns out to be a non-tragedy like the Hebrew Bible; it likewise has a small closed canon. In two respects it *breaks* with both Israel and Hellas: in principle it has no need for a definition of insiders, and therefore ultimately no need for a definition of outsiders; its enlarged lan-

38. Colin H. Roberts and T. C. Skeat, *The Birth of the Codex* (London: British Academy, 1983), 38–41. They list eleven Christian biblical papyrus manuscripts that they judge to be of the second century C.E.; all are in codex form.

39. Saul Levin, "From Scrolls to Codex: The Ancient and the Medieval Book," *Mediaevalia* 12 (1989 [for 1986]) 1–12, esp. 4.

guage about God goes beyond both. Its use of the Greek language reflects a later development in Hellas: not just as the common tongue of the Greek city-states, but the new function of Greek as the instrument of imperialism, first of Macedon, then of Alexander's successors, then finally of Rome.

Translatability of Hebrew and Greek Texts

What does it say about a text in one language that its key features are translatable into another—easily? with difficulty? hardly at all? I have heard that the Russian of Tolstoy and Dostoyevsky is not so essential as to render the English versions seriously defective; certainly the story line comes through with abundant clarity. It might seem that the elegant linguistic structure of Shakespeare renders him less translatable. But the German version of August Wilhelm von Schlegel and Ludwig Tieck (1796–1833) has so won the day that Germans tend to think of Shakespeare as a poet of their own language! For one thing, all agree in the supremacy and variety of his characterization, which no translation can spoil. But further, this is also because "die Stammes-verwandtschaft des deutschen und englischen Idioms mächtig zu Hilfe kam"[40] ("The historical connection between German and English idiom helped a great deal [in the translation]").

> And like the baseless fabricke of this vision
> The Clowd-capt Towres, the gorgeous Pallaces,
> The solemne Temples, the great Globe it selfe,
> Yea, all which it inherit, shall dissolue,
> And like this insubstantiall Pageant faded
> Leaue not a rack behinde: we are such stuffe
> As dreames are made on; and our little life
> Is rounded with a sleepe. . . . (*Tempest* IV.i Folio)

Schlegel:

> Wie dieses Scheines lockrer Bau, so werden
> Die wolkenhohen Türme, die Paläste,
> Die hehren Tempel, selbst der grosse Ball,
> Ja, was daran nur teil hat, untergehn;
> Und, wie dies leere Schaugepräng' erblasst,

---

40. Wilhelm Dechelhäufer, *W. Shakespeare's dramatische Werke,* übersetzt von August Wilhelm von Schlegel und Ludwig Tieck, 13th ed. (Stuttgart: Deutsche Verlags-Anstalt; ca. 1891), xi.

> Spurlos verschwinden. Wir sind solcher Zeug
> Wie der zu Träumen, und dies kleine Leben
> Umfasst ein Schlaf. . . .

The two metrics run parallel, with an extra syllable at the end where the vocabulary warrants it. The most conspicuous loss is the Latinism *insubstantiall,* which German has no good parallel for. On the same grounds, both Greek prose and verse ought to have been quite translatable into Latin. And in fact, the meters of verse were taken over and, if anything, improved; but Roman writers and poets set themselves other tasks than the translation of Greek.

For the Greek church of the East, the Bible is the Septuagint plus the Greek New Testament, in uneasy coexistence with the texts of pagan Hellas. For the Latin church of the West, the Bible is Jerome's Vulgate, in uneasy coexistence with the texts of pagan Rome. Jerome's Old Testament is a more adequate and nobler version than the Septuagint; his Gospels often unconsciously restore the lapidary brevity of the underlying Aramaic. In both Testaments his excellence springs from his guilty knowledge of the Latin classics.

Greek texts were never fully translated into Latin: the Western Middle Ages knew Aristotle best. The key event was the capture of Constantinople by French and Venetian crusaders in 1204 C.E. It appears that from there Greek manuscripts were brought west as far as to England. The victors set up Latin principalities in Hellas and appointed their own bishops there, and the land was opened to Western scholars. The Britisher John Basingstoke took lessons in Athens from one Constantina, to whom remarkable psychic powers were attributed, daughter of an archbishop of Athens. On his return he translated a Greek grammar into Latin (*Donatus Graecorum,* not extant?); in 1235 he was Archdeacon of Leicester and a friend of Robert Grosseteste, bishop of Lincoln, who probably learned Greek from him.[41] From some such underground source the Fleming William of Moerboke also learned Greek, became the pope's contact with the Eastern church, and at the end of his life (ab. 1278–86) was the Latin archbishop of Corinth.[42]

The *Nicomachean Ethics* of Aristotle were first completely translated by Grosseteste about 1245; the *Politics* by Moerboke (who had previously trans-

41. *Dictionary of National Biography* (Oxford: Oxford Univ. Press, 1917), 1:1274–75.
42. L. Minio-Paluello, s.v. "Moerbeke, William of," in *Dictionary of Scientific Biography* (New York: Scribner's, 1974), 9:434–40.

lated most of Aristotle's works on logic) about 1260. There is a large manuscript tradition of these medieval translations. When Thomas Aquinas quotes rather than paraphrases Aristotle we can mostly pinpoint the version. Thus he quotes[43] the *Eth. Nic.* 1132a22 as *iudex est iustum animatum*; "for the judge wishes to be as it were living justice," where Grosseteste[44] *iudex enim vult esse velud iustum animatum*. Elsewhere[45] he quotes *Pol.* 1252b28 as *perfecta enim communitas civitas est*; "the perfect partnership composed of several villages is the polis," where already the imperfect translation attributed to Moerboke has *ex pluribus vicis communitas perfecta civitas.*[46] When the Clerk of Oxenford has

> Twenty bookes, clad in blak or reed,
> Of Aristotle and his philosophie

these are expensive bound Latin manuscripts of Moerboke's versions, for the subject is *logyk*.

In the three hundred years after Grosseteste and Moerboke, Greek achieved an overwhelming role in education. Roger Ascham was tutor to princess Elizabeth (born 1533) as a teenager from 1550–52; and speaks of her later:

> . . . Our most noble Queen Elizabeth, who never took yet Greek nor Latin grammar in her hand, after the first declining of a noun and a verb; but only by this double translating [to English and back again] of Demosthenes and Isocrates daily, without missing every forenoon, and likewise some part of Tully [Cicero] every afternoon, for the space of a year or two, hath attained to such a perfect understanding in both the tongues, and to such a ready utterance of the Latin, and that with such a judgment, as they be few in number in both the universities, or elsewhere in England, that be in both tongues comparable with her majesty.[47]

43. *Summa Theol.* Secunda Secundae, quaest. 58, art. 1 ad quintum.

44. *Aristoteles Latinus* xxvi.1—3.3 p. 234.

45. *Summa Theol.* Prima Secundae, quaest. 90, art. 2 ad finem.

46. *Aristoteles Latinus* xxix.1 p. 5. The full Latin translation of the *Politics,* unquestionably done by William of Moerboke, is critically edited from the manuscripts by F. Susemihl parallel to the Greek in his major edition, *Aristotelis Politicorum Libri Octo cum uetusta translatione Guilelmi de Moerbeka* (Leipzig: Teubner, 1872). For the translation is so exact that the readings of the underlying Greek manuscript are mostly discernible—an excellent witness, several centuries older than our extant manuscripts.

47. In his *Schoolmaster,* ed. Giles, *Whole Works* (London, 1864), 3:180 (repr. New York: AMS, 1965).

(But Ascham might not have reported it if the princess ever sulked, or played hooky, or muffed a translation.) He runs through her praises at the time in a letter to Sturm, April 4, 1550 (Old Style),[48] in which he speaks of her *ingenium sine muliebri mollitia, labor cum virili constantia* ("talent without feminine softness, labor with masculine firmness"); and adds that the morning began with the New Testament and included Sophocles.

For an age when both Hebrew and Greek texts were translated into a vernacular we go to that same sixteenth century. In the later Middle Ages there was a thin stream of knowledge of Hebrew, mostly derived from Jewish converts; it was much augmented when the Jews were expelled from Spain, 1492. Northern Europe is the key; for there the Latin Vulgate is rejected in favor of new translations, which, above all in England and Germany, formed the basis of a renewed vernacular literature. The rediscovery of the Bible in the Protestant Reformation of northern Europe comes nearly at the same time as the Italian Renaissance of classical, and in particular Greek, learning.

Luther's German New Testament was published in 1522 and his complete Bible in 1534. Parts of William Tyndale's Old Testament (with some use at least of the Hebrew) were published in 1530 and 1537, parts copied by Myles Coverdale in 1535. Genesis 3 in Tyndale's version will show how it set the standard for all that followed:

> But the serpent was sotyller than all the beastes of the felde which ẙ LORDE God had made / and sayd unto the woman, Ah syr [!] / that God hath sayd / ye shall not eate of all manner trees in the garden. And the woman sayd unto the serpent / of the frute of the trees in the garden we may eate / but of the frute of the tree ẙ is in the myddes of the garden (sayd God) se that ye eate not / and se that ye touch it not: lest ye dye.[49]

The successive versions won the heart of English-speaking people, both as the newly provided text of the religion they had long professed, and as the standard of their own language.

The Gospels and the Revelation of John, as sharing the Semitic substructure of the Hebrew Bible, found equal resonance in English; Acts as a flowing narrative presented little difficulty either. Paul's letters and especially Romans, in spite of Luther's championing of them, are true Greek texts and

---

48. Giles, *Whole Works,* 1:191.

49. David Daniell, ed., *Tyndale's Old Testament . . . in a Modern-Spelling Edition* (New Haven: Yale Univ. Press, 1992); I restore Tyndale's spelling from Daniell's plate of the Pentateuch of 1530.

difficult ones at that, and in many versions come out crabbed. A few classical Greek *prose* texts found adequate translations at nearly the same time as the English Bible and remained influential. North's Plutarch (1579, secondhand from a French version) underlies Shakespeare's *Julius Caesar* and *Antony and Cleopatra* and contributes much to their elegance. Sometimes the poet had nothing to do but an easy versification:

> Furthermore, there was a certaine Soothsayer that had geven Caesar warning long time affore, to take heede of the day of the Ides of Marche, (which is the fifteenth of the moneth) for on that day he shoulde be in great daunger. That day being come, Caesar going unto the Senate house, and speaking merily to the Soothsayer, tolde him, The Ides of Marche be come: So be they, softly aunswered the Soothsayer, but yet are they not past.

Thomas Hobbes published his translation of Thucydides in 1629; he found much in the Greek (we may assume) that he already believed, and took more from it. A recent study finds Thucydides deeper than his translator:

> Is it realistic [with Hobbes] to assume that all people act predictably, that they are always guided strictly by self-interest, that all other motivations are a sham—or, if genuine, so rare that to take them into account is useless? . . . According to Thucydides, human beings are multifaceted, so that it becomes necessary, for example, to examine individual leaders and to listen seriously to their reasons for acting a certain way.[50]

But Hobbes so resonated with the historian that his interpretations continue to hold the field. See Hobbes's manly version of the Melian Dialogue (5.105.1):

> For of the gods we think according to the common opinion; and of men, that for certain by necessity of nature they will every where reign over such as they are too strong for. Neither did we make this law, nor are we the first that use it made: but as we found it, and shall leave it to posterity for ever, so also we use it: knowing that you likewise, and others that should have the same power which we have, would do the same.

---

50. Laurie M. Johnson, *Thucydides, Hobbes, and the Interpretation of Realism* (De Kalb: Northern Illinois Univ. Press, 1993), 201–3.

In English (I cannot speak for German) the translations of Greek *verse* accentuate the peculiarities and faults of each age. Chapman's *Iliad* (1616), which Keats found a "pure serene," for us is Elizabethan bombast with its seven-beat lines and rhyme:

> Achilles' banefull wrath resound, O Goddesse, that imposd
> Infinite sorrowes on the Greekes, and many brave soules losd
> From breasts Heroique—sent them farre, to that invisible cave
> That no light comforts; and their lims to dogs and vultures gave.

Here "resound" replaces *aeide* ("sing"), "breasts" is padding, *Aidi* gets a popular (but uncertain) etymology, and "lims" replaces "themselves" *(autous)*. Pope's version (1715) is hardly a translation, but a whole new construction of images, built distantly on the Greek narrative: "It is a pretty poem, Mr Pope, but you must not call it Homer."[51]

> Achilles' wrath, to Greece the direful spring
> Of woes unnumber'd, heav'nly Goddess, sing!
> That wrath which hurl'd to Pluto's gloomy reign
> The souls of mighty chiefs untimely slain:
> Whose limbs, unburied on the naked shore,
> Devouring dogs and hungry vultures tore. . . .

"Limbs" and "vultures" show that Pope had Chapman before him. Homer is read today through translations that are at least accurate, line by line, and idiomatic, like Richmond Lattimore's (1951), but hardly memorizable:

> Sing, goddess, the anger of Peleus' son Achilleus
> and its devastation, which put pains thousandfold upon the Achaians,
> hurled in their multitudes to the house of Hades strong souls
> of heroes, but gave their bodies to be the delicate feasting
> of dogs, of all birds. . . .

But here *hurled* still reflects Pope.

English versions of tragedy in the late eighteenth and nineteenth centuries are even more precious and mannered than of epic, today even less singable or

51. Richard Bentley, in Samuel Johnson's *Life* of Pope.

memorizable.[52] Still, only in the twentieth century did educators feel obliged to make Greek books widely available to the cultivated reader, whereas in the sixteenth century there was a growing cry for Hebrew books (along with the Greek New Testament) to be accessible to men, women, and children in the pews. And it is intrinsically harder to spoil Hebrew than Greek. To our ears the Septuagint did its best to spoil Hebrew, but the New Testament writers—all steeped in the Septuagint—turned it into a people's mode of expression. Modern versions of the English Bible have successively watered down the elevation of the Authorized Version, and the vogue of inclusiveness has rejected the goal of accuracy that originally motivated the new translations. Greek epic and tragedy until recently brought out the worst instincts of translators; today, only their incapacities. The structure of Hebrew narrative comes from the unavoidable sequence of events; Greek adds antitheses and (in epic) the verse pattern. My own translations in this volume follow the least objectionable patterns available, and strive for nothing more than a mediocre accuracy.

What does this tell us about Hebrew and Greek texts in the worlds of their origination? The only narratives in Ugaritic are mythical verse; Hebrews surely rejected any models they might have found in Akkadian literature. If we imagine Hebrew narrative coming out of hill villages remote from Canaanite cultural influence, we can only conclude that isolation and a dawning sense of freedom brought into being a wholly new level of transcription for popular stories and sagas. The figures of Hebrew narrative are archetypes we instantly recognize: apart from a few abstract terms of psychology or ethics, the vocabulary is of concrete nouns and verbs whose translation into other languages is as near as possible automatic. The Greek of the New Testament narratives, in view of its Semitic background, has many of the same features. Only at the end of a long Greek prose development did Plutarch approach a comparable level of simplicity. The excellence of Hobbes's Thucydides is a shining exception.

Besides its built-in difficulty, Greek verse had complex antecedents. Behind the Homeric epics we can discern a background of shorter lays in somewhat different dialects, but in the same old metrical form, though not as such known elsewhere in Indo-European. The elaborate structure of Greek drama, both tragic and comic, with its variety of meters, dialects, and styles, requires an extensive prior history. In Hebrew, lack of defined syllables,

52. See T. S. Eliot's critique of translations in "Euripides and Professor Murray," in idem, *Selected Essays 1917–1932* (New York: Harcourt Brace, 1932), 46–50.

meter, vowel harmony as vehicle of expression means that *less is lost* in translation (for there is less to be lost). Likewise, the New Testament is eminently translatable for the same reason as Plutarch. This does not mean that the Hebrew Bible is less deep or universal than Greek works, just that it has fewer secrets. (But I should add that there are many more Hebrew phrases we simply do not understand, for want of parallels.) Thus a paradox: the clannish and isolated Hebrews produced a more generally accessible work than the outgoing Greeks! Hebrew verse texts, though less memorizable than Greek, are more translatable.

But it is not the sole (though the final) task of literature to show what humanity may become; a necessary preliminary task is to define also what humanity is. While people in readiness to hear the biblical texts hear them correctly, and pattern their lives according to them, people not so ready, or with distorted psyches, hear them incorrectly and do much damage. Indispensable to undoing the damage is the laborious work of scholarship, trained (normally) on other texts, classical or indigenous. So a further item in the complementarity is the relative accessibility (in translation) of the books of Israel (including the New Testament), and the greater precision of the texts of Hellas, necessary in training people how to read such books.

Reciprocal Takeover of Attributes

Although today in the West the heritage of Israel is seen as religious faith, and of Hellas as scientific reason, this was not so clear in the first centuries of our era. Directly after the formation of the New Testament, each society takes on features of the other. Thus the large fact of *Greek religion* has a sociological continuation in the church. The cathedral of Syracuse incorporates the Doric columns of the temple of Athena Nike of the fifth century B.C.E.; the Romans built the columns into walls; the Christian basilica changed at least internal arrangements; under Islam a minaret was built;[53] the eighteenth century added a rococo facade. Each successive cult involved processions, singing, vestments, a contrast between leaders and people.

More generally, Greek civilization is built on the necessity of *myth*. Much more strongly than Hebrews, Greeks needed to find a sequence of better lands, offering blessedness first to heroic figures, then to all. Plato ends his major dialogues with a myth concretely supporting the theoretical conclusions of the discussion. The myth of the *Phaedo* agrees in two contrasting ele-

---

53. That is my recollection from a visit in summer 1960, but I cannot easily verify it.

ments with Israel: human beings around the Mediterranean like ants or frogs around a marsh; over against them a better world of jasper and emerald. And wherever we can make a comparison like this, it is always Hellas that has fantastic elements, merging true and ideal geography, while Israel retains a dignified realism in descriptions of the earth, and a sober transcendence about its God.

As Greek ultimate affirmations rest on Mediterranean myth, parallel to Hebrew-Phoenician ones and in part derived from them, so rabbinic exegesis rests on a basis parallel to Greek logic and Roman law, perhaps derived from them. To give the Greeks exclusive credit for an inheritance of Reason ignores the logical principles developed by the rabbis to interpret the Torah.[54] Some themes they pick up are illustrated in Plato *Laws* 7.793AB (Daube 243). It begins with a distinction between "unwritten customs" and "written laws";[55] and goes on that "very old ancestral customs when properly founded and become habitual, acting as a shield hold subsequently written laws in full safety." A heathen asked Shammai (*b. Shabb.* 31a), "How many Torahs do you have?" and he answered "Two, written and oral." 'Aqiba (*Ab.* 3.14), defining more closely *m. Ab.* 1.1, said, "Tradition is a fence to the Law."

The seven exegetical principles of Hillel (*t. Sanh.* 7:11; *Sifra* introd.) owe something to Hellenistic-Roman logic. In particular the first, *qal waḥomer* "Light and Heavy," that is, *a minori ad maius* (from lesser to greater): "If P holds in the trivial case A, *how much more so* in the weighty case B." Again at *b. Shabb.* 31a Hillel brings a proselyte to reason *qal waḥomer* on Num 1:51: a stranger (where Hillel includes even king David) who approaches the tabernacle is put to death, and the proselyte concludes, "how much more one like myself!" At about the same time the logic appears in pagan Greek: when fictitious mythology about Hades begets piety, "how much more does history, the prophetess of truth and metropolis of all philosophy," build character (Diodorus 1.1.2)![56] It is striking in the New Testament: "If God so clothes

54. Lee I. Levine, *Judaism and Hellenism in Antiquity: Conflict or Confluence?* (Seattle: Univ. of Washington Press, 1998), 113–16, briefly discusses two positions on the degree to which the rabbis borrowed from Greco-Roman thought. He calls Saul Lieberman a "minimalist": *Hellenism in Jewish Palestine* (New York: Jewish Theological Seminary of America, 1950); "Rabbinic Interpretation of Scripture," 47–82. He calls David Daube a "maximalist": "Rabbinic Methods of Interpretation and Hellenistic Rhetoric," *HUCA* 22 (1949) 239–64.

55. Aristotle (*Rhet.* 1.13.2 = 1373b5) divides law *(nomon)* into unwritten *(agraphon)* and written *(gegrammenon)*. Rabbinic borrows the first word in a whole Greek sentence, unattested in Greek and perhaps parodied or misunderstood, i.e., "For the King, the law might as well not have been written down, he need only observe it if he wishes to" (*j. Rosh hash.* 57a75 bottom).

56. See Josephus, *War* 2.365.

the grass of the field, how much more you?" (Luke 12:28 [cf. 11:13]). "If the fall [of the Jews] is the wealth of the world . . . how much more their fulfill-ment?" (Rom 11:12). The New Testament usage is often taken as reflection of the rabbinic logic; but I suggest that both it and the rabbinic ultimately are from Latin: "How much more [*quanto . . . magis*] would you have marveled if you had heard [Demosthenes] in person?" (Cicero *de Oratore* 3.213). Still, rabbinic logic, whatever its source, was deeply internalized.[57] The European Jewish community, its intellect practiced by those centuries of exegesis, led the modern world in various enterprises: rational philosophy with Spinoza, economics and sociology with Marx, psychology with Freud, physics with Einstein.

Faith and Reason

Today the polarity between Israel and Hellas is mostly seen as one between religion and science, faith and reason. An influential and in places helpful treatment of the theme "Faith and Reason" appears in an encyclical (Septem-ber 15, 1998) of John Paul II.[58] The contrast is partly a simplification in view of the realms where each society trespasses on the presumed monopoly of the other. The two concepts nearly fall together in Hebrew, where "truth" (*'emeth*) comes from the root *'mn* ("be reliable") as is clear from the form Ps 91:4 *'amittô* ("his [God's] reliability"). Thus at 1 Kgs 22:16 Ahab says to Micaiah, "How many times shall I adjure you that you should speak nothing to me but the truth in the name of Yahweh?" Greek *alēthēs* ("true") does not have the modern connotation of something's being in conformity with the real world, but of its unavoidability, "that which cannot escape notice."

Still, current perceptions are historical facts with their own legitimacy. Until recently in Europe and the United States, "faith" *meant* the profession of Judaism or Christianity; and still today communities here adhering to Islam, Buddhism, Hinduism are seen as to some degree alien. And even more so "reason" *means* the habits of thought derived from Greek philosophers—as filtered through Latin understanding. To discuss the truth or falsity of the

57. A parallel development of legal logic leads from the case-by-case style of the Roman XII Tables and the Covenant Code of Exodus to the codifications, contemporary with each other, of the Roman lawyer Gaius and the Mishnah.

58. Printed in *Origins,* CNS Documentary Service, vol. 28, no. 19 (October 22, 1998). The English translation is by the Vatican and appears to have the same authenticity as the Latin original *Fides et Ratio,* which I have not looked up.

insights in the ancient Near Eastern empires would be wasted effort; we know too much about their restricted social systems. Does that mean that Hebrew or Greek insights likewise should be considered outmoded? It might seem that the question arises principally with Jewish-Christian faith; and that the process of reasoning, once grasped by the Greeks, is mandatory and unchanging. But our theme of complementarity suggests that the two should be more nearly parallel.

Today relations are the exact opposite of what they were in the later Middle Ages. *Then* society was based on a generally accepted system of belief, and secular Greek rationalism was only just making its way. *Today* Christian (and Jewish) belief is marginalized as a private choice, while Greek rational thought seems everywhere triumphant. In the United States, government must everywhere permit, but nowhere authorize, the places of worship where a transcendent source of justice is proclaimed. And even though the study of the classical languages has retreated, Greek literature in translation is the solidest part of the university canon (such as it is), with the English Bible as a very optional extra.

If we take the present situation as a permanent state of affairs, the whole enterprise of this volume is put under a cloud. For it would mean that the breakout of Israel from the ancient Near East, though admirable in many ways, was still darkened with the uncritical beliefs of its origins; and that only the Greeks were sufficiently distant to throw off their pantheon, god by god, and (with much backsliding into myth!) move toward a full reliance on reason. Here our historical study throws us back to look at ourselves. In *my* best understanding, does reason, carried through sufficiently far, demand to be completed by an affirmation of faith? or does it leave faith as an optional or arbitrary supplement to itself?—the position that faith occupies in all of American law, and in much American practice. (But presidential candidates usually must belong to a Christian church; most weddings are performed by clergy; department stores, if they wish to end the year in the black, play Christmas carols in December.)

We may here settle for a minimum definition of faith: affirmation of a providential God watching over events. For early Israelites with an indefinite future ahead, it was enough to affirm that continuance of their family in ongoing time was thereby secured. In the formative period of Judaism and the New Testament, when the final destruction of the Temple and the dispersal of the Jewish people were in the cards, Providence required further a symbolism of the resurrection of the body. For us likewise, with the certainty that life on this planet, even if prolonged for millions of years, will eventually be wiped out by a dying sun, it may still require something more than even the continuance of history over that period. To affirm the values in a secular-ized Hellenism or Judaism, celebrating their human cultures but rejecting what they say about God or the gods, blessed lands, or the restoration of the dead is much less than they affirmed about themselves. If that is all our famous Greco-Roman or Jewish-Christian heritage amounts to, we are being given a much-reduced inheritance by the probate court of history. We do not have a long enough view to know whether either tradition will continue to blossom if it is so far cut off from its roots; or whether humanity will be psy-chically able to continue its enterprise if all it can see ahead, near or far, is a blank wall.

The enterprises of those two old societies are continued among us in two places: classroom and congregation. They teach and pass on, respectively, the use of logic and the use of trust. In a kind of meta-logic and meta-trust, let us ask what functions they perform in our society. They are parallel and con-trasted: each relies on books handed down from its mother society to train contemporaries in urgent tasks likewise inherited from it. They are equally inevitable structures of our society. In their graciousness they freely make those books available for private study, and many people do learn calculus and read the Bible on their own, or home-school their children. People in a soci-ety without classrooms or congregations would not have those options. The teaching may be poorly or well done; the congregation may be formed on too narrow or broad a basis. But if a community abandons traditional formats, it must improvise, and its improvisations will not be better than what they replaced. And classroom and congregation each has a style. While the style can be learned by self-study, it is the group that preserves and carries the style on. We have near-universal agreement that the style of the classroom is indeed indispensable for approaching the problems and tasks of our society with commitment and understanding. Is the style of the congregation equally a necessary prerequisite for something?

It used to be taken for granted that membership in the congregation was the necessary prerequisite for a sound family structure, training children (and parents too) in responsibility. Today families alienated from the old congre-gations, or unaware of them, are doing about as well as the meeting-goers. Perhaps everything would run downhill if the congregations simply disap-peared—an unlikely event, as most sociologists would agree. It used to be taken for granted that the congregations were the organ of society from which aid went out to the poor, hungry, sick, suffering. Since then government first took on those tasks, then dropped a number of them, asking the congregations to fill in the gap. But the homeless, hungry, mentally disturbed walking the streets present a bigger task than congregational charity can easily take on.

Marx in the last of his eleven Theses on Feuerbach says: "The philosophers have only interpreted the world in various ways, but the main thing is to change it" ("Die Philosophen haben die Welt nur verschieden *interpretiert,* es kömmt drauf an, sie zu *verändern*").[59] The world is changed in many ways by many agents—governments, corporations, wars, revolutions. The changes that do the least damage, and have the brightest future, are those brought by people working out of faith communities by nonviolent direct action for new levels of justice. Susan B. Anthony (1820–1906) out of a Quaker heritage participated in the three great women's tasks of the nineteenth century: temperance to rescue their menfolk from drunkenness; abolition of slavery; their own suffrage. Gandhi from his Hindu background (with a little help from British thought) discovered a peaceful way for a people to recover its autonomy. The American revulsion against the war in Vietnam elicited Buddhist allies who thought as we did. César Chávez carried the banner of the Lady of Guadalupe to campaign for the rights of farmworkers. Martin Luther King Jr. out of the black church, Dorothy Day and the Berrigan brothers out of Irish Catholicism, did what we know. As technology, law, physics, healing only arise from a place where reason is allowed free play, so the grassroots commitment to peace, justice, and the integrity of creation (in the formula of the World Council of Churches) only arise from the heart of faith communities. That is less a theoretical doctrine than an observational fact. Direct action on a purely secular base tends to be grim, austere; faith adds an indispensable *joy.* People have the option of dispensing with the classroom and the faith communities in their own lives; society as a whole will either nurture both or do without their products.

With respect to the ancient Near Eastern empires, we saw, the two societies of Hellas and Israel grew up, respectively, just outside and just inside. Since nothing ever fully dies, modern states to some degree inherit the status of those empires: our law and the very concept of law is Roman; Rome historically continued the imperialist techniques invented by those regimes. Correspondingly, then, the two free traditions ever since maintain something

59. Written in 1845, not published until 1888 (by Engels); often taken as a summary of Marx's essential insights.

of their original stance of opposition over against the inheritors of those original empires here. The Greek tradition of reason looks at our institutions in guidance and critique as from the *outside*; the Hebrew-Christian tradition of faith in guidance and critique as from the *inside*.

We have been so well trained by the classroom and our Hellenic tradition of logic generally that the first thing we ask, when we come to face the Hebraic tradition of faith in the congregation, is "Is it *true*?" That question is more in the style of the classroom than of the congregation. But also, the validity of scientific theories developed in the laboratory and classroom is judged by their results: Does relativity or the proposed structure of DNA explain observed facts? Then it should be fair to say, The validity of an insight nurtured in the congregation of faith is judged by its results—the campaign for change that flows from it. If such campaigns for change are necessary for the continuance of our society in justice, and if (as seems to be the case) they emerge primarily from faith communities, the faith of such communities is a necessary structure of our society.

CHAPTER 2
Divine Kingship, Civic Institutions, and Imperial Rule

꧁꧂꧁꧂꧁

The Mediterranean city-state was a transient political structure. Its institutions emerged under a quasi-divine king: partly as progressive limitation and dispersal of his power; partly from its own necessities, in particular his dependence on a civic militia. Its Canaanite sites, on the rain-watered periphery of the irrigated societies, Egypt and Mesopotamia, during precious centuries held out against imperial advances while they perfected their own institutions. Greek resistance kept Persian power to the eastern shore of the Aegean. But the greatest energy of the city-states went into defending themselves against others of the same kind.

Throughout Greece the independent city-state, whether fully constitutional or under a limited residual kingship, was ended by the rise of new imperial powers with a different structure—Persians and Macedonians. These were Indo-European peoples with no fixed civic base, organized as a hereditary kingship commanding a people's army under an elite officer corps. But while taking away real independence from the old city-states, they left the formal constitutions of magistrates, senate, and assembly intact. The literary texts and cultural forms developed under freedom were preserved under a relatively benign imperial overlordship.

In Italy a single city, Rome, passing from a legendary kingship to a Greek-style constitution, while progressively modifying but not discarding its political structures, gradually extended citizenship to the whole peninsula. Beginning in its struggle with Carthage, a wealthy naval power also able to recruit land armies, Rome further extended its power to overseas "provinces," at first seen as conquered territory under military control, later as new areas of citizenship. As it turned to the east, the successor kingdoms of Alexander—Antigonid, Attalid, Seleucid, Ptolemaic—were no match for it; but Iran, under successive dynasties, constituted a permanent barrier.

The military success of Rome ended its true civic structure. Ambitious proconsuls, commanding armies with a provincial base, caught the vision of a personal monarchy, going beyond the annual consulate and the collegial authority of the Senate. The Hellenistic monarchs offered an enticing model. Carthaginian generals like Hannibal likely aspired to the same goal, but their political situation at home remains obscure. The name of king, *rex*, remained unacceptable at Rome, and Julius Caesar was killed partly because he did not dissociate himself from it firmly enough.

Augustus, after full power fell into his hands, consolidated it in a style consistent with Roman tradition. At first he held the quasi-monarchical office, the consulate, in successive years. But later he perceived that all power necessary was available through offices of the Senate and Assembly: to them he added sacral functions old and new. Thus a new single rule with political powers and divine sanctions more powerful than those of any previous kingship was created out of the forms of the Republic.

Among many mysteries of the Roman constitution is the fact that the king must be an outsider;[1] the patricians were seemingly not eligible. Cornell 148 sees the latter kings of Rome in the guise of Greek tyrants, populist and anti-aristocratic figures. Vergil in his survey of Roman history describes Ancus Marcius (*Aeneid* 6.816) as "taking too much pleasure in popular favor." In the first act of L. Iunius Brutus (Livy 2.1.9), "he forced [the people] to take an oath that they would allow no one to reign as king in Rome." Cornell 150: "What was truly repugnant to the nobles was the thought of one of their number elevating himself above his peers by attending to the needs of the lower classes and winning their political support." It was the patricians to whom the name of *rex* was unacceptable. This suggests that in the kings of Israel and Judah deemed bad by the Deuteronomic editor of Kings we may see populist leaders, practicing the cults that found favor among the people who built "*bamoth* and pillars and *asherim*" (1 Kgs 14:23), as over against the official cult of the priestly aristocracy.

In Rome as in Athens, to a late date the old office of the king was kept with largely sacral functions (but in Athens the *basileus* presided at trials for homicide); the old dual kingship hung on in Sparta even when its power was mostly gone. In Israel a new regal dynasty arose with the Maccabees, continued partly as client kings under Rome, partly as a high priesthood. The sentiment of a Davidic kingship remained in strata of the people with no allegiance to Rome, to the high priesthood, or to the client kings. The story

---

1. T. J. Cornell, *The Beginnings of Rome: Italy and Rome from the Bronze Age to the Punic Wars (c. 1000–264 BC)* (London: Routledge, 1995), 142.

of Jesus has suggestions—no more—of a failed political Messianic uprising. The opposition between Christ and Caesar arose from the fact that they fell heir to opposite aspects of the old divine kingship.

Moses Finley's valuable but oblique study of ancient politics is helpfully summarized in the Cambridge paperback edition:

> Finley . . . argues that politics come into play only in societies in which binding public decisions are made by discussion followed by a vote. The participants and the voters need not be the whole adult (or male) population but they must extend well beyond the small circle of a ruler (or junta), his family and his intimates. These qualifications narrow the practitioners of politics in the ancient world to the city-states of Greece and to Republican Rome.[2]

Those criteria exclude ancient Israel. But if we look beyond the process to the results, Israel has as good a claim as Greece and Rome to the merits arising from their politics: dispersal of power; a demand for justice by spokesmen for the poor, worked out to some degree in real history; preservation of that history in widely accessible texts. Although the two states of Israel retained kings until their conquest by eastern empires, their law embodies restrictions on his possessions; Deut 17:16-17 specifies horses, wives, and money, perhaps from a bad experience under Solomon. That law at least in theory goes beyond Greece and Rome in providing for periodic manumission of slaves and cancellation of debts; for needs of orphans and widows; for exemption from military service (Deut 20:5-8); for limitations on a scorched-earth policy (Deut 20:19-20).

Unlike Greece and Rome, Israel did not bequeath an adaptable form of political government to the modern world, other than the Puritan theocracies of Geneva and Massachusetts. But it bequeathed a model of a humanistic people, whose virtues, still carried by its physical descendants, are complementary to those of Greece and Rome. During its independence, it retained a kingship with attributes patterned on the High God, whereas Greece and Rome underwent a political evolution with only fading memories of an original divine kingship before written record. But the institutions by which Israel dispersed power under the umbrella of kingship in many ways run parallel to those which Greece and Rome developed to fill the gap left by the lack of kingship.

---

2. M. I. Finley, *Politics in the Ancient World* (Cambridge: Cambridge Univ. Press, repr. 1984), inside front cover.

Among "Mediterranean city-states" I include legendary ones, Homeric Troy and the Homeric Achaeans (an ad hoc city); and historical ones, Jerusalem, the Phoenician cities, Athens and Sparta (with other Greek *poleis*), Rome and Carthage. All from time to time used their city-base to build an extended territory. Troy, Jerusalem, and Phoenicia had full kingships; Roman tradition claimed *reges*; the Achaeans had heroic leaders *(basilēes)* and some true kings at home *(anaktes)*; Athens (like later Rome) had a vestigial *basileus*; Sparta had *two* hereditary kings with limited powers; Carthage had two annually elected *sufetes* whom the Greeks called *basileis*. In Jerusalem, Rome, and the Greek states (with their legendary Achaean ancestors) the dispersal of power is clear. Legendary Troy has a well-developed council of elders. Carthage, whatever its internal freedom, is a special case of a Semitic state that developed a Senate, Assembly, and magistracies—like Palmyra long afterwards. The historians of the city have in general not recognized any special status of those that developed an alphabetic literature of self-analysis; Hammond says, "Nor did [the Hebrews'] cities, particularly Jerusalem, represent any advance in the idea of the city."[3]

A peculiar agreement among the city-states is the *ceremonial military force of three hundred men*. Gideon (Judg 7:6) reduced the army of Israel to three hundred so that the victory would be to Yahweh alone. Sparta and Argos had a battle of three hundred picked men each (Herodotus 1.82). The three hundred of Sparta may have been the king's personal bodyguard, which Leonidas led to Thermopylae; Herodotus 7.205.2 calls them "the regular three hundred." Livy says that Romulus "had three hundred armed men whom he called the Swift to protect his person, not only in war but also in peace" (1.15.8). Brutus raised the Senate to the same number of three hundred (Livy 2.1.10). There was a supposed conspiracy of three hundred against Porsinna (Livy 2.12.15). The private army of the Fabii numbered 306, "a notable Senate at any period" (Livy 2.49.4). When Rome demanded three hundred hostages from Carthage in 149 B.C.E. (Polybius 36.4.6), they were to be "sons of the members of the *synklētos* and of the *gerousia*."[4]

It is natural to speak of Mediterranean cities in the same breath. Tertullian's contrast "What, therefore, does Athens have to do with Jerusalem?"

---

3. Mason Hammond (with L. J. Bartson), *The City in the Ancient World* (Cambridge: Harvard Univ. Press, 1972), 89. Nor is Jerusalem given any special status in Frank Kolb, *Die Stadt im Altertum* (Munich: Beck, 1984).

4. These are evidently separate bodies. The *synklētos* was larger, for at Carthago Nova (Polybius 10.18.1) captives included two of the *gerousia* and fifteen of the *synklētos*. Hence in Palmyrene (*PAT* 0290) and rabbinic (*Exod. Rabbah* 46.4).

Quid ergo Athenis et Hierosolymis?[5] recognizes that they are two of a kind. Aristotle's comparison of the Carthaginian *politeia* to Crete and Sparta brings together Semitic and Greek models. Deger-Jalkotzy observed that Homer's Troy was for Greeks the type of an Oriental city.[6] Priam was a true king, for Troy was "the city of King Priam" (*Iliad* 2.373). And its features rest on a historical foundation; for Greeks had lingering memories of the Hittite empire. In the Hittite texts "Millawanda" is probably Miletus and the "Ahhiyawa" Achaeans, although the territory meant is unclear, whether the Greek mainland or Rhodes.[7] Further, it is plausible to equate Achaeans/Ahhiyawa with the Hebrew "Hivites."[8]

Most persistent among echoes of the Hittite world in Greek is King Muwatallis II (1295–1272 B.C.E.),[9] whose treaty with Alaksandus of Wilusa has reminded many of Alexander/Paris of Ilion/Troy.[10] Stephanus 554 records a "Samylia: city of Caria, a foundation of *Motylos* who received Helen and Paris."[11] This presumes the travels of Helen and Paris on their way from Sparta to Troy (*Iliad* 6.290). The founder of Mytilene on Lesbos is said by some to have been one Mytilēs.[12] Lesbos is surely Hittite Lazpas, controlled by King Mursilis II (1321–1295), the father of Muwatallis.[13] Again, we must recognize Mursilis in Myrtilos, charioteer of Oinomaos and of Pelops the

5. Tertullian, *de praescriptione haereticorum* 7.9.

6. Sigrid Deger-Jalkotzy, "Homer und der Orient: Das Königtum des Priamos," *Würzburger Jahrbücher für die Altertumswissenschaft,* n. F. 5 (1979) 25–31. See further her thesis: Sigrid Deger, "Herrschaftsformen bei Homer," Dissertationen der Universität Wien 43 (Vienna: Notring, 1970).

7. So Frank H. Stubbings in CAH III.2.186. There is a summary of the Ahhiyawa problem as of 1981 in "The Hittites and the Aegean World," *American Journal of Archaeology* 87 (1983) 133–43, with contributions by Hans G. Güterbock, Machteld J. Mellink, and Emily T. Vermeule; see now Trevor Bryce, *The Kingdom of the Hittites* (Oxford: Clarendon, 1998), 59–63.

8. For the identification, see Othniel Margalith, *The Sea Peoples in the Bible* (Wiesbaden: Harrassowitz, 1994).

9. Bryce, *The Kingdom of the Hittites,* 13.

10. Translation of the treaty in John Garstang and O. R. Gurney, *The Geography of the Hittite Empire* (London: British Institute of Archaeology at Ankara, 1959), 102; now also by Gary Beckman, *Hittite Diplomatic Texts* (Writings from the Ancient World 7; Atlanta: Scholars, 1996), 82–88. Discussion in Bryce, *The Kingdom of the Hittites,* 394.

11. Samylia is an old Anatolian toponym, for it has the same name as Zinjirli (*KAI* 216.2), whose king "Panamuwa" also has a Carian counterpart in *Panamyēs* (Meiggs-Lewis no. 32.30) and elsewhere in Anatolia.

12. Stephanus 465. But Diodorus 5.81.7 says the city was named after a woman of the same name, daughter of Makareus of Achaia.

13. Hittite texts cited by Garstang and Gurney, *The Geography of the Hittite Empire,* 95.

Lydian.[14] The Hittites themselves may appear as the *Kēteioi* (*Odyssey* 11.521, with variants *Kēdeioi* and *Chēteioi*), companions of the Mysian Telephos, who reminds us of the Hittite king Telipinus (1525–1500). On the Hebrew side, Gen 14:1 has one Tidal king of "goyim" who bears the name of the four Hittite kings Tudhaliyas (possibly also in Greek *Tantalos*). Suppiluliuma I (1344–1322) is known at Ugarit as *tpllm mlk* (KTU 3.1.16) along with its own king Niqmad, *nqmd mlk ugrt* (3.1.24). Priam can be seen[15] as Indo-European "First," beside Latin *prīmus*; a similar name is borne by Pir'am, Canaanite king of Yarmuth (Josh 10:3).[16]

This chapter falls into four parts. First we outline features of an old divine kingship in the Mediterranean city-state. But from the beginning it was limited by the necessary structures of the state, in particular the power of the citizen militia; and (whatever the eventual status of the king) it was progressively hemmed in by the threefold structure of magistrates, council of elders, and people's assembly. At the end of the process, as the city-state lost independence, the old royal ideology reasserted itself in two ways: in Caesar and Augustus, by reappropriating the old prerogatives of Council and Assembly and the sacral powers of kingship; in Christ, by reaffirming the old sanctity of the Davidic king, now divorced from political and military power.

Divine Kingship[17]

In early texts, the king, real or legendary, is notoriously of divine character, "godlike." For Homer, kings generally are "nurtured by Zeus" (*Iliad* 2.445),

14. For Myrtilos see Apollodorus *Epit.* 2.6–9 with Frazer's notes in the Loeb. Candaules king of Sardes also had the name *Myrsilos* (Herodotus 1.7.2), and Alcaeus had a contemporary *Myrtilos* at Lesbos.

15. Hans von Kamptz, *Homerische Personennamen: Sprachwissenschaftliche und historische Klassifikation* (Göttingen: Vandenhoeck & Ruprecht, 1982), 343.

16. Several items here are drawn from the large body of speculations in Richard D. Barnett, "Ancient Oriental Influences on Archaic Greece," in *The Aegean and the Near East: Studies Presented to Hetty Goldman,* ed. Saul S. Weinberg (Locust Valley, N.Y.: Augustin, 1956), 212–38. Hans G. Güterbock ("Troy in Hittite Texts? Wilusa, Ahhiyawa, and Hittite History," in *Troy and the Trojan War,* ed. M. Mellink, 33–44 [Bryn Mawr, Pa.: Bryn Mawr College, 1986], repr. as pp. 223–28 of *Perspectives on Hittite Civilization: Selected Writings of Hans Gustav Güterbock,* ed. H. A. Hoffner [Assyriological Studies 26; Chicago: Oriental Institute, 1997]) regards the equation of Muwatallis and Motylos (like the others of his title) as plausible but unproven. Mērinē, the *therapōn* of Idomeneus and perhaps his charioteer (*Iliad* 23.113), bears the name of an Akkadian "charioteer," *mariannu* (see EFH 612); CAD x. 1.281.

17. The human kingship of Hellas and the Near East is analyzed along somewhat different lines by West (EFH 14–19); its divine coloration is treated EFH 132–37.

and so in particular Menelaus (7.109). Odysseus is *"diogenēs"* (born of Zeus; *Odyssey* 2.352). Paris, a king's son, is "godlike" (*Iliad* 3.16); and likewise his father Priam—but only in the book (24) of his humiliation, an ironic touch that shows the poet much in control of inherited formulas. Priam was in the seventh generation from Zeus (*Iliad* 20.213ff.) and Achilles the fourth. Rhea Silvia named Mars father of Romulus and Remus (Livy 1.4.2), *Martia proles* (Ovid, *Fasti* 3.59). Yahweh says of David's son, "I will be his father, and he shall be my son" (2 Sam 7:14), a formula of royal "adoption" (Pss 2:7; 89:26-27).

Drews maintains that during the age of Geometric pottery (900–720 B.C.E.) "the Greek *poleis* were not ruled by kings"—with the possible exception of Athens;[18] but the *ethnē* of the Peloponnesus retained weak monarchies from an earlier age. He proposes that for Homer *basileus* meant "a highborn leader who is regularly flanked by other highborn leaders" (p. 129). But *anax* in Homer does mean "king"; Nestor is *"anax* of sandy Pylos" (*Iliad* 2.77), and when Agamemnon is described as *"basileus* of golden Mycenae" (7.180, etc.), this clearly means "king" also. The weakest part of Drews's argument is his failure to explain how Homer formed an idea of kingship when there was no such institution available in his time. Here it is not critically important for us to determine whether the supposed powers of early kingship are historical memories or idealized constructions.

The early city-states recognized a High God in the sky, and on earth a king of semidivine character with limitations on his power, while the monarchs of Egypt and Mesopotamia have in principle unlimited powers. Thucydides 1.13.1 contrasts the age of tyrants with an earlier pattern of "hereditary monarchies with *fixed* prerogatives." The High God is in charge of rain with all else in the sky; as such he makes the city-state possible. He is also king over a pantheon of other gods. After the battle of the gods with the Titans (Hesiod *Theog.* 883) the other gods urged Zeus to "reign and rule" over them. Thenceforth he was "king of the gods" (*Theog.* 886); Pindar enlarges his title to *"great* king of the gods" (*Olympian* 7.34). In a beautiful parallel Yahweh is "a great god, and a great king above all gods" (Ps 95:3).[19] Surely this parallel reflects the Old Persian regal formula: Darius at Behistun[20] calls himself

---

18. Robert Drews, *Basileus: The Evidence for Kingship in Geometric Greece,* Yale Classical Monographs 4 (New Haven: Yale Univ. Press, 1983). His title is, however, misleading since (as he holds) *basileus* in Homer and subsequent poets did not mean "king."

19. See my article "Kingdom of God," in *Encyclopedia of Religion* (New York: Macmillan, 1987), 8:304–12 (with addenda 16:482), esp. 8:304–5. Jerome *iux. Hebr.* peculiarly translates the first clause *quoniam fortis et magnus dominus.*

20. Kent 116.

"great king," and Herodotus 1.188.1 refers to the Persian monarch in general as "the great king."

In the West Semitic world the High God is "Master of the heavens": in Phoenician *b'l šmm* (*KAI* 4.3, Byblos), in Aramaic *b'lšmyn* (*KAI* 202 passim and often); Philo Byblius[21] "Beelsamēn, which is 'lord of heaven' among the Phoenicians, Zeus among the Hellenes." So in the Aramaic of Dan 4:34, "king of heaven" (in the mouth of Nebuchadrezzar). Likewise Hesiod *Theog.* 71, "And [Zeus] is reigning in heaven"; Euripides *Iph. Taur.* 749, "the lord of heaven, holy Zeus" (EFH 108).

The kingship of the High God might seem only a projection from the status of the human king. But the opposite may be the case: fading memories of a legendary absolute human kingship were reinforced by the ongoing cult of the God. Here, then, I outline powers of the Mediterranean king so far as they run parallel to the attributes of the High God. Ideally, each item will show that an attribute is possessed by a Semitic and classical High God, and by a Semitic and classical king or his successor.

In two features, by the nature of the case, absolute attributes of the early king are not shared by the High God. (a) He has special inviolability: "It is a fearful thing to kill one of royal descent" (*Odyssey* 16.401–2); so 2 Sam 1:14, "How is it that you were not afraid to put forth your hand to destroy the anointed of Yahweh?"[22] (b) A king in his youth kills a giant:[23] David kills Goliath; Nestor remembers killing Ereuthalion (*Iliad* 7.133–60). At *Iliad* 7.135 Nestor says that the combat was "at the streams of Iardanos." This river name, which also lies behind the Palestinian Jordan, marks the theme as from epic repertory.

The King, like the High God, Owes His Power to the Fall of a Previous Dynasty[24]
At Ugarit, Baal after his death and resurrection may take over the functions of the older god El, although the texts do not affirm this unambiguously. Before Yahweh could proceed with creation or history, he had to slay the sea dragon, variously named; only after he crushed the heads of Leviathan, it seems, did he establish "light and the sun" (Ps 74:14-16). Kronos castrates his father Ouranos (Hesiod, *Theog.* 180–81), and Zeus in turn overcomes *his* father Kronos in a struggle strangely censored (cf. *Theog.* 73). The dynastic

---

21. *FGH* 790 frag. 2.7.

22. So Cyrus H. Gordon, *Before the Bible: The Common Background of Greek and Hebrew Civilisations* (London: Collins, 1962), 255.

23. Hugo Mühlestein, "Jung Nestor jung David," *Antike und Abendland* 17 (1971) 173–90.

24. The "succession myth" is now treated in detail by West, EFH chapter 6.

transition from Saul to David is Yahweh's doing: Samuel says to Saul, "Yahweh has torn the kingdom of Israel from you this day, and has given it to a neighbor of yours, who is better than you" (1 Sam 16:26-28, cf. 28:17); and likewise from David to Jeroboam (1 Kgs 14:8; 2 Kgs 17:21). In legend the Spartan kings owed their power to the takeover of the Peloponnesus by the Dorians with the Heraclidae after the fall of Troy (Thucydides 1.12.3). After Cyrus conquered Astyages the Mede, the Persians held that "Zeus gives the Persians hegemony" (Herodotus 9.122.1).

The King, like the High God, Controls Fertility
Thunder is the voice of the High Gods Yahweh, Zeus, and Jupiter. Shamanistic figures imitate thunder and lightning: Salmoneus (Apollodorus 1.9.7) claimed to be Zeus, and produced thunder and lightning in his chariot; the trumpets and torches of Gideon's men seem mimetic of thunder and lightning (Judges 7). Related words (Gk. *lampas,* Heb. *lappid*) mean both "torch" and "lightning." Samuel through Yahweh calls up thunder and rain out of season (1 Sam 12:17). In a beautiful parody, Aristophanes (*Acharnians* 530–31) says that "Thence in wrath Olympian Pericles made lightning, made thunder, created confusion all over Hellas." Milton picks up the exact phrase (*Paradise Regained* 4.270) of Greek orators generally, "and fulmin'd over Greece."

The High God whose voice is thunder also more gently brings the rain on which the crops depend. The nonagricultural Cyclopes still rely on wheat and barley (along with the vines), "and the rain of Zeus increases [all these] for them" (*Odyssey* 9.111). Yahweh says, "And I will give the rain of your land in its season, the former rain and the latter, that you may gather in your grain and wine and oil" (Deut 11:14). Odysseus compares Penelope to a blameless king by whose justice "the black land bears wheat and barley" (*Odyssey* 19.114). Job as a near king presumes that if he has improperly used land, he can confidently say, "let thorns grow instead of wheat, and stinkweed instead of barley" (Job 31:40). And in the days of the just Israelite king there will be "abundance of grain in the land" (Ps 72:16). This quasi-magical view of the king's powers rests on his kinship with the High God who controls rain and fertility of the land.[25]

The king's power over fertility extends from the natural to the human world, so that the king, like the High God, is *the father of heroes.* It seems natural to us that the king is permitted sexual license and so becomes the father

---

25. Vergil calls Augustus "author of crops and powerful over the seasons," *auctorem frugum tempestatumque potentem* (*Geor.* 1.27), perhaps following a Hellenistic model (Mynors *ad loc.*).

of many; but for the ancients this is no less a sacral function than his power over the fields. His return from battle as victor also celebrates his sexual prowess. If the king can no longer beget heroes he is no longer king. So, if we take 1 Kgs 1:1-5 in sequence, the pretext for Adonijah's claim to the throne is that David cannot have relations with lovely Abishag. There are hidden indications that the God of Israel fathers heroes. Perhaps the original conception of Samson was when a "man of God came to me [Manoah's wife]" (Judg 13:6). The "sons of Elim" or the "sons of Elohim" (Gen 6:2) may have been seen more literally as procreated by the High God. The Hebrew writers and editors downplayed indications of divine paternity. Thus the son of Rehoboam king of Judah is called Abiyahu "Yahweh is my father" at 2 Chron 13:20-21 (or Abiyah) but is totally disguised as Abiyam in Kings (1 Kgs 14:31; 15:1-8).[26]

Notoriously, Zeus is the father of many heroes by mortal women: of Heracles by Alcmena (Hesiod, *Shield* 56); of Sarpedon by Laodamia (*Iliad* 6.198); and a multitude of others. Hesiod lays out his paternity of the gods; for Homer (*Iliad* 1.544) Zeus is the "father of men and gods,"[27] combining the attributes of Yahweh with respect to men and to the "sons of Elim."

Just as notoriously, Israelite judges and kings from their harem beget a company of sons. Gideon had seventy sons (Judg 8:30); David had six by as many wives (2 Sam 3:2-5), with eleven more at 2 Sam 5:13-16; Solomon had seven hundred wives and three hundred concubines (1 Kgs 11:3), although no catalog is given of his sons. Deger-Jalkotzy sees Priam's kingdom as an Aegean outpost of the Oriental realm with its harem.[28] Priam tells Achilles (*Iliad* 24.495–96) that he had fifty sons, nineteen by Hecuba alone. Hector boasted (5.474) that he could support the realm just with his brothers-in-law and brothers, where the latter presumably includes half brothers. The concubine is known by a common name; and the act by which a son claims his father's throne is to "go in" to the concubine.

The King, like the High God, Is Associated with Animals

The king, like the High God, is *enthroned on griffins.* Greek *gryps* and Hebrew "cherub" must be the same word; structurally they are identical, each can represent a lion with head and wings of an eagle. Yahweh "rode on a cherub

26. Besides the adoption formula of the Israelite king (2 Sam 7:14; Ps 2:7), for God as father see Deut 32:6; Jer 3:19; 31:9; Exod 4:22; Isa 63:16; Mal 2:10. But Moshe Weinfeld, *Promise of the Land: The Inheritance of the Land of Canaan by the Israelites* (Berkeley: Univ. of California Press, 1993), 241, considers David's sonship a "forensic metaphor."

27. A Sumero-Akkadian bilingual hymn to Sin the moon god addresses him "O father begetter of gods and men" (*ANET*[3] 385).

28. But note Edward Said's caution against assuming a uniform "Orientalism."

and flew" (Ps 18:11) and sits on cherubim (1 Sam 4:4); the cherubim of the sanctuary are described at 1 Kgs 6:23. Aeschylus (*Prometheus Bound* 803–4) calls griffins the "dogs of Zeus." King Ahiram of Byblos or a predecessor sat on a griffin or "cherub" throne, shown on his sarcophagus; in the theater of Athens the priest of Dionysus sat on a throne with a relief of griffins fighting men. The throne room of Knossos has two griffins (improved by Sir Arthur Evans) flanking the throne.[29]

Likewise, both king and High God are *identified with a bull*. Of Joseph it is said, "his horns are the horns of a wild ox" (Deut 33:17); at *Iliad* 2.481 Agamemnon is like a bull. The old names both of the bull and its horn are the most undeniable and ancient contacts between Indo-European and Semitic.

Also the king, like the High God, is *seen as a lion*. At Amos 3:8 the voice of Yahweh is like a lion's roaring. Hosea 13:7-8 has Yahweh act as a leopard, a bear, and a lion: "I will devour them like a lion." Heracles, who bridges the characters of gods and men, after killing the lion of Kithairon, "dressed himself in its skin and used its gaping mouth for a helmet" (Apollodorus 2.4.10)—as he and Alexander are represented in art. In the song of Jacob "Judah is a lion's whelp" (Gen 49:9), and so Gad and Dan in the song of Moses (Deut 33:20-22). The Apocalypse adopts this as a title of the Christ, "the Lion of the tribe of Judah" (Rev 5:5), in the twentieth century the proudest boast of the kings of Ethiopia. Homer compares the Achaean kings to a lion: Menelaus (*Iliad* 3.23), Diomedes (5.161). The Mediterranean names of the "lion" are related, though of varying form.

The King, like the High God, Has His Seat on the Citadel

Not merely may Zeus have his temple on a citadel: his golden throne is on Olympus (*Iliad* 8.442–43), it is "the seat of the gods" (*Odyssey* 6.42); the "golden house of Zeus" (Euripides, *Hipp.* 68) must be Olympus. Not merely is the "house of Yahweh" (1 Kgs 6:1) on the citadel: his home is on a mountain, where he "sits on the throne of his holiness" (Ps 47:9); "on the mountain of thy inheritance, the place, Yahweh, which thou hast have made for thy seat" (Exod 15:17, cf. Ps 68:17). With Exod 15:17 we may then compare the Homeric formula, "the seat of the gods, steep Olympus" (*Iliad* 5.367). Alternatively, Hebrew may speak of the "house of God," where *'elohim* sometimes may have been a true plural; at one time it was in Shiloh (Judg 18:31); Micah had one such (Judg 17:5); Bethel (Gen 28:17) "is none other than the house

---

29. Anna Maria Bisi, "Il Grifone: Storia di un motivo iconografico nell' antico oriente mediterraneo," Univ. di Roma—Centro di Studi Semitici, *Studi Semitici* 13 (Roma 1965) Tav. VII. (She doubts, however, that the biblical cherubim are griffins [70–71].)

of God, and this is the gate of heaven." Plato (*Phaedrus* 247A) says that, when the other Olympians go out, Hestia the homebody alone remains "in the house of the gods," where "gods" is of course a true plural.[30]

So of the pretender Heylel or Lucifer, "I will set my throne on high, I will sit on the mount of assembly" (Isa 14:12-13). Of human kings, the "house of Priam in Troy" (*Iliad* 22.478) is on the citadel (7.345–46). The house of a Roman king may have been on the Palatine, where later the imperial "palaces" stood. Solomon's palace (1 Kgs 7:2) stood on the citadel south of the Temple. The house of both gods and kings is surrounded by a precinct with a common name: Lat. *templum*, Gk. *temenos*, Heb. *timnat*.

The King Gets the Best Cuts of Meat in the Sacrifice
Here the king (who may conduct the sacrifice) comes out *better* than the god, who is mostly fobbed off with inedible parts. When Adonijah sacrifices, the guests of honor are David's sons, Joab the chief of staff, and Abiathar the priest (1 Kgs 1:25); surely the pretender was served first. At a Homeric banquet Agamemnon "honored Ajax with the long steaks from the back" (*Iliad* 7.321). Herodotus (6.56) among the privileges of the two kings of Sparta includes their receiving "the hides [for leather] and the backs [for meat] of all sacrificed animals."

The King, like the High God, Goes to War for His People
Thus the king is armed with a defensive panoply. Yahweh is a "man of war" (Exod 15:3). As such "he put on righteousness as a breastplate, and a helmet of salvation on his head" (Isa 59:17); the "panoply of God" (Wisd 5:17-20; Eph 6:11-17; see 1 Thess 5:18) retains the sense of armor once worn by God. Zeus likewise is the "steward of war" (*Iliad* 4.84). Athena for war (*Iliad* 5.736, etc.) "put on the tunic of Zeus" (apparently a special military item), along with thorax, "aegis" (shield?), and helmet. Goliath, in the same phrase used for Yahweh, is a "man of war" (1 Sam 17:33); so is David (1 Sam 16:18; 2 Sam 17:8). Hebrew has a static description of the panoply (1 Sam 7:5), with Goliath in the four defensive items, helmet, thorax, greaves, and shield. Homer actively describes the hero putting on armor, in the order greaves, thorax, sword and shield, helmet.

Likewise the king, as the Hebrew High God, is shepherd of his people. (This theme is imperfect in that Greek gods are hardly so designated.)[31]

30. Levin (SIE 51–58) links Heb. *beth* and Greek *oikos* through the Sanskrit and Avestan forms of the latter.
31. But note Anacreon 3.8 (*PMG* 177) of Artemis *poimaineis* (West EFH 553, 227). West further (EFH 154) cites *Beowulf* 610, 1832 *folces hyrde* "folk-herd, shepherd of the people."

Yahweh is the "shepherd of Israel" (Ps 80:2). Israelite leaders or prophets are so described: "[the people] are afflicted for want of a shepherd" (Zech 10:2); "I will give you shepherds after my own heart" (Jer 3:15); Ezekiel 34 on the "shepherds of Israel"; also foreigners, "Your shepherds are asleep, O king of Assyria" (Nah 3:8). Hence of Christ (Heb 13:20; 1 Peter 2:25); of a "pastor" (Eph 4:11). So Agamemnon and other kings are "shepherds of the people" (*Iliad* 2.243, etc.). The image is less of a people being passively led than actively protected from enemies. For one job of the shepherd up on the mountain is to kill or fend off wild animals that threaten the flock.

Finally, the king, like the High God, rides out to battle in his chariot. The High God, to our surprise, drives his chariot over the *sea*. "Thou didst trample the sea with thy horses" (Hab 3:15); otherwise, Yahweh rides on a cloud (Isa 19:1) or on the cherubim (Ps 18:11). "For behold, Yahweh will come in cloud, and his chariots like the stormwind" (Isa 66:15); his chariot (hardly distinguishable from himself) is described at Ezekiel 1. At *Iliad* 13.21–27 Poseidon drives in his chariot across the waves; so Euripides *Andromache* 1011–12, also of Poseidon, "And you of the Sea who drive a chariot of grey mares over the sea." Likewise the kings of Israel and Judah go out to war, each in his chariot (2 Kgs 9:21); as the Achaean and Trojan heroes do constantly.

The King, like the High God, Determines Justice for His Subjects

The Israelite and Greek High Gods are guarantors of justice. The theme hardly appears with the historical kings of Israel or Judah: they mostly did not warrant it; and it is mostly reserved for the ideal future descendant of David. Thus (Isa 11:4) it is said of the "shoot of Jesse" that "with justice he shall judge the poor." So "he shall reign as king and deal wisely, and shall execute justice and righteousness in the land" (Jer 23:5 = 33:15); "May he judge thy people with righteousness, and thy poor with justice" (Ps 72:2).

Similarly, it is almost unique when the poet says of Sarpedon that "he defended Lycia by his just pronouncements" (*Iliad* 16.542). More typical is the theoretical definition of monarchy, *Iliad* 2.204–6: "Let there be one ruler, one king, to whom [Zeus] . . . has given a sceptre and judgments *(themistas)* by which he expresses his counsel." Hesiod has a critique of current kings (*Opera* 263–64): "Gift-eating kings, make straight your words, put crooked judgments altogether from your thoughts."[32]

---

32. At *Iliad* 16.387–88 the making of "crooked judgments" is on the contrary ascribed to a plurality in the Agora.

The King's Power in Theory May Be Limited Only by the High God
We may summarize the godlike character of the king out of Grotius, who in his *De Iure Belli et Pacis* (1625) more than any other author before or since takes the Hebrew Bible and classical authors with equal seriousness as indications of actual political structures. For kings "not subject to the will of the people even taken in its entirety" (1.3.7.8) he cites 1 Sam 15:1 where Yahweh through Samuel anoints Saul as king over Israel; Horace *Carm.* 3.1.5–6: "The power of kings who are to be feared is over their own flocks; the power of Jupiter is over kings themselves"; and a saying of Marcus Aurelius, "for only God can judge about absolute rule."[33] For such rule Grotius (1.3.20.1) adopts the coinage of Aristotle (*Pol.* 3.10.2, 1285b36), "absolute monarchy" (*pambasileia*), and of Sophocles *Antig.* 1163 (*pantelē monarchian*).[34]

Structure of the City and Dispersal of the King's Power

Before the Mediterranean city-state could do anything else, it had first of all to survive. Since it was not part of a larger imperial power, its citadel and wall could only be defended by a citizen militia; with the availability of iron, every able-bodied man must have a weapon in his hand. As in Switzerland today, the soldier's weapons and armor were his personal property; we hear little of an armory from which they were carefully issued by the state. David has no bronze armor, and when he is lent Saul's he cannot deal with it (1 Sam 17:39). Men were rated by the level of the equipment they could afford to provide. In Rome, Cicero notes (*Rep.* 2.40), "Servius named the lowest class 'proletarians,' on the grounds that from them, it seemed, [only] offspring could be expected," *{Seruius} proletarios nominauit, ut ex eis quasi proles . . . expectari uideretur;* Gellius 16.10.13 does add that in times of crisis "arms were given them at public expense," *armaque eis sumptu publico praebebantur.* Servius Tullius was credited with reorganizing Roman citizens in "centuries" (Livy 1.43, Cornell p. 199): apparently both to strengthen the army and to give the rich a near monopoly of the vote. Cornell p. 189 refers to "the context of an ancient city, in which military service was not the specialized preserve of a professional group, but on the contrary was an integral function of citizenship."

33. Dio 71.3.3, printed as Saying no. 10 in the Loeb edition of Marcus by C. R. Haines (1930), 364.

34. Barbeyrac *ad loc.* (in the edition of Grotius by William Whewell (Cambridge: Cambridge Univ. Press, 1853), 1:146, elegantly notes: *Faciunt enim . . . Tragici regnum Thebanum simile regnis Phoenicum, unde orti erant* ("The tragedians give the Theban monarchy the same [absolute] character as the Phoenician monarchies from which [in the legend of Cadmus] the Thebans sprang").

In Athens a knight or *hippeus* was drawn from the class of those "who could raise horses" (Aristotle *Ath. Pol.* 7.4) by having enough high-quality farmland. Perhaps in the distant past the same was true of the Roman *eques*. But at the earliest period we can reach, many but not all such were assigned *equi publici* (Livy 5.7.5), and it was a punishment to serve *equis priuatis* (Livy 27.11.14). In Israel perhaps Solomon begrudged subordinates land to raise horses, and cavalry mounts were provided by the state (1 Kgs 10:26–29). But throughout the Mediterranean in the historic period until Alexander, while horse ownership remained prestigious, infantry arms decided battles. However strongly men adhered to the civic god or gods and their agent the king, effective power in the state lay with the militia; its members were identical with the citizen body, and its fighting power meant that it could not be simply ignored.

The one exception to the identity of soldier and citizen was the body of men too old to fight or even to command, the "elders." But they had previously fought, and had since then reflected on the conditions for the state's survival. They were the repositories of the society's wisdom. The army was only itself when it was mustered in force; and so a gathering of the citizen body, which was nothing more or less than a mustering without arms, must also be in force. That was not the case with the elders; a deliberative body drawn from among them could afford to be representative. Among them, the prestige of wealth or aristocratic descent meant more than in battle, where all were at equal risk of their lives, whatever their officer or line status. Thus the social divisions of wealth and influence, minimized in the army or citizen assembly (except as skewed in Rome), were maximized in the council of elders.

Therefore the mere fact that a city existed, and had managed to survive over the years, implied of itself that it was structured by a citizen assembly and a council of elders. In the *Iliad* the besiegers acquire nearly as much civic structure as the besieged. When the Achaeans arrive, "[the Trojans] were holding an assembly at the gates of Priam, all gathered together, both young men and elders" (2.788–89). Here the elders join the citizen body. But when the army goes out to fight, the elders remain (3.146–50): "those around Priam . . . the elders of the people were sitting at the Scaean gates, withdrawn from war by old age, but excellent counsellors, like cicadas." *Demogerontes* suggests again that the elders are an agency of the people rather than fully independent; Philo[35] uses the same word of Jewish elders.

---

35. Philo, *Life of Moses* I.86 (LCL ed. vi.320).

Earlier, Agamemnon had commanded the heralds "to call to an assembly the flowing-haired Achaeans" (*Iliad* 2.51). But prudently, "*first* he held a council of the great-hearted elders" (2.53). The Achaean "elders" were mostly younger than the Trojan, for they serve as commanders, though perhaps we should think of some as purely deliberative. It is hard to believe that in both cases the poet did not have in mind a city of his own age with a *Boulē* of elders and an Agora of the people at large.

Although an assembly of the gods can be either limited or inclusive, the same language is used in any case. Just as Hector "made an assembly" of the Trojans (8.489), so Zeus "made an assembly of the gods" (8.2), where only Olympians appear. A more representative assembly including rivers and nymphs is spoken of also after the human pattern as (20.4, 16) "to the *agorē*." The Olympians do not act as an inner Senate or executive committee for the larger body.

We are not to think of either body at the early period in the modern sense as ordered by a constitution with fixed times of meeting and regular officers; they gather on call, from the structure of the state, as need arises. So, in the crisis of the Israelite state at the death of Solomon (1 Kgs 12:3), Jeroboam "and all the assembly of Israel" come to Rehoboam, asking for concessions. Then "king Rehoboam took counsel with the elders" who had stood before Solomon his father (1 Kgs 12:6), who advise conciliation. But instead he follows the advice of the hotheaded "young men" (12:8) who had grown up with him, and splits the state. These seem a temporary party, for elsewhere just people and elders appear. Ruth 4:11: "Then spoke all the people who were at the gate and the elders, 'We are witnesses'" (where we would expect the elders rather to be at the gate). Psalm 107:32 gives the contrast we would expect: "Let them extol [God] in the assembly of the people, and in the session of the elders praise him." Joel 2:16 has parallel phrases, including "gather the people; sanctify the congregation; assemble the elders," but it is not clear which are equivalent. More common is "elders of the people" (Lev 4:15, etc.), as if they were agents of the people as a whole like the Trojan *dēmogerontes*—an exact equivalent!

In the historical period, it is taken for granted in the West that decisions are made by the council of elders and the assembly of the people. In Latin and Greek the name of the "old man" gives a name to the council: *senex* makes *senatus*, *gerōn* makes *gerousia*. From the fifth century B.C.E. on, Athenian documents begin "It was decided by the Council and People."[36] Many sources

36. E.g., Meiggs-Lewis no. 71 (424/3 B.C.E.).

(e.g., Aeschines 3.125) show that any measure to be approved by vote of the Ekklesia of the people first must have preliminary approval of the *Boulē*; the traditional formula, however, hides the reality that the People was more influential. In Rome Cicero attests the parallel formula *Senatus populusque Romanus* (e.g., *pro Plancio* 90), which here hides the opposite reality that true power lay in the Senate.

While Greek and Roman writers attest (below) that Carthage likewise had a senate and assembly, no formula yet discovered in its very numerous Punic inscriptions so reads; nor is even a plausible word for "Senate" or "senator" attested. But in a Punic–Latin bilingual from Lepcis (*KAI* 126, cf. 119) of 92 C.E., "before the nobility of Lepcis and the people of Lepcis," corresponds to *ordo et populus*.[37] Palmyra picked up the institutions of a Greek city: thus a lost equestrian statue has a bilingual dedication of 171 C.E. (PAT 2769) "by decree of the Boule and Demos." Probably both bodies did vote, since the Tariff (PAT 0259) has no mention of the *demos*. A Midrash has the same loan-words: at *Gen. Rabbah* 6.4 a king has two governors; "whenever the city governor goes out, the *council and people* go out with him."

Aristotle (*Pol.* 2.8.1 = 1272b27) compares the constitutions of the Carthaginians and Laconians (and Cretans), although the points of comparison are not fully clear. Elsewhere (*Pol.* 2.3.10 = 1265b36–40) he quotes others as holding that the Lacedaemonian (Spartan) constitution has elements of monarchy in the kingship, oligarchy in the elders, and democracy in the ephors; and this must be his analysis of Carthage also. For (2.8.2 = 1272b37) he says that the "kings" and *gerousia* at Carthage correspond to the kings and elders at Sparta; and (2.8.3 = 1273a8) that either kings or elders at Carthage can refer matters to the *demos*. Anyway, this is the understanding of Polybius 6.51.2, who lists the features of Carthage as the kings; the aristocratic, *gerontion*; and the people, *plēthos*. Aristotle never suspects that the Carthaginian "kings" are really the annual suffetes, and more comparable to the Spartan ephors.[38]

Polybius (6.11.12) sees the Roman constitution as composed of the same three elements: monarchic in the power of the consuls, aristocratic in the power of the Senate, democratic in the power of the people. So Cicero (*de rep.* 2.41) considers Rome, like Carthage and Sparta, balanced among three

37. W. Huss, "Der Senat von Carthago," *Klio* 60 (1978) 327–79. He cites Livy 34.61.15 *seniores ita senatum uocabant*. But zqn is unattested in the Punic inscriptions.

38. For the Carthaginian constitution, see Stéphane Gsell, *Histoire Ancienne de l'Afrique du Nord,* vol. 2 (Paris: Hachette, 1918), 183–233; Werner Huss, *Geschichte der Karthager* (Munich: Beck, 1985), 458–66.

powers, *regali et optumati et populari*. The Roman chancery assumed that any city or people it dealt with had a proper government of magistrates, Senate, and people, just as the United Nations today assumes that we are all organized as sovereign nations; and very likely then as now governments accommodated themselves to what they had been told was the correct pattern. Thus in 47 B.C.E. Caesar writes in Greek to the "magistrates, council, people of the Sidonians" (Josephus *AJ* 14.190); and Claudius in 45 C.E. to the "magistrates, council, people of the men of Jerusalem" (*AJ* 20.11). Here, then, in sequence we consider the parallel features in these three structures: magistrates, the council of elders, the assembly of the people.

The Highest State Office Comes to Be Collegially Shared by Two Men

When the functions of the king are taken over by one or more officers in Greece, Rome, and Carthage, this in itself suggests no relationship. Livy 1.8.3 says that among the Etruscans a "king" was created by vote of the twelve peoples, but the political realities are at present impenetrable. What does suggest a relationship is when the officers are precisely two in number and share their office collegially rather than with distinct functions. At Rome the tradition briefly has two collegial kings, Romulus and Titus Tatius the Sabine (Livy 1.13.8), replaced by two annually elected consuls.[39] Sparta had two hereditary kings who held office for life (Herodotus 6.51–59), supposedly descended from twins, with the family of the firstborn twin Eurysthenes having the preeminence. Aristotle (*Pol.* 2.8.2) compares the kings at Sparta and Carthage: but he mentions neither the point of similarity, that each were two, nor the point of difference, that the Punic "kings" were elected for a year only, but the Spartan as hereditary served for life.

For at Carthage the persons called "kings" by the Greeks (since Herodotus 7.165–66, who has a "king of the Carthaginians," that is, Amilkas, surely *Hamilcar*) were chosen annually.[40] It is doubtful that there was ever a lifelong hereditary kingship there as at Tyre.[41] The two were called by the Cartha-

<hr>

39. Livy 2.1.7 says that liberty arose "more from the fact that the consular power was made annual than that anything had been subtracted from royal authority."

40. So Zonaras 8.8.2 "annual rule," and Nepos *Hannibal* 7.4.

41. Our only account of early Carthage is in the late epitomator Justin, who cannot be relied on for constitutional details; for Justin, the great founder of a Carthaginian dynasty was Mago, whom he calls *imperator* (18.7.18–19); his predecessor Carthalo was "accused of seeking the kingship," *adfectati regni accusatus*. Even if the legend that Carthage was founded by a queen Dido (Deidō Timaeus *FGH* 566 F82) was historical, the monarchy cannot be shown to have survived her death. Carthage always maintained close ties to Tyre; in 162 B.C.E. a Carthaginian ship took firstfruits to Tyre (Polybius 31.12.11–12) shortly before the final fall of Carthage.

ginians "judges" (i.e., Hebrew *shopheṭim*) and by the Romans *sufetes* (Livy 28.37). Some Punic inscriptions are dated "in the year of the suffetes M and N." Thus *KAI* 77: "in the year of the suffetes Adnibaal and Adnibaal son of Bomilcar." (It has been much discussed[42] why the first judge is given no patronymic.)[43] And so a partly illiterate Latin inscription from North Africa under Hadrian (*CIL* 8.12286) is dated *anno sufetum (H)onorat{i} Fortunati {f(ili)} . . . et Fl(aui) Victoris Similis {f(ili)}*. At *CIS* 1.5510 they are not called suffetes: "In the month [P]ʻlt of the year of Eshmunamas son of Adnibaal the *rab* and Hanno son of Bostar son of Hanno the *rab*." It seems less likely that the two suffetes are designated *rab* than that the genealogy of each is carried back until a *rab* is reached; I presume that the *rab* designates a general. Krahmalkov[44] feels that *CIS* 1.5632, which he considers very old, chronicles the actual introduction of the office of suffete: "In the twentieth year of the [rule?] of the suffetes in Carthage." This is one of the rare texts containing the actual name of the city of Carthage.[45]

Drews[46] held that the Spartan dual kingship was an adaptation for lifetime tenure of the Semitic pattern at Carthage and perhaps at Tyre also. Roman historians saw the more obvious parallelism between the two annually elected magistrates at Rome and Carthage: so Nepos, *Hannibal* 7.4 *ut enim Romae consules, sic Karthagine quotannis annui bini reges creabantur,* "as the consuls at Rome, so at Carthage every year two annual 'kings' were created." By Livy 3.55.1 and Varro *de lingua latina* 6.88 the consuls are called *iudices,* "judges." Hence R. Yaron concluded[47] that the Roman consulate was modeled on the Carthaginian pattern.[48] But the opposite may have been the case. The

And the closer the ties of Carthage to Tyre, the less likely it would have been to set up an alternative kingship. W. Ameling (*Karthago* . . . [Vestigia 45; München: Beck, 1995], 67–97) thinks there were actual kings at Carthage; but the absence of *mlk* from the inscriptions is decisive.

42. Werner Huss, "Zu punischen Datierungsformeln," *Welt des Orients* 9 (1977/8) 249–52.

43. Forms of this annual dating are further attested at *KAI* 80, 81 (twice), 96; *CIS* 1.4824, 6053.

44. C. Krahmalkov, "Notes on the Role of the Softim in Carthage," *Rivista di studi fenici* 4 (1976) 153–57.

45. But the *iudicum ordo Carthagine* (Livy 33.46.1) appears to be a body of regular court judges.

46. Robert Drews, "Phoenicians, Carthage and the Spartan *Eunomia*," *AJP* 100 (1979) 45–58.

47. R. Yaron, "Semitic Elements in Early Rome," 343–57, in A. Watson, ed., *Daube Noster: Essays in Legal History for David Daube* (Edinburgh: Scottish Academic, 1974).

48. The name *Rōma* itself might be the Phoenician form of Heb. *ramah* "high," and the temple of Heracles in the Forum Boarium at Rome might have been a Phoenician foundation.

Phoenician colonies, which eventually turned into cities, were in a situation unique for West Semitic civilization. Practically, they were independent powers, engaging in trade and war, facing internal strains and dissension; but sentimentally they were still attached to the Phoenician homeland with its kings. Thus there is no clear evidence that they developed an autonomous kingship; and in the vacuum thus created, it seems equally possible that they developed magistrates after the pattern in Greece and Rome, where kingship (in contrast to Phoenicia) early faded out.

However, in some sense the Carthaginian suffetes must be inheritors of the old Canaanite pattern represent by the Hebrew book of Judges *(shopheṭim)*, although there is no indication that any of those served at the same time or collegially. In an interim period in the history of Tyre, Josephus *(c. Ap.* 155–58)[49] records a series of "judges" *(dikastai),* including a period of six years when two judges served. After Alexander judges continued in the Phoenician homeland. About 200 B.C.E. the Sidonian Diotimus won the chariot race at the Nemean games, and the city honored him with a statue and inscription,[50] followed by twelve lines of elegiacs in Doric. He is a "judge." It has been suggested[51] that 2 Chron 19:11 is a parallel to the dyarchy of suffetes; but there it is a matter of a priest and a governor with separate functions. The closest Hebrew parallel to the Roman dual consulate, the Punic *sufetes,* and the Spartan dual kingship, is the dual kingship in Jerusalem and Shechem after the death of Solomon; for it seems that both kings of "Judah" and "Israel" claimed to be the true king of one people, or were thought of as joint kings over it.

No text explains the origins of the dual magistracy in Carthage. In Rome, Gantz[52] points out that both the first "consuls" (as later remembered) were Tarquins: L. Tarquinius Collatinus (Livy 1.60.4) and L. Iunius Brutus, son of Tarquinia a king's sister (Livy 1.56.7) and of M. Iunius (Dionysius Hal. 4.67.4). Gantz observes (p. 548):

> Livy seems not to notice the paradox inherent in the fact that the first two consuls of the Roman Republic after the expulsion of the Tarquins were themselves Tarquins. Nor does he remark that these courageous founders of the new government, Brutus and Collatinus, were precisely

49. = Menander Ephesius frag. 7 Jacoby *FGH* 783.

50. L. Moretti, *Iscrizioni agonistiche greche* (Studi pubblicati dall'Istituto Italiano per la Storia antica 12; Roma: Signorelli, 1953), no. 41, 108.

51. By Lipiński in DCPP 429 and elsewhere.

52. T. N. Gantz, "The Tarquin Dynasty," *Historia* 24 (1975) 539–54.

the Tarquins next in line for the throne after Superbus and his sons had been driven out. . . . Together the two of them engineered a revolution whose goal was not, I think, the abolishment of the monarchy, but rather the seizure of it.

But anyway, Roman annalists remembered them as the first of a new order rather than the last of the old. When Collatinus was forced to resign, P. Valerius Volesi filius (Publicola) was elected to take his place (Livy 1.58.6, 2.2.11); his name may stand in an archaic inscription from Satricum, POPLIOSIO VALESIOSIO.[53]

The Council of Elders May Be "Sitting at the Gate"

While in time the council of elders absorbs many of the functions of the god-like king, originally judgment is a perquisite of the king shared with the High God. Micaiah sees Yahweh on his throne, and the host of heaven standing on his right and left (1 Kgs 22:19-23); "God has taken his place in the council of El; in the midst of the gods he holds judgment" (Ps 82:1)—a Psalm where (as occasionally elsewhere) *Elohim* substitutes for the expected *Yahweh*. Further, "[Who] is like Yahweh among the sons of Elim? a God feared in the council of the holy ones?" (Ps 89:7-8). It is also "the council of Yahweh" (Jer 23:18), "the council of Eloah" (Job 15:8). Although his superiority is emphasized, "Who is like thee, Yahweh, among the Elim?" (Exod 15:11), nevertheless his colleagues were on hand when he raised up the wave of the Exodus; and when he thunders, those "sons of Elim" (Ps 29:1) give him praise. At Deut 32:43 the Hebrew has lost at least two lines preserved in the LXX, "You heavens, rejoice with him; and let all the sons of God bow down before him." So in Ugaritic,[54] '*dt ilm* "assembly of the gods," cf. Ps 82:1; KTU 1.65.3 *mpḫrt bn il* "assembly of the sons of El"; *KAI* 4.4 "the assembly of the holy gods of Byblos."

We saw above how (*Iliad* 8.2) Zeus "called an assembly of the gods." Earlier (*Iliad* 1.534) the others are in their seats at his "house," Olympus, awaiting his arrival. In Seneca (*Nat. Quest.* 2.41) from Etruscan traditions Jupiter has two levels of council, *consilium,* which he must consult before launching a second- or third-degree missile (it is unclear whether either includes the other).

---

53. *L'Année épigraphique* 1979.136. 61. It is a dedication by Valerius's *suodales,* "comrades"; Cornell, *The Beginnings of Rome,* 143, sees him as in a class of *condottieri,* leaders of private armies, among whom he counts Appius Claudius, Cn. Marcius Coriolanus, Lars Porsenna.

54. KTU 1.15.II.7 = *UNP* 24. Further discussion of these texts at EFH 177, 355.

In Israel a deliberative group of elders sits in the gates of any given city. Of the wise woman it is said: "Her husband is known in the gates, when he sits among the elders of the land" (Prov 31:23). Job boasts, "When I went out to the gate of the city . . . the elders rose and stood" (Job 29:7-8). The rebellious son (Deut 21:19, cf. 22:15; 25:7) is to be brought "to the elders of his city, even to the gate of his place." Amos (5:15, cf. 5:10-12) cries out, "Establish justice in the gate." These elders are obviously an inherited body, supplementing the king's authority, whether the city is Jerusalem or another.

In Troy—for Homer a model Oriental town—the council, as we saw, sits at a gate: at the gates of Priam (*Iliad* 2.788); at the Scaean gates (3.148–49), when the elders meet by themselves. Livy in book 1 assumes a class of *patres* under the kings, and calls them *senatus* when the last king is expelled. Thereupon the Senate becomes the dominant power in the state, providing from among its number the annually elected consuls (originally *praetores,* Livy 3.55.12) who take the king's place.

In the *rhetra* supposedly given to Lycurgus by Delphi at Sparta (Plutarch *Lyc.* 6.1) he is told to set up "a *gerousia* of thirty including the *archagetai,*" where Plutarch interprets the *archagetai* as kings. The Roman people once had three tribes divided into ten *curiae* each.[55] We saw above that at Carthage within the larger senate or *synklētos* there was a smaller body or *gerousia.* Drews[56] marshals evidence that the smaller body had thirty members. Livy 30.16.3 says that in 203 B.C.E. the Carthaginians sent for negotiation "thirty leading members from the elders; this group was a more influential council among them, a strong force in directing the Senate itself." It would be natural to identify it with the *gerousia.* Elsewhere also committees of thirty are mentioned (Livy 30.36.9; *Periocha* 49). At Polybius 1.87.3 the Carthaginians choose "thirty men of the *gerousia.*" A fragment (*CIS* 1.3917) of the sacrificial tariff (*KAI* 74)[57] fills out its initial line to create a complete text: "Table of the tariffs set up by the thirty men in charge of the tariffs." Committees of thirty then were standard at Carthage, and perhaps its Senate had a central committee of thirty. Drews assumed that it was the pattern for the *gerousia* of thirty at Sparta; but again, since it was the Phoenician colonists who had to be the innovators, perhaps they were dependent on Greeks.

55. Livy 1.13.6; Cicero *rep.* 2.14; Festus 113L; Cornell 114.

56. Footnote 46 above.

57. Latin "tariffs" from North Africa list seven to nine sacrificial animals offered to several divinities, always by a *sacerdos Saturni; CIL* 8.8246–47, 27763; E. Lipiński, ed., *Carthago,* Studia Phoenicia 6; Orientalia Lovaniensia Analecta 26 (Leuven: Peeters, 1988), 217, no. 53. See DCPP 440; D. W. Baker, "Leviticus 1–7 and the Punic Tariffs: A Form Critical Comparison," *ZAW* 99 (1987) 188–97.

When the messenger from Claudius came bringing his letter to the "magistrates, *boulē* and people of the men of Jerusalem" (Josephus *AJ* 20.11), if he had three copies, to whom did he deliver the copy for the *boulē*? Perhaps it was intended for the Sanhedrin, in effect the Hellenistic Senate of Jerusalem. Under the Maccabees (2 Macc 14:5) there was a *synhedrion* in Jerusalem (cf. Josephus *AJ* 14.167); at 20.20 Josephus calls it "of judges." It probably continues what earlier is called the *gerousia* (Josephus *AJ* 12.138). *M. Sanh.* I.6 calls the body in Jerusalem the "Great Sanhedrin"; being of seventy-one members it was identical with the *Beth Din* (*m. Sanh.* I.5).[58] The Hebrew *Sanhedrin* is then a loan of long standing; note its accurate record of the unwritten internal Greek *h*. At *BJ* 2.331 (cf. 336) Josephus must mean "the high priests and the Sanhedrin." At *BJ* 5.532 one Aristeus from Emmaus is "scribe of the Senate"; a session of the Sanhedrin (*m. Sanh.* IV.3) had two "scribes of the judges." Acts 5:21 is a unique witness to *two* bodies of elders at Jerusalem: "the Sanhedrin and the whole [evidently larger] *gerousia*." Joseph of Arimathea (Mark 15:43) was "a respectable member of the *Boulē*." The same word went into Palmyrene in a bilingual of 161 C.E. (*PAT* 1373) referring to a "senator" of Antioch.

The Assembly of the People Has a Spokesman with Sacral Immunity
To a large extent, Hebrew prophet, Hellenic reforming poet, and Roman tribune of the people have parallel immunity. In Rome the plebs was felt to be a state within the state; Livy 3.19 has a consul claim that the tribunes have made the plebs "like a part broken off from the rest of the people, your own fatherland, a separate republic," *partem uelut abruptam a cetero populo uestram patriam peculiaremque rem publicam.* From time to time the plebs was thought to "secede" to its own territory, *plebs . . . secessit in Ianiculum* (Livy *Per.* 11), although it is hard for lack of contemporary records to divine the underlying political realities.[59] What is plain is that the plebs was something less than the full body of citizens: its secession did not leave Rome without population. Cornell (339, etc.) insists that many or most Roman citizens originally were neither patrician nor plebeian; those names marked fixed points on a broad spectrum of social statuses.

58. Classically, *synedrion* appears in various connections: Diodorus 16.41.1 so names the Phoenician council at Tripolis before Alexander; Polybius 1.11.1 so names the Roman Senate, and 1.31.8 the Carthaginian.

59. Sallust (*Cat.* 33.3) has a dissident write: *Saepe ipsa plebes, aut dominandi studio permota aut superbia magistratuum, armata a patribus secessit;* "Often the plebs itself, either moved by the desire to rule or by the insolence of magistrates, has seceded under arms from the patricians."

In Athens the *dēmos* became the dominant power in the state, with the archon and other magistrates chosen by lot. In Israel any formal role of the people or *'am* is hard to document. Here again Carthage, partly anticipated by the Phoenician cities, is assimilated to the Greco-Roman pattern. Sznycer[60] finds three categories of Phoenician/Punic texts in which *'am* "people" has so formal a sense as to suggest the meaning "assembly."

(a) "People" as validating an era in dates. Thus, in an inscription of Umm el-'Amed (*KAI* 18), "In the year 180 [of the Seleucid era = 132 B.C.E.] of the lord of kings [Antiochus VII], year 143 of the people of Tyre." "People" must refer to a body that came into being at a definite date.[61]

(b) "People of Carthage." An enigmatic series of inscriptions from Carthage[62] are dedications, which may end in "people of Carthage." They may refer to manumissions; the general sense should be "by decree of the people of Carthage." This is the only series of texts other than *CIS* 1.5632 where the name of Carthage appears in Punic texts. Whatever the translation, the phrase suggests an organization of the people.

(c) People of another land, state, island. These come from Carthage proper, North Africa, and Sardinia; they are dedications by a man who is always from a different place than the site of the stone. Thus *CIS* 1.3707 (from Carthage), "Adnibaal son of Shaphat who belongs to the people of Rosh Melqart." The same appears on Punic coins from Sicily (Cephaloedium or Heraclea Minoa).[63] An African seamark *Mercuri promunturium* (Livy 29.27.8, Pliny 5.24) seems to have the same name;[64] and this raises the question whether *Mercurius* is elsewhere a Latinization of Melqart.[65]

As the Roman plebs constituted a state within the state, so in a sense did women, youth, and slaves (p. 140 below). Slaves were a collectivity with rights exercised on the annual Saturnalia: so Ausonius 7.23.15 defines the *Saturnalia* as the *festaque seruorum cum famulantur eri,* "the festival of the slaves

60. Maurice Sznycer, "L''assemblée du peuple' dans les cités puniques d'après les témoignages épigraphiques," *Semitica* 25 (1975) 47–68.

61. Similarly of the "people of Tyre," *KAI* 19; of the "people of Sidon," in a bilingual from the Piraeus (*KAI* 60); of the "people of Lapethos" (*KAI* 43); see *Lapathos* Strabo 14.6.3.

62. *CIS* 1.269–91, 4908–9; most fragmentary in part.

63. B. V. Head, *Historia Numorum,* 2d ed. (Oxford: Oxford Univ. Press, 1910), 136. For Rosh Melqarth, see DCPP 378.

64. So perhaps the "mound or tomb of Mercury," *tumulus Mercuri* (Livy 26.44.6) at Carthago Nova of Spain.

65. For these texts see also J. Teixidor, "L'assemblée législative en Phénicie d'après les inscriptions," *Syria* 57 (1980) 453–64.

when their masters wait on them at table." In legend Jerusalem, Rome, and some Greek cities of the West were founded by a community of slaves.

The Sacral Functions of the King (by Whomever Exercised) Survive His Political Power

The Maccabees called themselves "high priest" until John Hyrcanus (134 B.C.E.), and the Romans saw it in their interest to maintain the Jewish high priesthood. Athenian tradition records a long list of kings; at an uncertain date, it held, their political prerogatives were taken over by a polemarch and then an archon, later enlarged by six more to a total of nine (Aristotle, *Ath. Pol.* 3). So throughout the history of Athens there was a *basileus*; "we always have kings" (Plato, *Menexenus* 238D). By the fourth century B.C.E. he dealt principally with homicide and a range of religious matters, and was annually chosen by lot (*Ath. Pol.* 55.1); he often appears in the orators (e.g., Antiphon 6.38).[66] Livy (2.2.1) says that in the first year of the Roman republic the sacred functions previously filled by the kings were turned over to a *regem sacrificolum*, "king of the sacrifices," made subordinate to the pontifex so as not to hamper liberty. The *rex sacrorum* was forbidden political office (Livy 40.42.8). Down to the times of Cicero (*de domo* 38) there continued to be such a *regem sacrorum*. Another such is the *rex Nemorensis* at Nemi made famous by Frazer (Suetonius *Gaius* 35.3), who must be a fugitive slave who has killed his predecessor.[67]

Taboos Are Laid on the King and on the Priest of the High God

The law of Moses may be compared with regulations on the *flamen Dialis* or priest of Jupiter (Aulus Gellius, 10.15.19-25). (a) *Yeast.* "No cereal offering which you bring to Yahweh shall be made with leaven" (Lev 2:11); "It is not permitted for the flamen to touch flour mixed with yeast *{farinam fermento imbutam}*." (b) *Corpse.* "[The high priest] shall not go in to any dead body" (Lev 21:11); "[The flamen] never enters a place where there is a tomb; he never touches a corpse *(mortuum numquam attingit)*." (c) *Nakedness.* Aaron and his sons have linen tunics (Exod 39:27) "to cover the flesh of their nakedness . . . lest they bring guilt on themselves and die" (Exod 28:42-43); "The flamen never

---

66. Drews, *Basileus,* is uncertain whether that historical magistrate the Athenian *basileus* really (as Aristotle believed) is the inheritor of older sacral functions. But Aristotle *Ath. Pol.* 3.5 attests the "union" and marriage of the king's wife to Dionysus. She was the *basilinna* (Ps.-Demosth. 59.74).

67. For the "king" of Nemi see further Strabo 5.3.12, Servius on *Aeneid* 6.136.

takes off his inner tunic except under cover, lest he be naked under the sky as if under the eyes of Jupiter," *tunica intima, nisi in locis tectis, non exuit se, ne sub caelo tamquam sub oculis Iouis nudus sit.*[68]

Other restrictions on the high priest appear at *m. Sanhedrin* II, followed by privileges and restrictions attached to the king, based on Deut. 17:16-20.[69] "The king can neither judge nor be judged, he cannot act as witness and others cannot bear witness against him. . . . None may marry his widow. . . . None may ride on his horse and none may sit on his throne and none may make use of his sceptre. None may see him when his hair is being cut or when he is naked or when he is in the bath-house." Thus "the cuttings of the hair and nails of the Dialis must be buried in the earth under a fruitful tree." Shortly before his death Alexander the Great executed a deranged man who had sat on his throne (Plutarch *Alexander* 73–74).

Restoration of Divine Monarchy under Rome

Titles of the Emperor

At first there was an effort, in spite of antipathy to the title *rex*, to assimilate the new power of the Caesars to the old Roman kings. We all know how Antony says (*Julius Caesar* III):

> You all did see, that on the *Lupercall*,
> I thrice presented him a Kingly Crowne,
> Which he did thrice refuse. . . .

It was actually a *diadema* (Suetonius, *Julius* 79.2–3). Was it the influence of Caesar's eager adherents, or disinformation spread by the conspirators themselves, that the Sibylline books affirmed "the Parthians could only be con-

---

68. The words for "tunic" in these passages are probably related.

69. Whatever old materials this chapter contains, in its present form it is remarkably Latinate. (a) Thus (*Sanhedrin* II.1) at a banquet the high priest, unlike the people, sits on a "stool"; this is Latin *subsellium*, "bench," especially as reserved for the Senate (Cicero *Phil.* 5.18). (b) The king lives in his *paltorin* (*Sanh.* II.3), from *praetorium* with dissimilation and perhaps an echo of *palatium*. (c) The king may "heap up silver and gold" (Deut. 17:17) only to cover his soldiers' pay (*Sanh.* II.4 MS), from *opsōnion*, "pay" (but *opsonia* Pliny Jun. *Epist.* 10.118.2 is "pension"). So the Peshitto of Luke 3:14; the soldiers that John the Baptist met were of Herod Antipas, who, however, ran his little militia in Roman style. Thus the Mishna's idea of the king is colored with more recent memories of the Roman procurator of Judaea. For all these words see Samuel Krauss, *Griechische und lateinische Lehnwörter im Talmud, Midrasch und Targum*, vol. 2 (repr. Hildesheim: Olms, 1964).

quered by a king" *(Parthos nisi a rege non posse uinci?).*[70] Cicero *(Phil.* 2.85–87) describes the offer, and adds that M. Antonius made an entry in the *Fasti:* "Marcus Antonius the consul by command of the people offered Gaius Caesar, perpetual dictator, the kingship; Caesar refused it."

Initially, Octavian wished to be called "Romulus," but then saw that this created the suspicion he was aspiring to kingship and settled on "Augustus" (Dio Cassius 53.16.7). Still, in the Greek East, used to kingship, the emperor is occasionally called *basileus.* Josephus *(BJ* 5.563, cf. 3.351) "the kings of the Romans always honored and adorned the temple." Appian *Bell. Civ.* 2.86 calls Hadrian "king of the Romans"; and so at *IGRR* 4.341 (Pergamum) Hadrian (probably) is *despotēs basileus.* Then see 1 Peter 2:17 (cf 2:13): "fear God, honor the king." And further John 19:15, where the chief priests say, "We have no king but Caesar"; Acts 17:7: "They are acting against the decrees of Caesar, saying there is another king, Jesus." The fixation of Midrash on a "king of flesh and blood" can hardly refer to anybody but the emperor (mostly in Byzantium).

Julius Caesar stayed in power through continued holding the office of *dictator,* eventually as *dictator perpetuus,* as well as the consulate; but Octavian consistently refused the office of dictator (Dio Cassius 54.1.3, if the office then indeed existed). After the battle of Actium (31 B.C.E.) Octavian was consul annually until 23 B.C.E., when he resigned the office. He claims that in 27 B.C.E. *(Res Gestae* 34) "I transferred the state from my own control to the will of the Senate and the Roman people"; this was the first of two settlements, at which time he received the title Augustus. Dio (53.17.4) at his later date regards the normal title of the emperor as just that, *imperator* (in his Greek *autokratōr*); Augustus only refers to the twenty-one occasions when he was saluted as *imperator (R.G.* 4). He has in fact no standard way of referring to his status; when he is least self-aware he records the Temple of Janus as having been closed thrice *me princi{pe} (R.G.* 13) "while I was *princeps."* This was something both less and more than the title *princeps senatus,* which he held for forty years since 28 B.C.E. *(R.G.* 7).

The Proconsular Authority

The heart of Augustus's power, that which he received through membership in the Senate, is not attested in a fully satisfactory manner in contemporary

---

70. Cicero *(de div.* 2.110–12), writing after the Ides of March, begs the Quindecemviri *ut quiduis potius ex illis libris quam regem proferant,* "to bring anything at all out of the [Sibylline] books other than a king."

sources. Dio 53.32.5 says that in 23 B.C.E. the Senate gave him once for all a power, which must be in Latin *imperium proconsulare*; perhaps he had held something of the sort in the years after 27 B.C.E. For in 27 B.C.E. (Dio 53.12, cf. Strabo 17.3.25) he had divided the provinces into imperial and senatorial, retaining for himself the principal provinces in which there were standing armies; his new power was the grant of authority over those. At Tacitus *Ann.* 1.3 Tiberius becomes "(adopted) son, a colleague in his *imperium,* sharing in his tribunician power"; here *imperium* should refer to Augustus's full power.[71] Dio 53.32.5 also appears to say (although the language is vague) that Augustus held in addition a superior authority over the governors of the Senatorial provinces, which moderns call an *imperium maius,* a phrase apparently unattested in Latin. Under the Republic former consuls in the status *pro consule* were the normal governors of the provinces. Thus, while the honorific annual consulships were restored to the Senate, practical control over the far-flung provinces and the armies quartered there fell to him through the proconsular authority.

The Tribunician Power

The office of tribune had come down to the late Republic invested with a sacral immunity for its holder. At some point in his career (it appears) Octavian had been offered the bundle of privileges associated with the tribunate, but at first made no use of it.[72] In 23 B.C.E. the *tribunicia potestas* was made both perpetual and annual (*R.G.* 10, Dio 53.32.6). As a result his person was *sacrosanctus*; and by assuming the powers of the office he fell heir to the legislative privileges that the tribune proper had exercised on behalf of the plebs. (Technically he was not actually a *tribunus,* an office reserved for plebeians.) From 23 B.C.E. on, the annual *Fasti* are marked by the years of Augustus's tribunician power—and also by that of his designated successor. It is a special irony of history that the office intended to empower the plebs over against Senate and magistrates became the primary personal bulwark of a new monarch.

Sacral Offices of the Emperor

Augustus was made *pontifex maximus* in 13 B.C.E. upon the death of the triumvir Lepidus (*R.G.* 10). (The Vulgate of John 18:13-24 [but none of the other Gospels] translates *archiereus* of a specific Jewish high priest as *pontifex*.)

---

71. Later in the *Annals* Augustus seeks the *proconsulare imperium* for Germanicus (1.12), and Claudius for Nero (12.41), but these may be ordinary provincial commands.

72. I cannot easily document such an occasion.

In 2 B.C.E. Augustus records (*R.G.* 35) that "the Senate and the equestrian order and the whole Roman people" called him *pater patriae*, "father of the fatherland." The great founding event of his new age was the Ludi Saeculares in 17 B.C.E. Augustus's adoptive father Julius Caesar (like Augustus after him) was ascribed a formal cult as *diuus*, "deified," and Halley's comet conveniently appeared at his funeral games (Suetonius *Div. Jul.* 88). Thus the sacral offices, which both at Rome and Athens continued under the name of the old monarch, were added to the new monarch.

Christ and Caesar

Jesus is often called "son of David," in particular at what is called his "triumphal entry" into Jerusalem (Matt 21:19, but not in the other Gospels). Pilatus is put up by the Jerusalem authorities into asking Jesus, "Are you the king of the Jews?" (so all four Gospels); and so marks his *titulus* (in three languages, John 19:20). John, among other good pieces of tradition that he may not fully understand, records that after the feeding of the five thousand Jesus is aware that a movement is afoot "to make him king" (John 6:15). Both the God of the Decalogue and the Roman emperor ("Caesar"), in the line of the old loyalty oath, demanded exclusive allegiance; and the chief priests remind Pilatus of this, "We have no king but Caesar" (John 19:15). Then in the first century titles develop that more and more mutually assimilate the statuses of Christ and Caesar.

Evangelium, "Good News"

The letter of Paullus Fabius Maximus the proconsul of Asia, about 9 B.C.E. (together with decrees of the *koinon* of Asia), is the principal testimony for *euangelion*, "good news," in the imperial cult.[73] The first decree has (ii.40) "The birthday of the god [Augustus!] was the beginning for the world of the good news that exists on his account." We have fragments of a Latin version, but not of this phrase, and it is hard to guess Latin for *euangelion*.[74]

The word recurs with *kosmos* at Mark 14:9, "wherever the good news is proclaimed in all the world." In the Vulgate it is transcribed simply *euangelium*; and so occasionally in the Peshitto, Mark 1:1 along with "beginning."

---

73. Robert K. Sherk, *Roman Documents from the Greek East:* Senatus Consulta *and* Epistulae *to the Age of Augustus* (Baltimore: Johns Hopkins Univ. Press, 1969), no. 65, 328; *OGIS* 458.

74. A papyrus of 238 C.E. records the writer's pleasure at the "good news" that the son of Maximinus Thrax has been proclaimed Caesar (A. Deissmann, *Licht vom Osten* (4th ed.; Tübingen: Mohr, 1923), 314.

Thence into Qur'an 3.65 *'attawrātu wal' injīlu* "the Torah and the Gospel." In a text omitted from some editions of *b. Shabb.* 116a[75] the Greek is tendentiously distorted as "idol-scroll" and "sin-scroll." Scholars differ how far the New Testament usage has an imperial flavor. Nock[76] austerely thinks *euangelion* simply "the obvious Greek word both for [an emperor's accession] and for the news of the birth of Jesus." But Sherk[77] writes:

> Augustus was *sōtēr,* the savior of a war-torn and shattered world, the hope for the future, the bearer of *euangelia.* A title and an expression, these are keys to an understanding of the religious movements which were then taking shape.

"Savior of the World"

In an inscription from Myra of Lycia[78] Augustus has the titles "Divine Augustus, son of a god, Caesar, 'emperor' of land and sea, the benefactor and savior of the whole world." This text is exceptional, perhaps unique, in making Augustus *diuus* apparently during his lifetime. Already in 196 B.C.E., Chalcis set up a cult to T. Quinctius Flamininus for his proclaiming Greek liberty; it was still going on in the time of Plutarch, who quotes from the hymn in honor of "great Zeus, Rome, Titus, and the faith of the Romans" (Plutarch *Flam.* 16.4), ending "O savior Titus!" Luke 22:25 has Jesus correctly note that the great ones of the nations are called Benefactors, *euergetai.* In the Greek of the Rosetta Stone[79] earlier rulers, Ptolemy III and his sister Arsinoe, had the titles "Savior gods, Sibling gods and Benefactor gods." Philo (*Leg. ad Gaium* 148, LCL x. 174) calls Augustus *euergetēs,* but not as a full title.

"The savior of the world" in various forms is standard for the emperors after Augustus; see the summary by Koester.[80] A resolution from Narbo of Italy[81] on Augustus's birthday (in agreement with Paulus's letter) has a related formula: "September 23, on which day the good fortune of the age brought [Augustus] into being as the ruler of the world." Propertius 4.6.37, describing the battle of Actium, calls Augustus *mundi seruator,* but this is not

75. Cf. Jastrow i.27 and SVMB ii.379.

76. A. D. Nock, *Essays on Religion and the Ancient World,* 2 vols., ed. Z. Stewart (Cambridge: Harvard Univ. Press, 1972), 1:81.

77. Sherk, *Roman Documents,* 337.

78. Ehrenberg-Jones 72.

79. *OGIS* 90.4, 196 B.C.E.

80. Craig R. Koester, "'The Savior of the World' (John 4:42)," *JBL* 109 (1990) 665–80.

81. *ILS* 112A, 12/13 C.E.; Ehrenberg-Jones 100.

a phrase of the imperial cult. At John 4:42 (cf. 1 John 4:14) the Samaritans know that Jesus is truly "the savior of the world," Vg *saluator mundi*.

"Son of God"

The imperial title "son of the deified one" *(diui filius)* is regularly transcribed in Greek *huios theou*. The New Testament agrees in the Greek with a different connotation. At John 19:7 where the Ioudaioi (Jews? Judaeans?) say "because he made himself the son of God," Pilatus is afraid because the Greek sounds like an imperial claim. Again, most manuscripts of Mark 1:1 have "Son of God." In the neo-Punic of Lepcis (*KAI* 120, 8 B.C.E.) Augustus is *bn 'lm*. At Palmyra in the adulatory East, Hadrian even during his lifetime is *theou Hadrianou = hdryn' 'lh'* (*PAT* 0305).

"Lord"

Festus so refers politely to Nero, "I have nothing certain to write to the Lord," Acts 25:26. So it is mere politeness when Pliny the Younger writes to Trajan *ago gratias, domine* (*Ep.* 10.6). The Hellenistic monarchs were so addressed, in particular Herod the Great in Batanaea (*OGIS* 415). Cassius at Rhodes after Julius's assassination was addressed as "king and lord" *(basilea kai kyrion)* and replied, "Neither king nor lord, but slayer and chastiser of a king and lord" (Plutarch *Brut.* 30.2). Augustus prudently refused the title *dominus* (Suet. *Aug.* 73), though in papyri[82] he occasionally is addressed as *kyrios*. The identity *kyrios = dominus* is formal in a bilingual inscription under Trajan (*IGRR* i.1207) where AVG[VSTI] DOMINI N[OSTRI] = *Sebastou tou kyriou.*

Polycarp of Smyrna, bishop and martyr, refuses to say "Caesar is lord" *(kyrios Kaisar)* (*Martyrdom of Polycarp* 8.2). Domitian asked to be called "our lord and god" *(dominus et deus noster;* Suetonius, *Dom.* 13): Martial in a frivolous context (5.8.1) refers to an "edict of our lord and god" *(edictum domini deique nostri)*, but under Trajan rejects the title (10.72.8). And so at John 20:28 Thomas apparently makes a deliberate reference to the title, "My lord and my God." In Old Aramaic a king (*KAI* 216) calls himself "slave of Tiglath-Pileser, Lord of the four quarters of the earth." In Palmyrene (*PAT* 0291) Septimius Odainath is "illustrious consul *(hypatikos)*, our lord." Aretas of Nabataea (2 Cor 11:32) has the titles (*CIS* 2.201) "our lord Haretath, king of the Nabataeans, lover of his people." In the New Testament *kyrios* of God or of Christ comes out in Latin *dominus* and in Syriac *mr'*; in all three languages the usage echoes the imperial mode of address.[83]

---

82. E.g. *Aegyptische Urkunden aus den Königlichen Staatlichen Museen zu Berlin, Griechische Urkunden,* 15 vols. (Berlin, 1895–1983), 11:1200.

83. See the lengthy article by Foerster in *TWNT/TDNT* 3 with subtle distinctions.

Furthermore, the words for "lord" moved back and forth among the languages. *Domine* vocative becomes rabbinic *domine*. *Kyrie* becomes rabbinic *kîrî* and *qîrî*, "Sir,"[84] and in church usage enters Latin. Thus in the *Itin. Egeriae* 24.5[85] at the commemoration of the departed in the liturgy of Jerusalem: "And as the deacon speaks each individual name, many children (*pisinnus*, a very rare nursery word) stand responding each time *kyrie eleyson*, or as we say 'Lord have mercy.'" Above all the Aramaic came to be known. Paul writes to Corinth, without word dividers, *maranatha* (1 Cor 16:22); the phrase also appears at *Didache* 10.6, perhaps independently. Evidently the Aramaic and its meaning were familiar to Paul's correspondents. The word division is not quite certain, and the Syriac interprets *maran 'eta* "our Lord has come." It seems better to interpret with Rev 22:20 *erchou kyrie Iēsou* "come, Lord Jesus" (also at the end of a book) and divide *marana ta*. Still today a Beirut mother calls to her boy in Lebanese colloquial Arabic *ta'* "come" (but to a girl *tay*).

The god of Gaza was known as Marnas. Since the pagans under Porphyrius (bishop of Gaza 395–420 C.E.) believed (Marcus Diaconus) that "Marnas was god of the rains," it is natural to take his name as a title "our Lord." Philo *Flaccus* 36–39 (LCL ix.322) tells the story of the mock coronation (37 C.E. or later) of the lunatic Carabas by the Alexandrians: they hail him as *Marin*, which Philo states to mean "the lord" *(ton kyrion)* "among the Syrians." It was the mob's way of mocking the state visit of Herod Agrippa (I) "the Syrian." Carabas is given substitutes for diadem, cloak, and scepter. Compare Matt 27:28-29 with the same three items: the scarlet robe; the crown of thorns; and the reed in his right hand.

Thus both Caesar and Christ look back to ancient kingships. Octavian at first wanted to be called Romulus, and built his military powers on the (pro)consulate, the successor office to the regal. Jesus is called the "son of David." The dominion of each is extended from a city to the world; each is its savior; the birth of each begins good news *(euangelion)* to the world. Each is "lord and god" *(dominus et deus)*, each (in Greek) is "son of a god" *(theou huios)*. Each has exclusive claims made for him; the two are set against each other as objects of commitment. Here the comparison ends. Augustus achieved more power than any civic king dreamed of; Jesus' claim is through the renunciation of power. Between them the parabola from monarchy to constitution to monarchy is worked out in fully contrasted ways.

84. Texts in Krauss (note 69 above) 287, 539.
85. Ed. P. Marval, *Sources chrétiennes* 296 (Paris: Cerf, 1982), 240.

CHAPTER 3

The Mediterranean Seer and the Shaman

S*haman* properly means the Siberian figure so named in Tungus and other Altaic languages of Central Asia.[1] Tungus *šaman* is often thought derived from Pali *samaṇa* (Sanskrit *śramaṇa*).[2] The Pali is frequent in the *Dhammapada,* where it has been strongly ethicised: thus 184 (cf. 142, 254–55, 264–65): "nor is he an *ascetic* who harms others." I extend "shaman" to the Ainu and the North American cultures closely related to the Siberian, but not to comparable figures in other parts of the world. By "Mediterranean" seers I mean prophetic or charismatic figures primarily attested in Greek and West Semitic texts, supplemented by occasional artistic representations. Prehistoric religions and those of peoples without writing are a realm where everything can be compared with everything else. Here I strive for comparisons between cultures that commend themselves in as many ways as possible: through concrete details of cult or custom; in actual language attested in the texts; in artistic monuments.

There are several ways in which Mediterranean mantic figures *differ* from shamans.

---

1. For shamanism I originally followed the work of M. A. Czaplicka, *Aboriginal Siberia: A Study in Social Anthropology* (Oxford: Oxford Univ. Press, 1914), 197. I now supplement it with the survey by Mircea Eliade, *Shamanism: Archaic Techniques of Ecstasy,* trans. W. R. Trask (Bollingen Series 76; Princeton: Princeton Univ. Press, 1972). I draw illustrations further from Joseph Campbell, *The Way of the Animal Powers,* vol. 1 of *Historical Atlas of World Mythology* (San Francisco: Harper & Row, 1983), taking care to cite photos as close as possible to the restricted region defined above. The literature on shamanism is enormous and I make no claim to competency in it. My main point anyway is the *differences* between Mediterranean mantic figures and shamans strictly defined.

2. Discussion in Eliade, *Shamanism,* 495–96, who treats further the question how far Siberian shamanism takes up Buddhist/Lamanist influences.

(1) *The legendary element*. Shamanism, though extremely old in its origins, is also a contemporary phenomenon still being described and photographed by anthropologists. Our Greek and Hebrew texts describe charismatic figures, a Tiresias or Elisha, from what was already, for the authors of the texts (not to mention for us readers!), the legendary past. The principal exception is the Sicilian Empedocles, a personage apparently in the full light of history, although still in his poems making claims to divine status that in a few generations gave him too an aura of legend. Dodds:

> the fragments of Empedocles are the one first-hand source from which we can still form some notion of what a Greek shaman was really like; he is the last belated example of a species which with his death became extinct in the Greek world, though it still flourishes elsewhere.[3]

Thus he promises to one who learns from him:

> You will bring a needful drought for men out of black rain, and again you will bring sky-dwelling rains that nourish the trees from a summer drought; and you will bring the strength of a deceased man from Hades.[4]

In the sequel we shall find more rainmakers and raisers of the dead.

(2) *Historical period*. Siberian shamanism has coexisted for centuries with rational city life, and may well include broken-down practices from high religions such as Buddhism, *abgesunkenes hochreligiöses Gut*;[5] whereas Mediterranean prophecy was part of the matrix out of which civic freedom, high religion, and rational thought were to grow.

(3) *Climate*. In the arid Mediterranean, rainmaking is one of the functions of the seer. Around the Poles, rain or snow is the last thing the tribe needs to ask for. When the Ainu of northern Japan sacrifice the tame bear they have brought up from a cub, they instruct it: "You will tell the gods to give us riches, that our hunters may return from the forest laden with rich furs and animals good to eat, that our fishers may find troops of seals on the shore and under the sea, and that their nets may crack [cf. Luke 5:6!] under the weight

---

3. E. R. Dodds, *The Greeks and the Irrational* (Boston: Beacon, 1957), 145.

4. Empedocles frag 111, FVS[8] i.353.

5. K. Goldammer, "Elemente des Schamanismus im Alten Testament," 2:266–85 (esp. 284), in *Ex Orbe Religionum (Geo Widengren Festschrift),* Studies in the History of Religions 22 (Leiden: Brill, 1972).

of the fish."[6] No connection is made between the abundance of game and the weather. Only where Native Americans moved into agriculture in lands of uncertain rainfall, as in the southwest United States, did they take up the rain dance.

However, shamanism has been important as the label for attempts to look freshly at Mediterranean religion. Thus for Israel, A. S. Kapelrud was a pioneer.[7] Jepsen, operating with the model that the Israelites came from the desert into Palestine, concludes that the *nabi* was a role they first met in Palestine associated with a north Syrian or Anatolian stratum of the population.[8] K. Meuli explained striking elements in Hellenic prophecy as derived from contact with features of Scythian culture, beginning in the seventh century B.C.E., which he identified as shamanistic; thus "Skythische Schamanen bei Herodot."[9] So Dodds found appearing in Greece of the seventh century B.C.E. a "new religious pattern," which, "by crediting man with an occult self of divine origin, and setting soul and body at odds, . . . introduced into European culture a new interpretation of human existence, the interpretation we call puritanical."[10] He concludes that this was due to "the opening of the Black Sea to Greek trade and colonization in the seventh century, which introduced the Greeks for the first time to a culture based on shamanism."[11]

I begin this chapter by considering features of the Mediterranean seer that have good parallels in shamanism. I then go on to themes where Mediterranean prophecy has its own characteristic features, analogous often to shamanism, but distinct. Thus the birth of the seer takes place under divine auspices, perhaps directly by divine fatherhood; and upon birth he may undergo an ordeal such as exposure on the waters. In Mediterranean lands of uncertain rainfall, the seer is in charge of the withholding and granting of

6. A. I. Hallowell, "Bear Ceremonialism in the Northern Hemisphere" (Philadelphia: Univ. of Pennsylvania thesis, 1926), 126. For the bear cult among the Ainu, see Kazunobu Ikeya, "Bear Rituals of the Matagi and the Ainu in Northeastern Japan," in T. Yamada and T. Irimoto, eds., *Circumpolar Animism and Shamanism* (Sapporo: Hokkaido Univ. Press, 1997), 55–66. (The same volume has an environmental essay [pp. 3–7] by Masanori Toyooka Atuy, "Coexistence with Nature and the 'Third Philosophy': Learning from the Spirit of the Ainu.")

7. A. S. Kapelrud, "Shamanistic Features in the Old Testament," in C.-M. Edsman, ed., *Studies in Shamanism* (Scripta Instituti Donneriani Aboensis; Stockholm: Almqvist & Wiksell, 1967), 90–96.

8. A. Jepsen, *Nabi: Soziologische Studien zur alttestamentlichen Literatur und Religionsgeschichte* (Munich: Beck, 1934), 245–46.

9. K. Meuli, "Scythica," *Hermes* 70 (1935) 121–76 = *Gesammelte Schriften* (Basel: Schwabe, 1975), 2:817–80.

10. Dodds, *The Greeks and the Irrational*, 139.

11. Ibid., 142.

rain; here we find the common vocabulary of the *torch* imitating lightning. As the shaman is in close touch with the animal world, and in particular the bear, the Mediterranean seer in his mysterious disappearances and appearances takes on features of the hibernating and risen bear. An eventual death is less final for him than for others, he remains powerful even in the realm of the dead. A mantic woman, a Circe, Sibyl, or witch of En-Dor, controls access to him. Such a prophetic pattern might have been transmitted between Israel and Hellas through the travels of the Gergithians or Girgashites.

Shamanistic Traits of the Mediterranean Seer

The Seer as Third Sex

Czaplicka says that it is common for male shamans to take up women's dress, exchange the lance and rifle for the needle and skin-scraper, and as "soft men" occasionally to be married to another man. Less common but not unknown is such a reverse case as the Chuckchee[12] widow with children:

> Following the command of the "spirits," she cut her hair, donned the dress of a man, adopted the masculine pronunciation, and even learned in a very short time to handle the spear and to shoot with a rifle. At last she wanted to marry and easily found a young girl who consented to become her wife.

Hence Czaplicka rejects the theory that all shamans were originally female and represented a vestige of an original matriarchy; she concludes rather:

> Socially, the shaman does not belong either to the class of males or to that of females, but to a third class, that of shamans. Sexually, he may be sexless, or ascetic, or have inclinations of homosexualistic character, but . . . may also be quite normal. And so, forming a special class, shamans have special taboos comprising both male and female characters.[13]

Campbell from other authors reports both changes; adapts from Hermann Baumann a global map of peoples with a "ritualistic permanent sex change"; and reproduces (his fig. 303) from Knud Rasmussen a "'soft man,' transvestite, or transformed shaman of the Chuckchi" wearing ordinary animal skins and boots.[14]

---

12. A tribe living just on the Siberian side of the Bering Strait.
13. Czaplicka, *Aboriginal Siberia*, 249–53.
14. Campbell, *The Way of the Animal Powers*, 174–75.

Herodotus (4.67, cf. 1.105) among the "prophets of the Scythians" includes the "androgynous Enarees." Here as in *oiorpata* (Herodotus 4.110) he seems to transmit a genuine Indo-European word, *a*- privative + *nar* "man," that is, "unmanly." Hippocrates (*Airs* 22) records impotence, transvestitism, and adoption of a feminine dialect among Scythian males: "Most of the Scythians become 'eunuchs,' take on women's work, [dress?] like women and speak likewise; such are called Anaries." Aristotle attests *malakia* (hereditary effeminacy?) among Scythian kings (*Eth. Nic.* 1150b14).

The mantic figure of early Hellas above all is Tiresias, more a class name than that of an individual, "reader of portents" *(teirata),* and a dialectal variant of *teratias* (Diodorus 34/35.2.8). He was Odysseus's guide in the underworld (*Odyssey* 10.492-3), "Tiresias of Thebes, the blind seer." Hesiod in his lost *Melampodia*[15] told how Tiresias saw two snakes copulating, wounded them, and was turned into a woman; then after seven years (according to Ovid) saw them again and was turned back into a man. Once Zeus maintained against Hera that the woman enjoyed intercourse more than a man and they called Tiresias in as experienced arbiter. He rashly answered: "Of ten parts a man enjoys only one, but a woman enjoys the full ten parts in her heart." Wherefore Hera blinded him, but Zeus bestowed on him the mantic art.[16] Ovid tells the story and adds: "for the loss of his sight [Jupiter] granted him to know the future, lightening the penalty by the honor" (*Metam.* 3.322–38): Zeus also gave him seven times an ordinary lifetime: "to live for seven generations of mortal men."[17] Tiresias, "old man with wrinkled dugs," is the narrator in *The Waste Land* and, as with Zeus and Hera, foresuffers the union of the typist and the "young man carbuncular."

The Hebrews found transvestites of both sexes in Canaan, and the practice caught on sufficiently to be forbidden: "The things of a man shall not be on a woman, and a man shall not put on a woman's mantle" (Deut 22:5). The prophet Ahijah wore one such (1 Kgs 11:29); of a woman, "the smell of your mantle is as the smell of Lebanon" (Song 4:11). Of Yahweh it is said: "wrapping himself in light as a mantle, spreading out the heavens like a curtain" (Ps 104:2). To put on such a garment from the opposite sex suggests some sort of functional interchange. In particular the earliest Hebrew documents attribute

15. Hesiod frag. 275, Merkelbach-West from Apollodorus 3.6.7 and other sources; see Frazer's notes *ad loc.* in the LCL.

16. But others (Apollodorus, ibid.) said that he saw his mother the nymph Chariclo naked while she was bathing, and was struck blind by Athena.

17. Hesiod frag. 276, Merkelbach-West from Tzetzes; the editors count the seven generations as: Cadmus, Polydorus, Labdacus, Laius, Oedipus, Eteocles, Laodamas.

to prophetic women the martial lifestyle thereafter exclusively masculine. Thus Miriam the prophetess (Exod 15:20) with her tambourine celebrates the victory over Egypt; Deborah the prophetess celebrates the slaying of Sisera by Jael (Judg 4:4). The only later prophetess we hear of is Huldah (2 Kgs 22:14); Noadiah (Neh 6:14) appears a false prophetess; at Isa 8:3 "prophetess" (*nebî'ah*) is just the prophet's wife.

The Seer as Handicapped

The shaman is one unfitted for standard vocational roles. Czaplicka interprets shamanism as a process of healing for the person involved: "to be called to become a shaman is generally equivalent to being afflicted with hysteria; then the accepting of the call means recovery." Her description points less to physical defects than to psychological deviance: "the expression of a shaman is peculiar—a combination of cunning and shyness; . . . it is often possible to pick him out from among many others."[18]

In early societies, where every able-bodied man is needed in time of peace for hunting or agriculture, and in time of war to take up arms, the sedentary occupations are reserved for the handicapped. Hephaestus the metalsmith was lame (*Iliad* 18.397), as a result (it was said) of having been thrown from Olympus by Zeus (1.591–93); but rather, a lame boy would normally be apprenticed to a smith. Teutonic Wayland the smith is lame.[19] But Charles thinks that Hephaestus "reflects the traditional view of the unhealthiness of the smith's craft stemming mainly from the use of the early arsenical materials,"[20] in particular the copper-arsenic alloy arsenical bronze found in early tools and weapons, which would have produced, among other symptoms, "muscular atrophy and polyneuritis"; in this view lameness is the effect, not the cause, of the trade.

The Phoenician priests of Baal "limped around the altar" (1 Kgs 18:26); and Elijah mocks them in the same language (18:21) "Why do you limp between two opinions?" Perhaps they were not doing a ritual dance step but really were lame, either from birth or having been made so for the priesthood. (But in Israel lameness, like other defects, disqualifies for the priesthood,

---

18. Czaplicka, *Aboriginal Siberia,* 172–74.

19. K. R. Crocker, "The Lame Smith: Parallel Features in the Myths of the Greek Hephaestus and the Teutonic Wayland," *Archaeological News* (Tallahassee) 6 (1977) 67–71; comparing the representations of the two in the François Vase from Chiusi, painted by Cleitias ab. 570 B.C.E.; and the Anglo-Saxon Franks Casket, eighth century C.E., now in the British Museum.

20. James A. Charles, in T. A. Wertime and J. D. Muhly, eds., *The Coming of the Age of Iron* (New Haven: Yale Univ. Press, 1980), 178.

Lev 21:18). Jonathan's son Mephibosheth, whose true name was surely Meribaal (1 Chron 9:40b), is lame (2 Sam 4:4, etc.), and perhaps this accounts for his apparent devotion to Baal (which here may be something more than a mere title of Yahweh).

Lameness also qualified a man, surprisingly, as a lover. The Amazons were said to cut off the hand or foot of their male children. The Scythians offered themselves as husbands, perfect and unmutilated, to which Antianeira the leader of the Amazons answered, in a formula that became proverbial, "the lame man does it best."[21]

Even in the modern world blindness can bring the compensation of a heightened ear for language; we need only remember the blind or near-blind writers Milton, Joyce, Thurber. As with Tiresias (above), the *Odyssey* (8.63–64) says of the bard Demodocus, in verses that make us think twice about the favor of the gods, "Him the Muse loved very much, and gave him good and evil; she deprived him of his eyes, but gave him sweet song." He is propped against a pillar (v. 66) to orient him, as Samson in the temple (Judg 16:25). The *Homeric Hymn* to Apollo (3.172) says, apparently in reference to Homer, that the sweetest of singers is a "blind man" of Chios.

The Hebrew prophets describe themselves as poor speakers, in language that sounds real and not deprecatory. Isaiah is "unclean in his lips" (Isa 6:5); Jeremiah "does not know how to speak" (Jer 1:6). Especially Moses is no "man of words" but "heavy of mouth and heavy of tongue" (Exod 4:10); he is "uncircumcised of lips" (Exod 6:12-30). Perhaps he had a stutter or the like. Yahweh recognizes and overrides Moses' protestation: "Who has given man a mouth? Who has made him dumb or deaf, seeing or blind?" (Exod 4:11).

The Seer as Madman or Hysteric
Czaplicka believes that Siberia has a high incidence of nervous disorders hardly known elsewhere.[22] She ascribes this spectrum of "arctic hysteria" to the "dark winter days, light summer nights, severe cold, the silence, and the general monotony of the landscape." Central is "imitative mania," "with its characteristic symptom of imitating unconsciously all gestures and sounds." Campbell (p. 156) states that the powers credited to the shaman "are believed to be derived from his intercourse with envisioned spirits; this intercourse having been established, usually in early adolescence, by way of a severe psychological breakdown of the greatest stress and even danger to life." But Eliade

---

21. M. L. West, *Iambi et Elegi Graeci,* 2 vols. (Oxford: Clarendon, 1971), Mimnermus frag. 21a, from a manuscript of proverbs.

22. Czaplicka, *Aboriginal Siberia,* 320–24.

insists, "the shaman is not only a sick man; he is, above all, a sick man who has been cured. . . . The shamans, for all their apparent likeness to epileptics and hysterics, show proof of a more than normal nervous constitution."[23] Campbell has a most impressive photo of a masked assemblage mirroring the faces on the totem poles behind them:

> On the brink of madness, the Kwakiutl Indians of the North Pacific Coast enact in spectacular mystery plays the violence and brilliance of shamanic visionary ordeals. A youth undergoing initiation here will be seized and possessed by a cannibal spirit, become cannibalistic himself, and dash about crying "Eat! Eat!" while snapping and biting at those who strive to restore him.[24]

The Greeks for once correctly etymologized prophecy, *mantikē,* as derived from madness, *maniē.* Plato so explains the *mantikē* at Delphi, at Dodona, of the Sibyl (*Phaedrus* 244 A-C). Plutarch, in contrast to Sappho's charming words, quotes Heraclitus: "The Sibyl with her raging mouth speaks words without laughter, beauty or perfume, yet reaches the age of a thousand years by her voice by means of the god" (*Moralia* 397A). Tiresias says of the new god Dionysus: "This divinity is a *mantis*; for Bacchic frenzy and madness contain much that is mantic" (Euripides, *Bacchae* 298–99). The contagious female Maenadism described in the *Bacchae* is attested still in the Roman period as a real cult practice.[25] Plutarch has one of his speakers describe as if real and current "ill-omened and gloomy days, in which occur eating of raw flesh, rending of victims, fasting and beating the breast" (*Moralia* 417C). Again Plutarch, describing the effects of cold,[26] mentions how the capes were frozen "of those who climbed Parnassus to help the Thyiades, when the women were caught in a strong wind and snow." The reference is both so casual and circumstantial that we must take it exactly at face value.

Eating raw flesh has a parallel at 1 Sam 14:32 where the fasting Israelite army kills animals "on the ground" and eats them there, although what struck the narrator was that they ate "with the blood." The prophets of Baal (1 Kgs 18:28) cut themselves "with swords and lances" like the Galloi of Hierapolis.[27] The Hebrews cut themselves in mourning for their own dead

23. Eliade, *Shamanism,* 27, 29.

24. Campbell, *The Way of the Animal Powers,* 190, fig. 316, from Edward Curtis.

25. Dodds, *The Greeks and the Irrational,* 270–82.

26. Plutarch *de primo frig.* 18 = *Mor.* 953D. Pausanias 10.32.7 speaks as if in his own times Parnassus is where "the Thyiad women rave in honor of Dionysus and Apollo."

27. Lucian *de dea Syria* 50, LCL ed. iv.402.

(and conceivably for dead gods too), for the practice is frequently forbidden (Lev 19:28; 21:5; Deut 14:1; Jer 16:6).

Samuel predicts approvingly what will happen to Saul (1 Sam 10:6) "Then the spirit of Yahweh will come over you, and you will 'prophesy' with them, and you will be turned into another man." It does indeed come out so (1 Sam 10:9-13). Another account of a similar or the very same episode occurs at 1 Sam 19:18-24, where first Saul's messengers, then Saul himself, catch the contagion of "prophecy" and eventual nakedness. Such prophecy can bring the impulse to violence, going beyond that of the Kwakiutl (above): on the day after a triumphal entry (1 Sam 18:10), "an evil spirit from God came over Saul, and he prophesied." In his prophetic fit Saul tries to kill David. It seems plain that the earliest sense of the root *nb'* involves ecstatic dancing and perhaps unintelligible speech. Sophocles represents the hero uttering ominous and evil words "which a daemon and no human being taught him" (*Ajax* 243–44)—some kind of glossolalia. The Pythia at Delphi once when the consultation went badly was filled with "a dumb and evil spirit,"[28] that is, one that refused to tell its name. Compare, in a different context, Mark 9:17: "spirit of dumbness."

The Spirit Journey of the Seer

The typical shamanistic performance—to discover the cause of disease or defilement, to predict animal migrations, or for sheer bravado—takes the form of a dance and ventriloquism to illustrate a journey by air to consult a chief spirit, guided by a possessing spirit or animal. Campbell (pp. 158 and 167) reproduces maps by the shamans themselves of their spirit journeys, from Siberia and Eskimo lands; from other parts of the world (e.g., Bushman, pp. 94–95) he has actual photographs of the unconscious shaman as his soul travels.

The Journey on an Arrow. Dodds cites evidence that "the Tatar shaman's 'external soul' is sometimes lodged in an arrow."[29] Herodotus (4.36.1) in a fine display of *praeteritio* ("pretended omission") forbears to tell the story of Abaris the Hyperborean, "how he carried his arrow across the whole world without once eating." Porphyry says that Hyperborean Apollo gave him the arrow and that "carried on it he crossed rivers and seas and deserts, somehow walking on air" (*Vita Pythagorae* 29).[30] When Aristophanes has Socrates say "I

28. Plutarch *de defectu orac.* 51 = *Mor.* 438B.

29. Dodds, *The Greeks and the Irrational,* 141 and 161 n. 34.

30. Further citations in J. D. P. Bolton, *Aristeas of Proconnesus* (Oxford: Clarendon, 1962), 158.

walk on air" (*Nubes* 225, cf. 1503; denied by Socrates, Plato *Apol.* 19C), he is making him a shamanistic figure.

Catalepsy and Bilocation. To one Aristeas of Proconnesus, supposedly of the seventh century B.C.E., there was attributed a hexameter poem of which we have fragments,[31] describing what was perhaps a real voyage to Scythia, but remembered in the style of a spirit journey. Herodotus 4.14 describes his marvelous disappearances and appearances. Pliny 7.174–75 has a little anthology of such stories. "The soul of Aristeas was seen flying out of his mouth in Proconnesus in the form of a crow," and like Pythagoras he simultaneously appeared in widely separated places.[32] So Hermotimus of Clazomenae had a "soul which habitually traveled, leaving his body behind." But finally his enemies burned his body while the soul was absent, "and so deprived his soul on its return of what may be called its sheath." Elijah traveled no one knew how or where—"the spirit of Yahweh will carry you whither I know not" (1 Kgs 18:12)—and ran tirelessly after the contest on Carmel (1 Kgs 18:46).

Riding on a Bird. A Siberian shaman will sometimes portray his journey home riding on a goose.[33] The *Dhammapada* 175 has: "Swans travel on the path of the sun; men travel through the air by psychic knowledge." In a lost poem of Alcaeus,[34] Zeus gave the newborn Apollo a golden *mitra,* a lyre, and a chariot drawn by swans or identified with them; in it he traveled to the land of the Hyperboreans, gave them law for a year, and then returned to Delphi. Moses is to tell the Israelites in the name of Yahweh (Exod 19:4, cf. Deut 32:11-12) that they had seen what he did to Egypt, "and I lifted you up on eagles' wings" (Isa 40:31: "But those who trust in Yahweh shall renew their strength, they shall mount up on wing like eagles"). See the "wings of Dawn" (Ps 139:9) and Goethe: *"O dass kein Flügel mich vom Boden hebt. . . ."*

The Dangers of the Journey. Lindsay, in a speculative work, accumulates evidence from many cultures, including shamanist Siberia, that the entrance to the spirit world was guarded by a pair of rocks that clashed together, like the Clashing Rocks of the Argonauts that Odysseus must pass by, the Planktai (*Odyssey* 12.61).[35] The ordeal finds a Hebrew counterpart in the fiery sword "turning every way" (Gen 3:24) that blocked return to Eden; compare the

31. Edited by Bolton.

32. Porphyry *Vita Pyth.* 29; cf. Bolton 143.

33. Czaplicka, *Aboriginal Siberia,* 242.

34. Discussed by D. Page, *Sappho and Alcaeus* (Oxford: Clarendon, 1955), 244–52; *PLF* 307.1 (c) p. 260. We know it almost solely from a paraphrase by the sophist Himerius 14.10–11.

35. Jack Lindsay, *The Clashing Rocks: A Study of Early Greek Religion and Culture and the Origins of Drama* (London: Chapman & Hall, 1965), esp. chap. 14.

self-moving sword of Jer 47:6, which the prophet tells in vain "go back into your sheath."

The Seer's Drum

The drum or tambourine with its Mediterranean names, Greek *tympana* = Hebrew *tupim,* is an instrument of Dionysiac or ecstatic acts, with its near monopoly by mantic women or transsexuals. Here we only need to note that it is the instrument par excellence of the shaman. "It may be said that all over Siberia, where there is a shaman there is also a drum. The drum has the power of transporting the shaman to the superworld and of evoking spirits by its sounds."[36] Campbell has three photos of Siberian shamans with their drums, two in full raggedy regalia.[37] In most Siberian languages the drum is called *tüngür* or its equivalent, in Manchu *tunken;*[38] the words are both onomatopoetic and close to the Mediterranean ones. In Nichiren sects of Japanese Buddhism the mantra (the name of the Lotus Sutra in extended form, *namu-myoho-renge-kyo*) is always recited to the beating of the drum. Nichidatsu Fujii (1885–1984), called Guruji by Gandhi, the great international antinuclear activist, with his drumming reached out to Native Americans on a deep level.

The Birth and Death of the Seer

One of the prerogatives or duties of the divine king (as of the High God) was the begetting of heroes. It was notorious that Zeus was the father of many such. Mopsus the *mantis* in one version (Apollodorus *Epit.* 6.3) was the son of Apollo and Manto daughter of Tiresias. In Israel there is some ambiguity about the true father of the seer. Here, as often, ancient societies tremble on the verge of reckoning by matrilineal descent, since mostly there is never any doubt about a man's mother.

Who was Samson's father? Manoah's nameless wife says twice (Judg 13:6), "a man of God came to me" and again (v. 10) more simply, "the man who came to me [the other] day." The author initially says that "an angel of Yahweh *appeared* to the woman" (v. 3); but the second time uses the same language as the woman (v. 9), "and the angel of God came again to the woman, and she sitting in the field." Eventually (v. 18) Manoah learns that the "man's" name is wonderful (or Wonderful?); and in his ascension he is

36. Czaplicka, *Aboriginal Siberia,* 203.
37. Campbell, *The Way of the Animal Powers,* 176–79.
38. Czaplicka, *Aboriginal Siberia,* 215.

revealed to the couple (v. 20) as an "angel of Yahweh." Perhaps originally the woman simply reported to Manoah (v. 6) "a man came to me," as at v. 10. But Samson says, "I will go to my wife to the chamber," with the same idiom (Judg 15:1); "to the chamber" corresponds pretty nearly to 13:6, "and she sitting in the field." Nobody doubts that here the idiom means "go in to her sexually," as very often since Gen 6:4, "the sons of God came to the daughters of man, and they bore [children] to them." The author's use of the Hebrew language leaves open the possibility that the "man" is Samson's father.

Who was Samuel's father? First Samuel 1:19 seems straightforward: "And Elkanah knew Hannah his wife, and Yahweh remembered her." But later on (2:21) her further children are introduced simply by "For Yahweh visited Hannah," the same verb as at Judg 15:1: "and Samson visited his wife." The wicked sons of Eli "used to lie with the women who served at the entrance of the tent of meeting" (1 Sam 2:22). It is in the sanctuary that Hannah proposes to Yahweh (1 Sam 1:11) "And if you give your handmaid male offspring." So while the case here is not as clear as with Samson, the possibility remains that one feature of visiting the sanctuary was for the woman to have relations with the representatives of the god there. It may also be that in Israel of this date, as in other societies, the role of the male in procreation is not distinctly perceived, or is confused with the role of the god from whom children are requested.

When a child is exposed at birth there is some ambiguity about its mother also; and this is the case particularly with the two fateful figures Moses and Oedipus. Levin[39] pointed out parallels in their legends.

(a) *A male forebear who is a seer.* Moses' grandfather was Levi; for his mother Iochebed was Levi's daughter (Num 26:59); Oedipus's father was Laius, which from a name in *lawo-* was probably once *Lawios.* A Qumran fragment of Deut 33:8 has "give [masc. pl., in ref. to whom?] to Levi thy Thummim and Urim," in agreement with the LXX; thus Levi is a diviner. Oracles of Laius were extant (Herodotus 5.43).

(b) *A mother involved in incest.* While in Epic (*Odyssey* 11.261) Oedipus's mother is Epikastē, elsewhere as in Sophocles' plays she is Iokastē (Jocasta)—with no obvious etymology in Greek, hence probably older. Levin observes the parallel in its first syllables to (Heb.) *Iochebed.* Oedipus's marriage to his mother involves incest. Moses' father was Amram son of Kohath son of Levi; Amram married his father's sister Iochebed (Exod 6:16-20); thus Levi was also Moses' *great*-grandfather.

39. Saul Levin, "Greek Occupational Terms with Semitic Counterparts," *The First LACUS Forum* 1974, 246–63; "Jocasta and Moses' Mother Jochebed," *Teiresias Supp.* 2 (1979) 49–61.

(c) *Both were exposed at birth in an ark.* Thus Moses in the Nile by his mother (unnamed here) in an "ark" (*tebah;* Exod 2:3). A variant of the more familiar Greek story has Oedipus exposed on the sea in a chest: "Others say that [Oedipus] was put in a chest *(larnax)* and thrown out to sea; he came on shore at Sicyon and was brought up by Polybus."[40] Hyginus says that "Periboea the wife of king Polybus took up the exposed child while she was washing clothes in the sea" (*fab.* 66); in those days queens (or princesses such as Nausicaa) had the same tasks as any other wife. (But Pharaoh's daughter more elegantly comes down to the river to bathe.) All such stories appear to symbolize the dangerous passage from the amniotic fluid of the womb into the world.[41] In this case the "arks" assimilate the ordeal of the new child to the ordeal of all humanity in the flood; Noah's ark is *tebah* (Gen 6:14); Deucalion and Pyrrha rode out the flood in a *larnax* (Apollodorus 1.7.2). (The chamber in which Danaë was exposed was also a *larnax*.)[42] Romulus and Remus are floated in the Tiber (Livy 1.4.3). To the tale of Deucalion's flood (EFH 489–93) we can make additions: Plutarch attributes to "mythologians" the story that Deucalion "released a dove from the ark," which by its eventual failure to return predicted fair weather (*Moralia* 968F). Lucian[43] says that various animals entered the ark with Deucalion, "and whatever others live on the earth, *all by couples.*" It surely seems that both Plutarch and Lucian had heard the story of Noah from the LXX at one or more removes.

(d) *The graves of both were unknown.* Moses was buried by an uncertain party in Moab (Deut 34:6), "and no one knows the place of his burial until this day." None but Theseus must know the place where Oedipus dies (Sophocles, *Oed. Col.* 1522); the Messenger (1661–62) suggests that either a *pompos* from the gods received him, or the earth opened up.

The Seer with His Torch as Rainmaker

In the true Arctic shamanic realm, rain can be taken for granted. In the near-rainless river valleys of Egypt and Mesopotamia, crops can be grown through state-controlled irrigation, and only so. In the Mediterranean realm, a seer

---

40. Scholiast on Euripides *Phoenissae* 26,28 (ed. E. Schwartz, 1887, i.251).

41. Discussion in EFH 439–40; T. J. Cornell, *The Beginnings of Rome: Italy and Rome from the Bronze Age to the Punic Wars (c. 1000–264 BC)* (London: Routledge, 1995), 62.

42. Simonides frag. 543, *PMG* 284.

43. Lucian *de dea Syria* 12 (LCL iv.351).

who is thought to manage the withholding and granting of rain holds the keys of life and death. Greek *kleis* "key" went into Aramaic: at Luke 11:52 the "key of knowledge" becomes in the Syriac *qlyd' dyd't'*; see Rev 1:18 "the keys of death and Hades." See Matt 16:19 "the keys of the kingdom of heaven." The theme is taken up in Qur'an 39.63: "His are the keys *{maqālīdu}* of heaven and earth," where *maqālīdu* is the plural of *maqlīd*, an inner-Arabic extension of the Greek.

The rabbis agreed (*Gen. Rabbah* 73.4; *Deut. Rabbah* 7.6) that the Holy One had three keys: the key of the raising of the dead, for he says (Ezek 37:12), "I will open your graves"; the key of the womb, for it is written (Gen 29:31), "And he opened her womb"; and the key of the rain for it is said (Deut 28:12), "Yahweh will open to you his good treasure." But individually they are called in Greek style *'qlyd'*.

This doctrine provides a most ingenious exegesis of the history of Elijah (*b. Sanh.* 113a). He rashly predicted drought; in a weak moment the Holy One gave him the key of rain. He locked the rain up but couldn't reopen it. A Galilean said, "He is like a man who locked the gate and lost the key." The Holy One saw distress on the world and resorted to subterfuge. He sent Elijah to Sarepta where the widow's son was sick, and Elijah begged mercy to be given the key of the raising of the dead. The Holy One said, "Three keys have never been given to angel or seraph *{Deut. Rabbah}*; people will say, 'Two are in the hand of the *talmid* and one in the hand of the *Rab?*' Return that one and take this one." So he got the key of the rain back, and the storm at Carmel follows. But Elijah kept the key of the raising of the dead.

The vocabulary of rain mostly relates to the High God; here we look at the role of the seer. The displeasure of the god is made manifest by the withholding of rain. When the Pythia at Delphi tells the men of Thera to colonize Libya, and they refuse, "for seven years it did not rain on Thera" (Herodotus 4.151.1); the figure is conventional, cf. the "seven years of famine" of Gen 41:30 in Egypt. Elijah is abruptly introduced (1 Kgs 17:1) saying to Ahab, "As Yahweh the God of Israel lives, there shall be neither rain nor dew these years, except by my word." Yahweh in his brief against Israel (Amos 4:6-13) lists all his warnings, "yet you did not return to me"; he rains on one city or field and not on another.

The God can also carry out the alternate style of warning by bringing on unseasonable and damaging rain. Samuel (1 Sam 12:17) wishes to convey the anger of Yahweh when the people ask for a king; and he does it by sending thunder and rain at the time of the wheat harvest. In almost the same political situation, mortals in a violent assembly "pass crooked decrees and drive out justice" (*Iliad* 16.385–86); for in the parallel passage (Hesiod *Opera* 263–64) the problem, just as in Israel, is that "gift-eating kings" have been passing "crooked judgments." So what Zeus does is to "pour out much rain." However, the same god, through perhaps the same seer, is available under proper conditions to inflict the same weather damage on the state's enemy. When the weather-god is let out of his box or house, he can drown the enemy, Canaanites or Sabines.

The cosmos is set up to provide rain, primarily through the fact that the sky is "perforated" (Herodotus 4.158.3) like a sieve (Aristophanes *Clouds* 373); it has "windows" (Gen 7:11; Mal 3:10). But if God has reason to create a drought, it is a vain hope to ask (Job 38:37) "Who will lay flat the water-skins of heaven?" to let the rain flow out. The seer cannot hope for such direct access and must use what we would describe as sympathetic magic to bring down rain. Pausanias (8.38) describes Mount Lykaios, "Wolf-Mount" of Arcadia, with its precinct of Zeus Lykaios where no man or beast casts a shadow, and with secret sacrifices that he prudently did not investigate. In time of drought, the priest lets down an oak branch to the surface of the spring Hagno, "and the water being stirred, there rises a mist-like vapor, and in a little the vapor becomes a cloud, and gathering other clouds to itself it causes rain to fall on the land of Arcadia." So Elijah on Carmel hears a "sound of the rushing of rain"; he then "bowed himself down upon the earth, and put his face between his knees," and sent his servant seven times to look at the sea until the cloud appeared (1 Kgs 18:41-44). It seems that the fire from heaven that consumed the sacrifice was the lightning that precedes the rain. Is Elijah's posture one of forcing urination?

Herodotus says that the Thracian worshipers of Salmoxis "shoot arrows up to the sky against the thunder and lightning, and make threats to the god" (4.94.4). This must be weather-magic to bring on rain.[44] For Strabo 7.3.5 says that Zalmoxis was esteemed among the Getai for his "weather-predictions." Salmoneus of Elis, whose daughter Tyro Odysseus met in the underworld (*Odyssey* 11.236), has a name and attributes similar to that of Salmoxis. For Apollodorus says that he claimed to be Zeus: when he dragged hides and bronze kettles at his chariot wheels he was thundering, and "by throwing lighted torches at the sky he said he was lightning" (1.9.7).[45] But Zeus

---

44. Rhys Carpenter, *Folk Tale, Fiction and Saga in the Homeric Epics* (Berkeley: Univ. of California Press, 1946), 113–15, following Meuli.

45. From Hesiod, where frag. 30.1-14 Merkelbach-West was once an account of Salmoneus thundering.

turned the real thunder against him; and the Sibyl shows him to Aeneas among the Titans in Tartarus; no longer as before (*Aeneid* 6. 586) "While he imitates the flames of Jupiter and the sounds of Olympus." Originally perhaps he was a mantic king who brought on the thunderstorm by imitative magic; a fifth-century red-figured crater shows him holding a thunderbolt in his right hand and a sword in his left.[46] Conversely, the lightning is described as the torch that imitates it; see the usage of *lampas* in the *Bacchae* of Euripides.

Greek *lampas* and Hebrew *lappid* can both mean "torch" and "lightning." It might seem as if the equivalence would be more perfect if the Hebrew were **lappād*; but this form is reserved for nouns of agent, as with *gannāb* "thief," *rakkāb* "rider," *dayyān* "judge." The equivalence of the middle consonants is perfect as it stands. For Hebrew doubled stops (both voiced and unvoiced) correspond in Greek to (the coordinate nasal) + (the stop). Probably in fact the Hebrew "doubling" had a nasal element preceding the stop (SIE 456). Thus at 2 Sam 21:6 for the *Qeri yuttan* ("qal passive") "let there be given" the *Kethiv* has *yntn*, presumably **yuntan*.

Lampas has a corresponding verb that seems surely Indo-European, thus Lithuanian *lope*; it and Hittite *lapzi* "glow" seem to show a more basic root lacking the nasal of the Greek nasalized present. Thus the Hebrew, as corresponding to the Greek secondary form, must be derived *from* the Greek (or from an Anatolian Indo-European language with the same nasalization) rather than vice versa.

Gideon and each of his three hundred men had (Judg 7:16) "torches inside their jars"; it is a pity the Vulgate did not have, as it could have, **lampadas in cadis*. When they blew their trumpets, broke the jars to show the torches, and cried "[A sword] for Yahweh and Gideon!" the Midianites fled in terror. What did they think was happening? The legend of Salmoneus must give the answer: they interpreted the trumpets as thunder, the torches as lightning (same word!), and were convinced that the God of thunder and lightning was coming against them with his sword (as in the Salmoneus vase).

The Watchman in Aeschylus when he sees the beacon asks for "a welcoming shout to this torch" (*Agamemnon* 28). The prophet will not rest or be silent "until [Jerusalem's] vindication goes out as brightness, and her salvation as a burning torch" (Isa 62:1). In both passages the torch is seen as a beacon fire. In Hellas this use of the thing is institutionalized in the torch race. Plato initially describes it at *Rep.* 1.328A: "they will hold torches and pass them on to

46. *LIMC* vii.2.498 Salmoneus no. 6.

each other." In the *Laws* (6.776AB) he gives it a more definite application: a man must be "separated from his father and mother," and both man and wife must "bid farewell to mother and father and the wife's relatives . . . as if founding a colony," thus "handing on life as if a torch from one to another." Lucretius 2.75–79 shows how "the totality of things is perpetually renewed," "and in a brief space the generations of living things are changed, and like runners pass on the torch of life." The Olympic torch (in spite of all scandals) has become a precious symbol of the potential unity of the nations. Close to the phrase from *Laws* 6 is Gen 2:24, suggesting a Mediterranean formula, "wherefore a man shall leave his father and mother."

Deborah's general has the fulguric name Baraq "Lightning" (Judg 4:6) like a man of Palmyra, but probably not Hamilcar Barca "Blessed"(?). What does it mean that Deborah is "the *'ēšeth* of Lappidoth" (Judg 4:4)? The Vg *uxor Lapidoth* understands that Lappidoth is the name of her husband—another fulguric name, "Torches" feminine plural as an abstract. Or Lappidoth could be a placename. Or it could be no name at all, but rather descriptive, "a woman of lightnings"; the plural of *lappid* is elsewhere *lappidim,* the form of Judg 4:4 could be a dialectal variant. In any case she and Baraq belong together.

Baraq is comparable to the Cyclopes Brontēs and Steropēs "Thunder and Lightning," whose names by a shift of accent alone are derived from their attributes. The words in the accusative with final accent are feminines, Hesiod *Theog.* 707 "thunder and lightning and the shining bolt." When the accent recedes they become the masculine proper names of the Cyclopes, (*Theog.* 140), "Brontēs and Steropēs and tough-minded Argēs." In the first half of these two verses we have so to speak a unique epic formula indifferent to accent: if provided with the minimal final accent it denotes the natural phenomena in themselves as feminine; if with the distinctive next-to-final accent the phenomena are personified as masculine.

The poetry of Nahum 2:5 describing the fall of Nineveh to the Medes and Chaldeans runs parallel to the Salmoneus myth: "the chariots go mad in the streets, they rush to and fro in the squares; their appearance is as torches, they dart like lightning bolts." (Compare the tanks rolling through Baghdad in April 2003!) Divine agency is suggested but not definitely stated. The underlying symbol is of the thunderstorm seen as the god's chariot. So Isa 66:15, "For behold, Yahweh will come in fire, and his chariots as the stormwind." The vision of Ezekiel 1, which the rabbis call the Merkabah, includes wheels, living creatures (once horses drawing the chariot?), and fire all among them "like the appearance of the torches" (Ezek 1:13). The rabbis, to reconcile the vision with the more static one of the cherubim in the Temple (Isaiah 6), explained (*b. Hagigah* 13b), "All that was seen by Ezekiel was seen by Isaiah; Isaiah is like the city man who saw the king, while Ezekiel is like a villager who saw the king."

One of the kings of Midian was Ṣalmunnaʻ (Judg 8:5), who in several respects resembles Salmoneus. First, his name. Then, he may have been among those defeated by Gideon's thunder-and-lightning stratagem, as Salmoneus was defeated by Zeus's own thunder and lightning. As a Midianite he was one of the *bene-Qedem* (Judg 6:33; RSV: "sons of the east"). Salmoneus was related to Cadmus; for his brother Athamas (Apollodorus 1.7.3) married Ino, the daughter of Cadmus (3.4.2).

A Semitic water ceremony, which is specifically said to be for the purpose of getting rain, took place annually in the Jerusalem Temple at the feast of Tabernacles. "Why does the Torah say to pour out water on the Feast [of Tabernacles]? The Holy One, blessed be He, said, 'Pour out water before me on the Feast, so that the rains of the year may be blessed for you'" (*b. Rosh hashanah* 16a; see also *t. Sukkah* 3:18 [197]). According to other sources, Zech 14:16-17 was cited in this context. All former adversaries of Jerusalem are to go up annually to worship the King "and to keep the feast of Sukkoth." "And whoever from all the families of the earth does not go up to Jerusalem to worship the King, Yahweh of hosts, there shall be no rain upon them."

There is a beautiful contact with the story of Gideon in that the eight days of the festival also involved torches and trumpets. "Hasidim and men of good deeds (wonder-workers?) used to dance before [the assembly] with burning torches in their hands" (*m. Sukkah* 5.4). Two priests with (metal) trumpets blew prescribed blasts. Most remarkably, the torches were juggled.

> They said of R. Simeon b. Gamaliel[47] that when he rejoiced at the Rejoicing at the place ('house') of (water-)drawing, he would take eight burning torches and throw one and catch one, and one did not touch another. (*b. Sukkah* 53a)

Here is a beautifully exact parallel to that Salmoneus who threw lighted torches into the air.

The actual "libation of water" (*m. Sukkah* 4.9) was done with two silver bowls, one for water and one for wine, perforated in a prescribed fashion. Jesus' true "entry" into Jerusalem was on the autumn feast of Tabernacles (John 7:2). On the last great day of the feast (John 7:37-38) Jesus refers to the

47. This Gamaliel is either Paul's teacher Gamaliel (Acts 22:3, cf. 5:34) or a descendant.

water-theme of the feast by saying, "If any one is thirsty, let him come to me and drink" and cites an unknown scripture, "rivers of living water shall flow out of his belly."

The explicit testimony of the Talmud about the purpose of the pouring out of water suggests that pouring water out of perforated jars is elsewhere a ceremony of rainmaking. Delcor cites Lucian *de dea Syria* 12, where twice annually seawater is poured out in the temple of Hierapolis. Compare the leaking casks *(dolia)* of the Danaids, and see Horace *Carm.* 3.11.27 *inane lymphae / dolium.* They had to "carry water to a perforated jar," Xenophon *Oec.* 7.40; in Plato's Hades "they make certain ones carry water in a sieve" (*Rep.* 2.363D). Diodorus 1.97.2 reports that in Egypt near Memphis there is a perforated jar into which 360 priests, one for each day of the year, "carry water from the Nile"; this may be an adaptation to guarantee the annual rising of the Nile.

A final parallel involving the torch brings it into connection with a member of the bear and wolf clan, which figures in the next section.[48] Samson ties torches to the tails of three hundred (!) foxes and sets them loose in the Philistine grain (Judg 15:4-5).[49] In Rome the same was done ceremonially on the Cerealia; Ovid *Fasti* 4.681-2: "So I must explain the reason why foxes are sent out, carrying fire on their backs through tied-on torches."[50] So detailed a correspondence demands a historical connection, which is not easy to supply, though the Etruscans can be invoked as mediators. Perhaps the burning of the crops in Judges and Babrius is rationalization, and the foxes originally had the role of weathermakers. But their function remains ambiguous; do they carry the lightning-torches to assure rain on the growing crops, or to prevent rain at time of harvest?

The Seer as Hibernating and Risen Bear

Many of us grow up with a teddy bear, and around the Arctic Circle the bear is in special relation to human beings. Overhead circles a constellation known as *Ursa Major* (Germanicus, *Aratus* 164); or (*Iliad* 18.487–79 = *Odyssey* 5.273–75) "the Bear, which they also call the Wain, which circles there and watches Orion [its hunter], and alone has no share in baths of Ocean."

---

48. F. Bömer, "Die römische Ernteopfer und die Füchse im Philisterlande," *Wiener Studien* 69 (1956) 372–84.

49. Zech 12:6 speaks of Judah as a "torch of fire among sheaves."

50. Babrius 11 has a man punish a single fox by tying burning tow to its tail; but the fox runs straight into his grain field and burns it down.

So Vergil on both Bears: *Arctos Oceani metuentis aequore tingi* ("The Bears, which resist being dipped in the water of Ocean"; *Geor.* 1.246). In its upright posture the bear seems to have some relation to humanity. Mostly it is not specifically identified with human beings. In the materials gathered by Hallowell, the bear is object of hunt;[51] conciliatory speeches are made to it; it is treated as a tribal pet, killed and sent as an emissary to another world; there is elaborate disposal of its remains; poetry and saga grow up around it.[52] Still, in the kinship language addressed to the bear it is brought into some relationship with the tribe.

Maringer gives evidence for a bear cult in Palaeolithic Europe.[53] Thus during the last interglacial the Drachenloch cave at 8,000 feet altitude in the eastern Swiss Alps was used as a shelter or dwelling by (presumably) Neanderthal hunters,[54] whose principal quarry was the great cave bear; numerous skulls of cave bears were found set in its recesses and protected by stone slabs. *Homo sapiens* during the last glaciation apparently kept cave bears in captivity like the Ainu; for in the cave Hellmichhöhle of Silesia, dated by Aurignacian flints, the skull of a cave bear was found in which the canines and incisors had been filed down during life and the dentine had regrown—evidently to make the pet less dangerous. A bear's skull was carefully placed in the Chauvet cave.[55] Elsewhere Maringer proposes to interpret the late-Palaeolithic cave paintings of France in analogy with Siberian shamanism.[56]

Now, the Bering land bridge was open between Siberia and Alaska from c. 10,000 to 8,000 B.C.E., when there was also a corridor south between the Cordilleran and Laurentide ice sheets.[57] The Aleuts and Eskimos are proto-Mongoloid and made a coastal passage to North America; the American Indians went by land into the interior. The Aleuts and Eskimos are related to

51. Footnote 6 above. Hallowell's materials have been extended by David Rockwell, *Giving Voice to Bear: North American Indian Rituals, Myths and Images of the Bear* (Niwot, Colo.: Roberts Rinehart, 1991), with profuse illustrations.

52. Lauri Honko et al., *The Great Bear: A Thematic Anthology of Oral Poetry in the Finno-Ugrian Languages* (Oxford: Oxford Univ. Press, 1994). It includes stills from a color film of Siberian bear-hunt ceremonies in 1985 and 1988.

53. J. Maringer, *The Gods of Prehistoric Man,* trans. M. Ilford (London: Weidenfeld & Nicolson, 1960), 30, 69.

54. Photos and diagrams in Campbell, *The Way of the Animal Powers*, 54–56.

55. Jean-Marie Chauvet et al., *Dawn of Art: The Chauvet Cave* (New York: Abrams, 1996), 51.

56. J. Maringer, "Schamanismus und Schamanen in vorgeschichtlicher Zeit," *Zeitschrift für Religions- und Geistesgeschichte* 29 (1977) 114–28.

57. D. M. Hopkins, ed., *The Bering Land Bridge* (Stanford, Calif.: Stanford Univ. Press, 1967), 403, 411, 464.

Aurignacoid stone industries of Siberia about 13,000 B.C.E.; the American Indians (Llano culture) to Mousteroid industries with projectile points. It is difficult to imagine extended contact after 8,000 B.C.E.; accordingly, agreements between Native American and Siberian shamanism should point to the degree of development reached before that date.

Herodotus (4.95) continues his account of the Thracian devotees of Salmoxis by saying that Salmoxis, previously a slave of Pythagoras, held a feast for his fellow Getai, telling them that none present should die; meanwhile he constructed an underground chamber, into which he retired for three years, and then emerged to confirm the prediction. Zalmoxis and Abaris reappear at Plato *Charm.* 156–58; Socrates was in the army with one of the Thracian physicians of Zalmoxis, "who are said to grant immortality," 156D. Porphyry adds that the name "Zalmoxis" was taken from the Thracian word *zalmos* for a "hide," because the seer was dressed in a bearskin (*Vita Pyth.* 14–15), and that he was tattooed on the forehead. Carpenter observes:

> Surely it is not very difficult to read such a riddle. The *daimon* who wears a bear's hide, who feasts heartily, then retires to fast in a secret cavelike dwelling in the ground, vanishing from mortal ken to be given up for dead, yet after a time returns to life and his old haunts, can be no other than the hibernating bear, whose mysterious, foodless, midwinter sleep has everywhere made of him a supernatural spirit to the wondering mind of primitive man.[58]

Aristotle is aware of the bear's hibernation, and asserts that it lasts for forty days (*Hist. Anim.* 600b3). Again, at the sanctuary of Zeus Lykaios in Arcadia no man nor beast cast a shadow (Pausanias 8.38.6). Carpenter points to the role of the Germanic bear and (on Groundhog Day, February 2) the American woodchuck as prophesying fair weather from his lack of a shadow (and vice versa).[59]

The Greek seer who most closely realizes the traits of Salmoxis is the semi-legendary Cretan Epimenides, supposed to have purified Athens about 595 B.C.E. (Diogenes Laertius 1.109–14). He was longhaired. Looking for a lost sheep, he wandered into a cave and slept for fifty-seven years. It was said that the cave was of Dictyean Zeus in Crete, and that there he met with the gods.[60] But some said he had spent his time digging up roots. He was fed by the Nymphs, but never seen eating or evacuating. He kept the food from the

58. Carpenter, *Folk Tale, Fiction and Saga in the Homeric Epics,* 114.
59. Ibid., 135, 144–45.
60. Maximus of Tyre: FVS[8] i.32, Epimenides frag. 1.

Nymphs in a "cow's hoof" (D.L. 1.114)—perhaps a projection of the wide-spread belief that the hibernating bear receives nourishment by sucking its paws. Surely the gaunt hibernating bear appears in the riddle of Hesiod: "On a winter's day, when the Boneless One gnaws his own foot in his fireless house" (*Opera* 524–55). Epimenides' soul left his body and returned as often as he wished; at his death his body was found to be tattooed.[61] Noble Thracians were tattooed (Herodotus 5.6.2), and the Hebrews found tattooing in Canaan (Lev 19:28). I saw a Native American community organizer in the slums of Oakland with a bear tattoo on his forearm. Of all the ursine traits of Epimenides, the one best attested in shamanism is the long sleep that introduces the shaman's vocation.[62]

A "Cretan myth" which probably comes from Epimenides says that when the infant Zeus was being guarded in the Cretan cave, Kronos came by, and out of fear Zeus turned himself into a serpent and his nurses into bears; when he overcame Kronos, Zeus put a memorial of these events in the northern sky as Draco and the Bears.[63] Epimenides also treated another ursine myth in which the twin sons of Zeus and Kallisto were Pan and Arkas (frag. 16). Kallisto, daughter of Lykaon ("Wolfman"), was a companion of Artemis, wearing the same dress and sharing a love of hunting; Zeus fell in love with her, and (various reasons are given) Kallisto was turned into a bear (Apollodorus 3.8.2). Her son Arkas, eponym of the Arkadians, who surely seem to be the "Bear-people," saw her one day while hunting and was about to kill her, when Zeus took her up into the sky and made her the Great Bear (Ovid, *Metam.* 2.496–507). Polygnotus represented Kallisto at Delphi in a bearskin (Pausanias 10.31.10).

That Artemis herself was a bear-goddess is shown by the cult recorded in the Scholiast to Aristophanes' *Lysistrata* 645: ten-year-old girls in yellow-brown clothing played the role of bears in the cult of Artemis at Brauron of Attica.[64]

---

61. *Suda*, FVS[8] i.29, Test. 2.

62. Czaplicka, *Aboriginal Siberia*, 179–83. She does not mention the tattooing of shamans, but her plate 2 shows a young Ainu woman with tattooed upper lip.

63. FVS[8] Epimenides frag. 23.

64. Apparently at the conclusion of their ceremony or term of office the girls took off their brown clothes and finished naked, as they are represented in vases from the site. The vases are pictured in Ellen D. Reeder, ed., *Pandora: Women in Classical Greece* (Princeton: Princeton Univ. Press, 1995), 321–26. See Christiane Sourvinou(-Inwood) in *CQ* NS 21 (vol. 65, 1971) 339–42; and T. C. W. Stinton, *CQ* NS 26 (vol. 70, 1976) 11–13. In Aeschylus (*Agamemnon* 239) the suppliant Iphigeneia also drops her yellow-brown garment to the ground. *Brauron* may mean "Brownie, i.e., Bear" in some Indo-European language from the adjective represented in English *brown*; see Greek *phrynē* "frog" (Frisk), Latin *fiber* and English *beaver,* and Old High German *bero* "bear."

One story said that a tame bear was kept there, which clawed a girl and was killed by her brothers; Artemis sent a plague, and the Athenians decreed that every girl should play the role of bear to the goddess before she was married. Another story said that the attempted sacrifice of Iphigenia was not at Aulis but at Brauron, and that the girl was not replaced by a stag but by a bear. The "Pelasgians" took the women celebrating the cult of Brauron to Lemnos (Herodotus 6.138).

Carpenter compares the history of Odysseus with the widely disseminated folktale *Bearson,* which has apparently left traces also in *Beowulf.*[65] Panzer has gathered hundreds of versions in many languages.[66] I cannot forbear entering here the first paragraph of a version from Petznik gathered by Ulrich Jahn;[67] this work cannot be in many American libraries.

> It was harvesttime, when all people, young and old, were outside in order to bring home God's blessing from the field. Now the mayor received an important letter, and since he did not immediately have anyone else handy, he asked his young wife to carry the letter to the mayor of the next village. So she did that; but while she was in the forest, a large, strong bear fell on her, took her into its arms, and carried her into its cave; then it rolled a stone before the opening so that the woman could not escape, and trotted on its way again. In the evening it returned and carried a sheep in its jaws. Thus, after it had pushed the stone back, it went to the mayor's wife, tore off the best piece and gave it to her; and because she was hungry, she ate it raw. Throughout the night, she had to lie at the bear's side, and was warmed by the soft fur. When the morning came, however, it ran again from the cave and went out to pillage; but it did not forget to roll the stone in front of the entrance. Thus one day passed like the other, and the woman became familiar with the bear, and before a year had passed, she gave him a little son. He was rough over his whole body, but otherwise formed in fair human shape; but he grew faster than other children, and when he was seven years old, he had the size and form of a full-grown man.

Several items point to Odysseus's character as originally ursine. In particular he had a sister Kallisto (Athenaeus 4.158C) and a son Arkesilaos.[68] His

65. Pp. 128ff.

66. Friedrich Panzer, *Studien zur germanischen Sagengeschichte, I: Beowulf* (Munich: Beck, 1910 [repr. Wiesbaden: Sändig, 1969]).

67. Ulrich Jahn, *Volksmärchen aus Pommern und Rügen* (Forschungen, Verein für niederdeutsche Sprachforschung II; Norden & Leipzig: Diedr. Soltau, 1891), 135, "Der Bärensohn."

68. Eustathius on *Odyssey* 16.118.

grandfather on his mother's side had the wolfish name Autolykos (*Odyssey* 19.394). His grandfather on the other side, Laertes' father, has a sensational birth story, told in Aristotle's lost *Constitution of Ithaca*. Cephalus had no children. He consulted the oracle at Delphi, and was told that the first female he met would be the mother of his son; it turned out to be a she-bear, and by her he had Arkeisios, the father of Laertes.[69] (In the story Bearson, mostly but not always it is a male bear who has Bearson by a married but childless woman.) Heroes and heroines are properly nursed by animal mothers; a she-bear is specified for Paris (Apollodorus 3.12.5) and Atalanta (3.9.2).[70]

Yahweh is compared with (among other animals) a she-bear: "I will fall upon them like a bear robbed of her cubs" (Hos 13:8). David is compared to a "bear robbed of her cubs in the field" (2 Sam 17:8, with parallels in Gilgamesh and Homer). Having the day of that Yahweh come upon you is like fleeing from the lion and coming upon the bear (Amos 5:19); David compares the danger of the Philistine to the danger of the lion or bear (1 Sam 17:34-37). In these last two passages it is "*the* Bear," as if there were only one, appearing solitary and unforeseen at different times and places. The ultimate complaint against God is that he has been like "a bear lying in wait, or like a lion in hiding" (Lam 3:10). His ursine character comes out concretely when his prophet Elisha curses the boys in the name of Yahweh, and two she-bears come out of the forest and kill forty-two of them (2 Kgs 2:24). The indeterminate sex of the bear runs parallel to that of the shaman.

Elijah and Elisha are not merely in league with the Bear; in some sense they *are* the Bear. Elijah was "lord of hair" (2 Kgs 1:8), RSV "wearing a garment of haircloth." But the versions interpret as "hairy man." Whether the hair is his own or detachable, Elijah has a "mantle" with magical properties (2 Kgs 2:8-14), which can transfer his power to a new owner (1 Kgs 19:19; 2 Kings 2:13). It can cover his face (1 Kgs 19:13); the same word is used to describe the birth-hair covering Esau (Gen 25:25), the "hairy man" (Gen 27:11). (Jacob puts on himself goatskins, as it were making himself a satyr, to imitate his brother, Gen 27:16.) When Elisha takes up the mantle, the boys call him "Baldhead" (2 Kgs 2:23); this must be reverse mockery and imply that the hair mantle covers his head. Zechariah 13:4 explicitly defines the prophet's mantle as hairy. John the Baptist, who was understood as modeling himself on Elijah, gets himself up as a camel (Mark 1:6).

But the Baptist's diet suggests rather that he is identified with the bear, for he eats locusts and *wild honey* (Mark 1:6). Samson, another hairy figure and

69. Heraclides Ponticus 38 (Ithaca), FHG ii.223.
70. See further Cornell, *The Beginnings of Rome,* 62.

eater of honey (Judg 14:9), is associated with the fox as Elisha with the bear. Hebrews 11:32-38 specifies of "Gideon, Baraq, Samson, Jephthah, David, Samuel and the prophets" that they "went about in skins of sheep and goats" and lived in "dens and caves of the earth." That Elijah fasts for Aristotle's forty days (1 Kgs 19:8) may be the origin of the same figure for Moses (Deut 9:9), as it certainly is for Jesus. Elijah never dies, and it is appropriate that both he and Elisha have the power (like Jesus) of raising others from the dead; Jesus in effect compares himself with both (Luke 4:25-27). Elijah spends much time in caves and moves about magically (1 Kgs 18:12-46); like Abaris and Epimenides, he can get by with eating very little (1 Kgs 17:6); he has a special source of supply, the raven. He (or perhaps his successor John) was thought to have been raised from the dead as Jesus (Mark 6:14-15).[71]

Elijah and Elisha are a novelty in Israel. Did they take up attributes of the god they are fighting against?—the Baal of Tyre, namely (it seems clear) Melqarth.[72] His name is similar to that of the Greek mythical figure Melik-ertes. Ino mother of Melikertes is daughter of Cadmus and a sea-divinity (*Odyssey* 5.333–35). His father Athamas (the brother of Salmoneus the light-ning man) killed a third brother Learchus in the form of a deer. Ino threw Melikertes into a boiling cauldron and then jumped into the deep with him; they were renamed, she as Leucothea, he as Palaimon, and both help sailors in storms (Apollodorus 3.4.2). Melikertes was brought to the Isthmus of Corinth by a dolphin (Pausanias 1.44.8) where Sisyphus instituted the Isth-mian games in his honor. Palaimon has an underground *adyton* at the Isth-mus, where he lay concealed (Pausanias 2.2.1); at Tenedos children were sacrificed to him.[73] Carpenter compares the hiding place with that of Salmoxis; and suggests that Melikertes' name means "Honey-eater," compar-ing Homeric *keirō* in the sense "eat."[74] For in Slavic languages the bear has a taboo name, for example, Russian *Medved* ("Honey-eater").

In the original version of this chapter I explored the possibility that Melqarth (lacking a certain Semitic etymology) might be derived from Melikertes (which seems to have a good Greek one). But Melqarth seems too thoroughly rooted at Tyre to have come in from the outside; and the situation

---

71. The true relation of Jesus to John the Baptist comes out at John 4:2 "Jesus did not bap-tize, but only his disciples." Why? The natural conclusion is, that most or all of Jesus' original followers had, like himself, been baptized by John. What Jesus founded was, then, initially a further reform movement inside John's reform movement.

72. Philo Byblius, *FGH* 790 F.2.27.

73. Lycophron, *Alex.* 229.

74. Carpenter, *Folk Tale, Fiction and Saga in the Homeric Epics,* 124.

is rather that in the western Mediterranean Phoenicians transferred the attributes of Melqarth to Heracles. That both Melqarth and Melikertes have ursine character must then be explained by transfer, in one direction or the other, between divinities with coincidentally similar names. Or is Melikertes a folk-etymology of Melqarth? Anyway, in both lands the two figures, and their associates, make the hibernating and risen bear a symbol of life beyond death, which in Israel is realized as resurrection. Samson ate honey from the lion's carcass; the Baptist ate it regularly; according to one reading of Luke 24:42 the risen Jesus eats the honeycomb. It would naturally be assumed that honey, the bear's favorite food, is what gives him strength to rise again from his winter-long sleep. Then honey ought to be the "medicine of immortality."[75]

After the human mother has borne Bearson in the cave, "the bear prevents his captives from escaping by closing the entrance to his den with some large object, usually a boulder";[76] Carpenter compares the boulder that the Cyclops rolls against the door of the cave (*Odyssey* 9.240). In the folktale, "mother and son escape from the bear's den thanks to the Bearson's attainment of sufficient strength to roll the stone aside." In the Gospels a stone is rolled against the rock tomb of Jesus.[77] Perhaps this detail in the Bearson story is derived from the church rather than vice versa. Here the bear, from his residence in the realm of death, and perhaps from some reminiscence of the terrible cave bear *(Ursus spelaeus),* has become assimilated to the power of death, like the beast from the sea with bear feet of Rev 13:2; thus in some versions of the story Bearson kills his bear-father.[78]

The Seer as Insightful Even in Death

The dead continue in some relation to the living; the most obvious proof of this is that we *dream* of the dead. The *psyche* of Patroclus comes to Achilles in a dream (*Iliad* 23.65ff.) and gives instructions for his own burial. Achilles fails to embrace him, "for the soul went underground like smoke, twittering

75. Porphyry *Ant. Nymph.* 18 strangely calls honey "the type of death."

76. Carpenter, *Folk Tale, Fiction and Saga in the Homeric Epics,* 141.

77. At Jesus' burial the stone is described only by Mark 15:46 = Matt 27:60; but both Luke 24:2 and John 20:1 mention that the stone has been rolled or moved away.

78. The temporary transformation of men into "werewolves" (lycanthropy) is obviously related. Every member of the Scythian Neuri annually became a wolf for a few days (Herodotus 4.105). Damarchus the Arkadian became a wolf at the festival of Zeus Lykaios, and so remained for nine years (Pausanias 6.8.2). See further Plato *Rep.* 8.565D; Pliny 8.81-82; Augustine *de civ. Dei* 18.17; Petronius 62; Vergil *Ecl.* 8.97; Ovid *Metam.* 1.237. The Midian-ite Zeeb (Judg 7:25) is just "Wolf," along with his companion Oreb "Crow."

as it went" (23.100–101). The same verb is used for the souls of the suitors going underground and for bats (*Odyssey* 24.5,7). In Hebrew for a bird to "chirp" is *meṣaphṣeph* (Isa 10:14; cf. 38:14); then at Isa 29:4, "Your voice will come from the ground like a ghost, and your speech shall chirp from the dust."[79] At Isa 8:19 the wizards "chirp," where Vg almost Homerically *stridunt*. Achilles draws conclusions about the nature of death (*Iliad* 23.103–4): "Then there is some *psyche* and likeness even in the halls of Hades, but no *phrenes* [solid bodily organs? intelligence?] at all." So Propertius 4.7.1 of dead Cynthia *sunt aliquid Manes* ("The shades of the dead have some reality"). When Odysseus meets his mother in the underworld, "Three times I tried, for my spirit urged me to embrace her, three times she flew out of my hands like a shadow or a dream" (*Odyssey* 11.206–8). So Aeneas tries three times to embrace his father in the underworld (*Aeneid* 6.700–702): "Thrice the shade, vainly embraced, escaped his hands, just as light winds and most like winged sleep."[80]

In a common Mediterranean physiology, what makes the difference between a living person and a dead one is the breath. After Sarpedon's companions rescue him from the fray and push out the spear that pierced his leg (*Iliad* 5.696–98), "His *psyche* left him and a dark mist was cast over his eyes; but he got his breath back again, for the breath of the North wind revived him as he was painfully gasping out his *thymos*."[81] Again, when the widow's son approaches death, "there was no breath left in him" (1 Kgs 17:17). By sympathetic means Elijah brings it about (17:22) that "the child's spirit came back into him again, and he revived." What constitutes the life of animals is *ruaḥ*, Ps 104:29-30, inseparable from the wind (Gen 1:2; Ezekiel 37). In the original creation of mankind God forms them of dust and breathes into their nostrils the breath of life (Gen 2:7); at death "the dust returns to the earth which it had once been, and the *ruaḥ* returns to God who gave it" (Eccl 12:7; cf. Job 13:14-15).

Greeks and Hebrews agree on the ephemeral character of humanity, a creature of a day and "man the dream of a shadow" (Pindar *Pyth.* 8.96). Israel in its pessimistic mood sees life itself as no more than a dream (Ps 90:5) or a shadow (Ps 144:4: "Man is like a breath, his days are as a passing shadow"; see Job 8:9; 14:2; Eccl 6:12).

79. See EFH 163.

80. Similar comparison ibid., 151.

81. G. S. Kirk in the Cambridge Iliad *ad loc.* (ii.129): "thus the . . . main descriptions in *Il(iad)* of losing consciousness . . . draw in different ways on a formular terminology primarily designed for describing death."

The two nations agree in the miserable condition of the dead. The scenery of their land is described at Ps 18:5-6 = 2 Sam 22:56: "For the breakers of death encompassed me, the torrents of perdition assailed me; the cords of Sheol entangled me, the snares of death confronted me." Odysseus's mother points out to him the "great rivers and terrible streams" in the land of the dead, above all Ocean, and speaks of its "gloomy darkness" (*Odyssey* 11.155–58). So Ps 88:7: "You have put me in the pit of depth, in darknesses, in deep places." Cassandra describes the net in which Clytemnestra ensnared Agamemnon as a "net of Hades" (Aeschylus *Agamemnon* 1115); it is a "tunic without armholes or neckhole" (Apollodorus *Epit.* 6.23).

The inhabitants of Sheol are regularly called Rephaim, a word that ought to mean "healers" (but hardly can), and is so translated *iatroi* by the LXX of Isa 26:14; Ps 88:11. It corresponds to Ugaritic *rpum*, but the texts are not very informative about their true nature. A Latin-Neopunic bilingual from Libya (*KAI* 117, first century C.E.) has D(is) M(anibus) SAC(rum) = (Heb.) *l'l[nm] 'r'p'm* where Manes is an excellent version of "Rephaim." *Manes* plural can refer collectively to the shade of a single individual: Tibullus 1.1.67 "do not you harm my shade"; *Aeneid* 10.534 "the shade of father Anchises." Our *Manes* are our fate, for which our acts in life are responsible, but which comes to be seen as an entity independent of us: "Each of us suffer our own Manes" (*quisque suos patimur manis, Aeneid* 6.744). The meaning "shades" is clear for *repha'im* at Ps 88:11 "Do you work wonders for the dead? Do the shades rise up to praise you?" Mostly the LXX and Vg have either "giants" as here or transliterate. For what must be the same noun is applied to gigantic peoples left over from an earlier age.[82] At Deut 2:10 they are compared with the "Anaqim" and "Emim" as very tall. At 2 Sam 5:18 etc. the "valley of the Rephaim" in the LXX becomes "valley of the Titans." The two senses of powerlessness and power come together at Isa 14:9 "Sheol beneath is stirred up to meet you [the king of Babylon] when you come; it rouses the Rephaim [LXX *gigantes*] to greet you, all who were leaders of the earth; it raises from their thrones all who were kings of the nations." Since the Greek Titans were giants or elder gods banished to the underworld, the LXX versions are unusually perceptive. Deut 3:11 "For only Og the king of Bashan was left of the remnant of the Rephaim," with a note of the great size of his sarcophagus of iron. Hesiod (*Theog.* 133, 207) lists among Titans Ocean, whom Pherecydes[83] knows as *Ogēnos*. Joshua 2:10 makes the killing of Og parallel

82. See further EFH 117.
83. Papyrus, cited at FVS[8] 8 frag. 2.

to "drying up the water of the Red Sea," so that he could once have been an ocean figure.[84]

These tall peoples are not wholly legendary, for the earliest Greek contact with Palestinians shows them as a real folk. A fragment of Alcaeus, partially paraphrased by Strabo, has:

> "From the ends of the earth you are come, with your sword-hilt of ivory bound with gold" . . . Alcaeus says that his brother Antimenidas fighting beside the Babylonians accomplished "a great labor, and delivered them from distress, having slain a warrior who wanted only one palm's breadth of five royal cubits." (13.2.3)[85]

Another fragment of Alcaeus[86] brings together the names of Ascalon and Babylon. Thus it appears that Antimenidas fought on the side of Nebuchadrezzar against the Philistines of Ascalon (and perhaps against Jerusalem also). Goliath of Gath was "six cubits and a span in height" (1 Sam 17:4) but these cubits are not necessarily comparable. The historical Philistines, it seems, inherited their height from their semilegendary predecessors.

In principle the underworld is a "land of forgetfulness" (Ps 88:13); Plato *Rep.* 621A "the plain of Lethe" (only in Ovid does it become a river, *Metam.* 11.603).[87] For most mortals the breath that makes them a living being is fragile enough during life, and fails wholly at death; but the true seer has what Elisha asked from Elijah (2 Kgs 2:9), "a double share of your spirit on me." Samuel was exceptionally endowed with the Spirit, since he can dispense it to kings (1 Sam 10:6; 16:13), and from him it falls by contagion on the messengers and on Saul (19:18-24). Hesiod (*Theog.* 31–32) tells how on Helicon the Muses "breathed into me a divine voice, so that I might sing of things to come and that previously were." When Circe sends Odysseus off to consult the *psyche* of Theban Tiresias (*Odyssey* 10.493–95) "the blind bard," she testifies: "his *phrenes* are still sound; for even when he died, Persephone granted him alone the faculty of intelligence; the others flit around as shades."

---

84. For Og and Ogygos see: Joseph Fontenrose, *Python: A Study of Delphic Myth and Its Origins* (New York: Biblo & Tannen, 1974 [first pub. 1959]), 236–38; W. Fauth, "Prähellenische Flutnamen: Og(es)—Ogen(os)—Ogygos," *Beiträge zur Namenforschung* 23 (1988) 361–79; Scott Noegel, "The Aegean Ogygos of Boeotia and the Biblical Og of Bashan: Reflections of the Same Myth," *ZAW* 110 (1998) 411–26.

85. Denys Page, *Sappho and Alcaeus* (Oxford: Clarendon, 1955), 223–24; *PLF* 350.

86. Lobel-Page *PLF* 48.10–11.

87. EFH 160.

The "Witch" of En-Dor, Circe, the Sibyl

To get in touch with the shade of a (male) seer a female intermediary is needed, who herself plays a professional mantic role. The woman of En-Dor who brings up Samuel is a *ba'alath 'ob* (1 Sam 28:7), "mistress of an *ob*," LXX *engastrimython* "ventriloquist" (?!), Vg *habens pythonem*. As Samuel arises she says (1 Sam 28:13), "I see gods [plural!] coming up from the earth." It is unclear how the *ob* was conceived. The connection of LXX and Vulgate is explained by Plutarch:

> It is childish in the extreme to think that the god [of Delphi?] after the manner of ventriloquists, who used to be called "Eurykleis" but now 'Pythones,' enters into the bodies of prophets and prompts their speech, using their bodies and mouths as his instruments. (*Moralia* 414E)

The slave girl of Philippi has a "spirit of divination" (*pneuma pythona,* Acts 16:16). The same word went into rabbinic: "A [male] necromancer is a *pithom,* one who speaks from his armpits" (*m. Sanh.* 7.7). Here the Mishnah reflects a Hellenistic concept, rather than any original Hebrew one.

Likewise Circe, Odysseus's guide to Tiresias and the underworld, is of "many enchantments" (*Odyssey* 10.276) and has a magic wand (10.238).[88] The Sibyl of Cumae (*Aeneid* 6.65–66) is "a most sacred seer, knowledgeable about the future." West (EFH 551) has an elaborate table comparing the consultations of the spirits of Darius (in Aeschylus's *Persae*) and Samuel; I would suggest that rather Aeschylus is adapting *Odyssey* 10, to which he perhaps added some independent knowledge of Sibylline divination. Saul, Odysseus and Aeneas all in their different ways need to know what is coming; only the underworld seer can tell them; and only his female agent can reach him. Women normally stay at home and keep the house; in Greece they are "white-armed." Circe and the Sibyl in the big house of Hades, the witch of En-Dor with respect to Sheol, all play the role of *concierge*: you have to go through them to get into the inn in the first place, and then to find what room your prophetic party is lodging in. The act of consultation is dangerous, in Saul's case because he has declared it illegal himself, in all cases because of the danger of being trapped in the underworld. How shall we account for the com-

---

88. An Apulian crater of the fifth century B.C.E. shows Odysseus sacrificing with a slain ram at his feet, and the head of Tiresias emerging from the earth to drink the blood; see L. Brisson, *Le Mythe de Tirésias: Essai d'analyse structurale;* EPROER 55; 1976: Frontispiece; see now *LIMC* viii.2.826, Teiresias 11.

mon pattern of a seer in the underworld, to be reached only through a female intermediary?[89]

The story of Saul and the "witch" of En-Dor is isolated in the Hebrew Bible and so far as we know in West Semitic. While various forms of magic and necromancy are condemned, most fully at Deut 18:10-11, we have no picture how they were carried out except for the one tale. In contrast, Hellas has several stories of descents to the underworld, as with Odysseus and Orpheus, and a widespread cult of the Sibyl. The Sibylline phenomenon was well adapted to travel, for through its outpost at Italian Cumae it made a deep impression at Rome, both through the Sibylline books and as worked up in *Aeneid* 6. Here I propose a route by which it might have made its way to Palestine as well. The clue will be the accounts of the "returns" or dispersals of peoples, heroes, and seers from Troy.

A Sibyl was attributed a life of up to a thousand years: the ancients spoke as if, in every city with Sibylline activity, the same woman held the same position throughout all of time.[90] Some further ascribe Sibylline activity in different cities at different time to the same woman. Thus Pausanias 10.12 attributed it in Delphi, Marpessos, Samos, and Erythrae to a single woman, Herophile.[91] But the opposite tendency won out, canonized by Varro (as cited by Lactantius *Div. Inst.* 1.6.7-12), according to which the Sibyl of each such place was a distinct woman; Varro adds six more to Pausanias's list of four for a total of ten.[92] The Sibyl's spooky grotto at Cumae, which I walked through in 1960, has been excavated and fits well the ancient sources. Pausanias (10.12.7), a reliable observer, further records the tomb of Herophile at Alexandria near Troy.

At Erythrae of Asia Minor the actual Sibyl's grotto has been excavated, with a long elegiac poem put in her mouth (*IGRR* 4.1540). Verses 1-2 and 9-10 read: "I am the handmaid of Phoebus, the Sibyl who speaks in oracles, the

---

89. The stories of Saul and Odysseus are compared on literary grounds by Teresa Carp, "Teiresias, Samuel, and the Way Home," *California Studies in Classical Antiquity* 12 (1979) 65–76.

90. There is a very large literature on the Sibylline movement: survey by N. Horsfall in *Classical Review* 40 (1990) 174–75; see Martin Goodman, "The Sibylline Oracles," in SVMB iii.1.618–53.

91. He also names Sibyls at Cumae and Palestine.

92. Varro adds Sibyls of Persia, Libya, Cimmeria, Cumae, Phrygia, Tibur. Rzach (art. "Sibyllen," *PW* IIA.2073-2103), who conventionally follows Varro's model, has a grand total of nineteen. Michelangelo in the Sistine Chapel reduces Varro's list to five: the Libyan, Cumaean, Persian, Delphic, and Erythraean.

ancient daughter of the nymph Naias. . . . For thrice three hundred years of my life, an unwed maiden, I went over the whole earth." Italian Cumae was founded, according to Thucydides 6.4.5 (in "Opicia"), from Chalcis on Euboea, to which Dionysius Hal. 7.3.1 adds Eretria of Euboaea, and Strabo 5.4.4 Kyme—it is uncertain whether this Kyme is an obscure city of Euboea or the well-known one on the mainland of Asia. Varro gives Herophile as one of the names of the Cumaean Sibyl also.[93] Ovid (*Metam.* 14.137–38) records her unwise choice of a gift from Apollo: "I foolishly asked to receive as many years as the sand has grains," when (like Eos) she forgot to ask for youth as well. When Aeneas meets her she is already 700 years old and has 300 yet to run. Servius,[94] who identifies her with the Sibyl of Erythrae, adds that the gift had a condition, that she never again saw Erythrae; its people kindly freed her from her wretched old age by sending her a letter sealed with native clay.[95] Thus Cumae, from whichever cities it was founded, got its Sibylline institution from Asia Minor, where the original foci of the activity were Erythrae and the Troad.

Varro[96] says that his eighth Sibyl was "from the region of the Hellespont, born in a village Marmessus [elsewhere Marpessus] near the town *Gergithium*; Heraclides of Pontus testifies that she lived at the times of Solon and Cyrus." So Stephanus:

> Gergis, city of Troy . . . feminine ethnic Gergithia. From it the prophetic Sibyl is called Gergithia: she and a sphinx are stamped on the coinage of the Gergithians, so Phlegon in his *Olympiads*, Book I. They say that the tomb of the Sibyl is in the temple of Gergithian Apollo. (203)

Here we explore the extensions of "Gergithian" as an ethnic of the Sibyl, and the movements of the Gergithians and allied peoples.

Gergithes and Girgashites

The Gergithes were "the remnants of the ancient Teucrians" (Herodotus 5.122, cf. 7.43); Strabo 13.1.19 shows that they extended as far south as Aeolic Kyme, where there was another city of the same name, Gergis. Thus

---

93. In Lactantius *Div. Inst.* 1.6.18.

94. On *Aeneid* 6.321.

95. Eliot as motto to *The Waste Land* quotes Petronius 48.8, where the Sibyl of Cumae already is shut up in an *ampulla* and wishes only to die.

96. Lactantius *Div. Inst.* 1.6.12.

they are associated with two of the cities (Erythrae and Kyme) said to have founded Italian Cumae. Their relation to the Teucrians is further supported by a fragment of Arrian:[97] Dardanus the founder of Troy married the daughters of a King Teucer, Neso and Bateia; by Neso he had a daughter, Sibylla the mantis, from whom other prophetic women were named Sibyls. One testimony shows Teucrians as predating the Trojan war: Herodotus 7.20.2 has Mysians and Teucrians before the Trojan war invade Thrace and northern Greece. Strabo 13.1.48 regards the Teucrians as having come from Crete (before ever they arrived at the Troad?).

The Gergithians are attributed further migration, interpreted by our sources as "returns" after the fall of Troy; it is only part of a more extended migration told of the Teucrians and similarly interpreted. The Gergithes are traceable as far as Cyprus. Clearchus of Soli on Cyprus (early third century B.C.E.), who also attests the two cities Gergis near Troy and Kyme, respectively, describes a class of Cypriotes he calls Gergini: "One of the Gergini was a descendant of those Trojans whom Teucer[98] received as his share of the captives from Troy, and with whom he colonized Cyprus."[99] Again, Athenaeus (12.524AB), quoting Heraclides of Pontus (fourth century B.C.E.), names the lower class in Miletus as Gergithes, recounting incidents of a civil war between them and the oligarchy; they thus seem Anatolian natives reduced to serf status by Greeks like the Helots of Laconia.

The Teucer of Homer is the half brother of Ajax of the island Salamis near Athens (distinct from the Ajax son of Oileus of Locris), as being the illegitimate son of Telamon of Salamis (Iliad 8.284). Before the great expedition of Agamemnon, Troy had previously been captured and sacked by Heracles with only six ships (Iliad 5.640–51). On that expedition Telamon received as prize the daughter Hesione of king Laomedon king of Troy (Apollodorus 2.6.4, 3.12.7 with Frazer's notes); by her (but not as a lawful wife) he had Teucer. We are to assume that Teucer was so named from his mother's Asiatic ancestry. The tradition then takes him to be leader in migrations of his namesake people after the Trojan war, as if elected by them as a foreign prince of their line. Vergil (Aeneid 1.626) has Teucer call himself "descended from the ancient race of the Teucri." Herodotus at 2.118.2 has Egyptian priests call the Troad "the Teucrian land." But the Iliad nowhere so refers to it. Perhaps we

97. Arrian frag. 95 FGH 156, from Eustathius on Iliad 2.814.

98. Evidently the Achaean, discussed below, not the father-in-law of Dardanus the founder of Troy (above).

99. Athenaeus 6.256-7, from Clearchus's book Gergithios, named after a courtier of Alexandria descended from the Gergini.

are to think of the Teucrians after the war as having moved into the Troad, before they or a contingent of them traveled elsewhere.

At *Iliad* 8.303–5 Teucer kills Gorgythion, son of Priam, whose name surely echoes the Gergithes; the "Gergithes remnants of the Teucrians" are projected back into the heroic age as individual antagonists. The supposed travels of Teucer suggest movements of the Asiatic Teucrians after the war. Vergil has Teucer come to Sidon (*Aeneid* 1.619), meet Dido's father Belus who is attacking Cyprus, and, as we saw, praise the "Teucri" (Vergilian mostly for Trojans) from whom he himself is descended. Isocrates (*Euagoras* 18) has Teucer found Salamis of Cyprus and name it after the Athenian Salamis.[100] But Martin Bernal suggests that both Salamis of Cyprus (Herodotus 4.162.2) and the island near Athens (*Iliad* 2.557) are derived from *šlm* as "safe harbor," comparing the port Arabic *Dar es-Salām*.[101] If the name is Semitic, then the Cypriot city is surely the original. Teucer also went on to Spain, where his golden belt lay in the temple at Gades.[102] For Justin says that Teucer was rejected by his father Telamon and founded first Salamis on Cyprus, then Carthago Nova in Spain (44.3, cf. Strabo 3.4.3). Horace makes Teucer, expelled by his father, the type of eternal self-sufficient wanderers (*Carm.* 1.7.32). Olbe of Cilicia had a temple of Zeus founded by Teucer's son Ajax (named after Teucer's half brother), whose priest kings were alternately called Teucer and Ajax (Strabo 14.5.10).

If any of the travels of Teucer son of Telamon can be historicized as movements of Teucrians, or of their subdivision the Gergithes, after the supposed fall of Troy, we may think of the Teucrians and Gergithes as part of the shadowy Sea Peoples (if indeed such existed). Again, the Achaean seers at Troy, both those named in Homer and others, are regarded as having migrated to the east, either individually or as the leaders of actual peoples. Especially when they themselves play the role of seers powerful after death, they are plausible candidates to have brought necromancy and Sibylline prophecy to Palestine.

Herodotus 7.91 speaks of the Pamphylians as among those dispersed from Troy with Amphilochus and Calchas. The sixth book of the *Epitome* of Apollodorus recounts the returns or dispersals of the Achaeans other than Odysseus after the fall of Troy. Strabo 14.4.3 quotes Callisthenes: "Calchas

100. Pausanias 1.3.2 (and so Isocrates 9.19) regards king Euagoras of Salamis on Cyprus (435–374 B.C.E.) as descended from Teucer and the daughter of Cinyras; for Teucer in Salamis of Cyprus see Pindar *Nem.* 4.46.
101. Communication of January 1996.
102. Philostratus *Vit. Apol.* 5.5.

died in Claros, but the people with Mopsus passed over the Taurus; some stayed in Pamphylia, others were dispersed in Cilicia and Syria as far as Phoenicia." Either "Mopsus" like "Tiresias" was a generic name for a seer, or one man was thought to have outlived a number of generations—which come down to the same thing. For there was a *mantis . . . Mopsos* with the Argonauts (Pindar *Pyth.* 4.190). Calchas is well known from the Iliad; he appears in an Etruscan mirror divinized with wings as a sacrificing priest, studying the liver of the victim.[103] Apollodorus *Epit.* 6.1 lists those who after the war went from Ilion to Colophon: Amphilochus (below), Calchas, Leonteus, and Polypoites from Thessaly, and Podalirius the physician son of Asclepius (all but the first known from the Iliad).

The seers after the war found themselves in deadly combat. Calchas went to Claros of Asia Minor after the war with Amphilochus; there he was defeated by Mopsus in a contest of divination and died of chagrin.[104] Mopsus and Amphilochus, sons of Manto the daughter of Tiresias, were half-brothers, Amphilochus as son of Alcmaeon (Apollodorus 3.7.7), Mopsus as son of Apollo. In single combat at Mallus of Cilicia they in turn killed each other,[105] but after death were reconciled and became joint patrons of its infallible oracle (Frazer on Apollodorus *Epitome* 6.19, without noting that they were half brothers). Their posthumous expertise reflects the same prophetic psychology as with Tiresias and Samuel in the underworld. Vergil allows the role of seer to be taken up also by Anchises, who has almost the same name as Achish of Gath the Philistine.

The whole Sibylline phenomenon, and in particular the Sibyl of Cumae, has, as we saw, a good claim to be called "Gergithian"; Tibullus 2.5.67 connects the Cumaean and Marpessian Sibyls (the latter from next to Gergithium near Troy). The Gergithes and Teucrians are attested in Cyprus, and the witch of En-Dor has Sibylline traits. There is a beautiful parallel to the Greek *Gergithes* in the Hebrew Girgashites, always collective. In Ugaritic, *bn grgš* appears at KTU 4.123.15, 4.377.9, not necessarily as indigenous. They appear with the Qadmonites (Gen 15:19), the Hivites (Achaeans? see Deut 7:1, etc.), and the men of Arwad (Aradus), Arca of Lebanon, and Hamath (Gen 10:15-18).

103. *LIMC* v.2.601 Kalchas no. 1.
104. Strabo 14.1.27 = Hesiod frag. 278, Merkelbach-West. It had been foretold to Calchas that he would die if he met a *mantis* wiser than himself (Apollodorus *Epit.* 6.2). The later history of the oracle at Claros is discussed by Saul Levin, "The Old Greek Oracles in Decline," *ANRW* II.18.2 1599–1649, esp. 1628–37.
105. Strabo 14.5.16 = Hesiod frag. 279, Merkelbach-West.

According to the rabbis (*j. Shebiith* 6.1, 36c54–56, and elsewhere), Joshua gave the Canaanites three options: emigration, peace, and war. The Girgashites chose the first: "The Girgashites emigrated, for they believed the Holy One, blessed be He, and went to Africa." Somehow this tradition came to Procopius (43.10.17ff.), who says that the *Gergesaioi* (with Jebusites and others) at the coming of Joshua emigrated, first to Egypt, and then to Libya. He claims further that at Tigisis of Numidia there is an inscription in Phoenician, "We are they who fled from before Joshua the bandit, the son of Naue." He adds that the Carthaginians expelled them from their territory, and that they later became known as the Moors.[106] The story further recalls the western journey of the Teucrians.

En-Dor, where Saul consulted the seer, must be in some sense "the spring of Dor." There is some reason to conclude that Dor was named after the Dorians. It first appears surely in the narrative of Wen-Amon (eleventh century B.C.E.) who comes to "Dor a town of the Tjeker, and Beder its prince."[107] The Tjeker appear elsewhere in the catalog of the Egyptian "Sea Peoples": "Their confederation was the Peleset, Tjeker, Shekelesh, Denye(n) and Weshesh."[108] Identifications are much disputed. Wilson confidently identifies the Peleset with the Philistines; less confidently the Shekelesh with the Siculoi, the Denyen with the Danaoi, and the Tjeker with the Teucrians.[109] If the Teucrians reached not merely Cilicia and Cyprus, but Palestine also (along with "Mopsus"), we have additional grounds for identifying their tribe of Gergithes with the Palestinian Girgashites.

Dorians are not out of place in the eastern Mediterranean. Besides the possibility of their presence at Dor, the Pamphyloi through whom Mopsus led his people, and whom Herodotus knows as scattered from Troy with Amphilochus and Calchas (7.91), have the identical name of the Dorian tribe (Herodotus 5.68). In the mix of peoples in Crete (*Odyssey* 19.175–77)— Achaeans, true Cretans, Cydonians, Dorians, Pelasgians—each has some definable relation to Palestine.

---

106. Lipiński in DCPP 500 s.v. "Zarzis" of Tunisia suggests that the similarity of names underlies the story (see also the articles "Girgish" 190 and "Tigisi" 454).

107. *ANET*³ 26a.

108. *ANET*³ 262b.

109. But Hans Goedicke, *The Report of Wenamun* (Baltimore: Johns Hopkins Univ. Press, 1975), 182, thinks the Tjeker just Semitic "males," root *zkr*. Drews rejects the view that these Siculoi were eastern peoples who gave their name to Sicily; rather, they were the Sicilians themselves serving as mercenaries; *The End of the Bronze Age: Changes in Warfare and the Catastrophe ca. 1200 B.C.* (Princeton: Princeton Univ. Press, 1993), 70.

How shall we explain the parallels we have found? We can take it for granted that each Mediterranean society, like societies everywhere, had some sort of male seer or wonder-worker. In lands of uncertain rainfall, rainmaking again is an almost necessary function of such a personage. Pouring water on the ground is a natural magic to induce rain; the use of perforated buckets could have been independently devised. But the use of the *torch* with its common name to imitate lightning (along with the mysterious parallel of the torch-bearing fox) surely shows a connection. In what direction? The name of the "torch" seems Indo-European but not specifically Greek; both Israel and Hellas could have gotten it from Anatolia, where the root is attested in Hittite. The ursine character of the seer seems specifically due to boreal shamanism; there is no common vocabulary, and both Israel and Hellas could have gotten it independently from the North.

The theme of the seer as knowledgeable in the underworld, and accessible only through a female medium, is too close to be accidental, and not specifically boreal. It is attested in Israel only at En-Dor, a site with Mediterranean connections. The Sibyl can be called Gergithian from the town Gergis, and the Gergithes are part of a dispersal of peoples and seers in Asia Minor, Syria, and Phoenicia after the dramatic date of the fall of Troy; then the Canaanite Girgashites can be plausibly explained as a people migrating from Ionia. Thus I suggest that the prophetic powers of Samuel and the narration of the "witch" of En-Dor represent specific Sibylline influence.

CHAPTER 4
The Shifting Roles of Women

M arxism steered classical scholars in the former Socialist bloc, and by reaction scholars in the West, to the study of ancient slavery. Feminism has created a substantial literature on the status and roles of women, in both classical antiquity and the biblical world. But, as in other realms, classical and biblical feminist studies hardly intersect. Ideological battles over ancient slavery acted as proxy for battles over modern class structure. Ideological battles over the status of women in Israel and the early church are even more intense, because in the church the Bible still often stands as an authoritative model for contemporary structures.

Marxism and feminism each brought an embarrassing truth to light. The ancient societies that humanists and Christians had seen as the matrix of a new individualism and freedom—the Hellenic polis and monarchic Israel—are precisely those where restrictions on slaves and women (in spite of local variations among Greek cities) are clearest. In part, the notable restrictions reflect better documentation; in part, they are real. Gould points out that,[1] since we have no texts or monuments from classical Athens made by women,[2] we cannot "look at the world as it was seen by women"; we can only deal with "the dominant, male model of society." Roger Just, an anthropologist, adds that the "male view of society still retains its significance, for social reality is a social construct and what people think themselves and others to be remains a primary object of social enquiry."[3] No doubt Athens, Just goes on, had a

1. John Gould, "Law, Custom and Myth: Aspects of the Social Position of Women in Classical Athens," *JHS* 100 (1980) 39.

2. Apart from descriptions of their embroidery, e.g., in the robe carried up to the Athenian acropolis (Plato, *Euth.* 6C) with representations of struggles between the gods.

3 Roger Just, *Women in Athenian Law and Life* (London: Routledge, 1989), 3–4. This is the work on this subject that I have found most helpful.

different "social reality constructed by women"; but it is irrecoverable. Modern historians can only record "an important, but 'partial' in every sense of the word, truth about women: not what they were, but what men saw them to be. This is to limit the study of Athenian women and to reorient its findings; but it is no means to invalidate that study."

Exactly the same can be said about the status of women in Israel. But we may add: only through the eyes of the same male writers—and, in the Greek case, artists—can we discern the status of children, slaves (until Epictetus), sailors, or, for that matter, kings and rulers. In the historic breakthrough by which Israel and Hellas achieved a new self-awareness, that awareness is recorded by a small part only of the society. How could it have been otherwise? When a Hebrew or Greek book has come down to us, its author's understanding of society (whatever his limitations) must have been shared by some at least of those he was writing about, and writing *for:* otherwise it would not be in our hands at all. It is the place where its society's self-understanding is concentrated.

In this impressionistic survey, I prefix to the situation of classical Israel and Hellas what they document about an archaic state of their societies; and add as coda the situation after their loss of independence to new empires. In early Israel and Hellas, women had more power and freedom of action; but not such a freedom as would generate a permanent record of itself. In the classical independent states, which did generate such a record, the necessities (military and political) of maintaining independence reduced women's freedom of action, and sharply divided them into two categories: insider and outsider, housewife and harlot. When independence was lost to new empires (eventually to Rome), general freedom of action was reduced, and dependence was subsumed in a universal pecking order of debt. The restrictions on women (and on slaves) were reduced, and those remaining seemed by contrast less burdensome; and women's roles became more of a continuum.

Women's Freedom of Action in the Archaic Period

Women at Work

An anthropologist in a small village of southern France found that "both men and women in this peasant society actually work to maintain the idea of male dominance while not subscribing to it as a reality. Women's power is culturally muted but functionally active."[4] Meyers sees the figure of Eve in such a

---

4. S. C. Rogers, "Female Forms of Power and the Myth of Male Dominance: A Model of Female/Male Interaction in Peasant Society," *American Ethnologist* 2 (1975) 727–56, cf. p. 729

light in the hard frontier conditions of the Palestinian highlands, requiring full energies of both husband and wife. A longer text plainly reflecting women's freedom of action in a peasant society is the book of Ruth. We see only a little of the eighteen-year-old wife whom Hesiod recommends for the thirty-year-old farmer (*Opera* 695–98): but even the misogynist poet (*Theog.* 600) admits (*Opera* 702–3), "For a man wins nothing better than a good wife—and nothing worse than a bad one. . . ." For a lively Greek picture of women in village society we must go back again to Palestine, to the first two chapters of Luke.

In other archaic texts, no doubt idealized, a young girl has an idyllic freedom of action. Nausicaa has gone out with her handmaids to do the laundry, but feels confident to deal with the naked stranger thrown up by the sea and daydream (*Odyssey* 6.244–45): "If only some such husband as this should be called for me, one living here—and if this one were pleased to stay here." Rachel goes to the well with her father's sheep. When Jacob realizes that she is his cousin he rolls the stone away from the well; and she lets herself be kissed by him (Gen 29:11) before she in turn learns who he is.

Matrilineal and Matriarchal Societies

Through Bachofen and Engels the doctrine entered the Marxist schema of historical development that early society was matrilineal. What evidence there is comes from archaic societies on the fringe of the Greek world—as it happens, unattested in Israel. The best evidence for the Amazons defeated by Priam (*Iliad* 3.189) and Bellerophon (6.186) are the graves of "Sauromatae" (Herodotus 4.110) from the fourth century B.C.E. containing skeletons of women and horses, with spears.[5] Herodotus 1.173.4–5 says that the Lycians "name themselves from their mothers" and not their fathers; so that if a free woman lives with a slave, her children are counted freeborn; but if a free man has a foreign wife or concubine, his children are without status. We have

(not seen by me); cited by Carol Meyers, *Discovering Eve: Ancient Israelite Women in Context* (New York: Oxford Univ. Press, 1988), 42.

5. Mary R. Lefkowitz, *Women in Greek Myth* (Baltimore: Johns Hopkins Univ. Press, 1986), 22–23, citing T. David, "La position de la femme en Asie Centrale," *Dialogues d'Histoire Ancienne* 2 (1976) 129–62. She notes that the great river of Brazil was called the Amazon because the Spaniards saw native women there fighting beside their men. Herodotus does transmit (4.110) an apparently genuine Indo-European name for such given by Scythians, *oiorpata* "manslayers," (*androktonoi*); it should perhaps be "rulers over men," compare Latin *uir* and Greek *despotēs* ("master"). Ephorus (*FGH* 70 F 160) has that sense, the Sauromatai are "ruled by women" (*gynaikokratoumenoi*).

Lycian inscriptions, but their witness is unclear: Bryce thinks the Lycians may in fact have been matrilineal, but Carruba that Herodotus's informant misinterpreted Lycian grammar.[6] Glaucus the Lycian (*Iliad* 6.196–211) traces his ancestry along the male line; possibly Herodotus is just setting up one more "opposite of the standard practice of the Greeks."[7] But certainly Epyaxa, the wife of King Syennesis of nearby Cilicia, took the initiative in negotiating with the Persian pretender Cyrus, and perhaps slept with him (Xenophon *Anab.* 1.2.12).

Etruscan funeral texts name both father and mother: thus "Vel Partunu, son of Velthur and of Ramtha Satlnei, died at twenty-eight years."[8] Theopompus thought that the Etruscans had women in common,[9] and that the women "did not dine with their own husbands, but with whatever men happened to be present." But Warren,[10] showing by tomb paintings from Tarquinia that Etruscan (unlike Greek) husbands and wives dined together, thinks that Theopompus found this incredible and misinterpreted. In fact, the data are simply not there to determine the degree of sexual equality in Lycia or Etruria.

A true matriarchal society would consider as brothers those with the same mother. When the inherited Indo-European word for *brother* (cf. Latin *frater*) became *phrater* "fellow clansman" in Greek, Homer substituted *kasignetos* (origin unknown) and less common *adelpheos*. The latter corresponds exactly to Sanskrit *sagarbhya* "from the same womb." Homer in fact uses it for sons of the same mother; Zeus, Poseidon and Hades, sons of Rhea (*Iliad* 15.187); Hector and Alexander (Paris) (*Iliad* 7.2, etc.), sons of Hecuba (Apollodorus 3.12.5); Agamemnon and Menelaus (*Iliad* 2.586, etc.), sons of Aerope (Apollodorus 3.2.2). But the Sanskrit lexicon defines it as "a brother of whole blood;[11] one by the same father and mother"; and since Hellas and India are on the whole patrilineal, *adelpheos* is more likely to presuppose polygamy (as in Priam's Troy) to denote sons of one woman out of the many in the palace.

6. T. R. Bryce, "Two Terms of Relationship in the Lycian inscriptions," *JNES* 37 (1978) 217–25; O. Carruba, "Alle Origini del Matriarcato," *Istituto Lombardo, Rendiconti, Classe di Lettere e Scienze Morali e Storiche* 124 (1990) 239–46. P. Vidal-Naquet, "Esclavage et Gynécocratie dans la tradition, le mythe, l'utopie," 63–80, in *Recherches sur les structures sociales dans l'antiquité classique* [Colloque Caen 1969] (1970).

7. Lefkowitz, *Women in Greek Myth,* 20–21, citing other studies of the Lycian texts.

8. M. Pallottino, *Testimonia Linguae Etruscae* (1954) 128; discussed by Pallottino, *Etruscologia,* 6th Italian ed. (Milan: Hoepli, 1975) 402.

9. Jacoby *FGH* 115 F 204 = Athenaeus 12.517D.

10. Larissa Bonfante Warren, "The Women of Etruria," *Arethusa* 6 (1973) 91–102.

11. Monier-Williams 1125. Hesychius A 1061 (1.39 ed. Latte) understands that *adelphos* (brother) means "born from the same womb," since he is aware of *delphys* "womb."

An Athenian legend shows that somebody wished the city to have been matriarchal. Varro says that in the beginning king Cecrops consulted an assembly including women[12] on whether Minerva (Athena) or Neptune (Poseidon) should be the city's tutelary deity. The women, outnumbering the men by one, voted for Minerva; Neptune sent a flood, and the men imposed three penalties on the women: "that they should not again have the vote, that no child should take its mother's name, and the nobody should call them Athenian women."

One people—the Pelasgo-Philistines—was believed by both Greeks and Hebrews to be matriarchal and was feared for it. Apollodorus 1.9.17 says that at Lemnos, where the original population was "Pelasgian" (Herodotus 6.138), the women refused to honor Aphrodite, who in retribution made them all stink. So their husbands took Thracian mistresses; the Lemnian women, dishonored, killed their menfolk. Jason found them ruled by a queen Hypsipyle, who came out to meet him "in her father's armor" (Apol. Rhod. 1.638). The Hebrews gave Philistine women a bad name. Samson had three in all: the one of Timnah who extracted his riddle (Judges 14); the harlot of Gaza (16:1); and Delilah, who betrayed him (16:19).

The stories among them suggest a sensational etymology.[13] From Herodotus 6.138.2 "Pelasgian women" we can restore the singular *gynē Pelasgis* ("Pelasgian woman"). From the masculine "Philistine" (1 Sam 17:8) we can restore the feminine *(pᵉlištit)*. The woman of Gaza was a harlot, so Hebrew for "Philistine harlot" was *zonah pᵉlištit*. Yahuda,[14] among much that is fanciful, compared the two nouns; further, the whole phrases are comparable. A foreign word for *woman* would naturally designate a harlot. The Indo-European word came twice into English as *queen* and *quean* ("harlot"); Byron (*Don Juan* 6.96) describes the mistress of a harem as "This modern Amazon and Queen of queans." The frequent form *zonah* treated in the lexica as the participle of a root *znh* could in fact be the original form and the verb denominative.

Another international tale involves the death of the men in mass marriages, dealt with at length by Astour.[15] When Dinah has been taken by Shechem the "Hivite" (Gen 34:2), and his father Hamor asks for Jacob's

12. Varro, quoted by Augustine *de civ. Dei* 18.9.

13. John Pairman Brown and Saul Levin, "The Ethnic Paradigm as a Paradigm for Nominal Forms in Greek and Hebrew," *General Linguistics* 26 (1986) 100.

14. Joseph Yahuda, *Hebrew Is Greek* (Oxford: Becket, 1982), 46, 425.

15. Michael C. Astour, *Hellenosemitica: An Ethnic and Cultural Study in West Semitic Impact on Mycenaean Greece,* 2d ed. (Leiden: Brill, 1967), 1–112. Alternatively, the Danaoi are thought "river-men" from the widespread river-toponym *dan.*

daughters to be married to his men, Jacob insists that they must be circumcised; on the third day Simeon and Levi kill them. Apollodorus 2.1.4 (cf. Aeschylus *Sup.* 317–24) says that Egyptian Belus was father of Danaus and Aegyptus. Aegyptus has fifty sons; Danaus has fifty daughters, who for fear of the sons emigrated to Argos. The sons of Aegyptus follow them; Danaus makes a feast and gives his daughters daggers; they kill all of the fifty but one. There is an imperfect phonetic parallel between the descendants of Danaus (*Iliad* 1.42), and the Danites (Judg 13:2); as between Dinah (Gen 34:1), Danaë the mother of Perseus (Herodotus 2.91.2), and the Danaids of Aeschylus.[16] Perhaps underlying is a migration of "Danaoi" from Canaan or Egypt to Hellas, carrying with it the story of the mass marriage fatal to the husbands.

Matrilocal Succession

Succession to kingship may stay with the mother as "matrilocal": it goes to whoever marries the king's daughter. (However, the king also may be happy with this arrangement, for it allows him to select his heir.) Menelaus became king of Sparta, though not immediately, by having been chosen as Helen's husband (Apollodorus 2.11.2). When Oedipus solves the Sphinx's riddle (3.5.8), becoming king of Thebes and marrying Jocasta are parts of a single package. If Antinous could kill Telemachus and marry Penelope, he would become king of Ithaca (*Odyssey* 22.52–53). So it must mean that David is in line for the kingship that Saul twice offers him a daughter (1 Sam 18:17ff.). Song 3:4 (= 8:2) assumes a matrilocal society: "I held him, and would not let him go until I had brought him into my mother's house, and into the chamber of her that conceived me." Although no kingship is involved, Samson visits each Philistine woman only occasionally at the mother's house (Judg 15:1, etc.).

A "prenuptial ordeal"[17] is laid on a suitor where a woman's hand is kingship: thus the hundred foreskins that Saul asks from David for Michal (1 Sam 18:25).[18] After the king of Lycia fails to kill Bellerophon according to the secret message he brought from Proetus, the king retroactively treats

---

16. Astour further compares the *Dnnm* of the Azitawadd inscription (*KAI* 26.1.2, etc.), and *Da-nu-na* of Amarna 151.52. Any such connection is denied by H. M. Niemann, *Die Daniten: Studien zur Geschichte eines altisraelitischen Stammes,* FRLANT 135 (Göttingen: Vandenhoeck & Ruprecht, 1985), 288–91.

17. Sarah B. Pomeroy, *Goddesses, Whores, Wives, and Slaves: Women in Classical Antiquity* (New York : Schocken, 1975), 19.

18. Even better attested when no kingship but only the girl is involved. Thus with Caleb and Othneil. So Odysseus in one of his fictitious autobiographies (*Odyssey* 14.211–12); Othryoneus is promised Cassandra if he drives back the Achaeans (*Iliad* 13.365–67); Atalanta and her suitors.

Bellerophon's feats (like killing the Chimaera) as such an ordeal, *Iliad* 6.192–93, giving him his daughter and half the kingdom. In particular the ordeal may be a *riddle* containing more than meets the eye.

Did Oedipus in fact answer the Sphinx's riddle correctly? Just on the surface a better response would have been "Oedipus himself!":[19] more than other men going on all fours at birth because of his swollen feet; more than others walking on two feet at maturity because a king; more than others using a cane or third foot in old age because blind. The riddle was not tailored for every comer, but for Oedipus alone. If the Sphinx was truly prophetic she should have seen that his answer only led the more surely to his destruction; then her suicide itself was just a ruse to lure him on.

But we may discern yet another layer underneath. The name *Oidipous* is supposed to mean "Swellfoot" from his pierced ankles when he was exposed at birth; but they did not bother him as a man. If we did not know that story, from the comic adjective *peoidēs,*[20] we would take it as "with swollen penis"; its fluctuating declension (LSJ) suggests that both nouns *pous* "foot" and *peos* "penis" are at work. The preserved riddle (*Anth. Pal.* 14.64), which says nothing about three stages of life, has ". . . and three-footed; for it alone changes its shape" of all creatures. Then the third foot can also be seen as the penis of the one man potent enough to take his mother to wife.

Samson's riddle-contest was also once a nuptial ordeal, since when he loses it, the woman is given to his best man (Judg 14:20). The "companions" are really suitors: *re'im* (Judg 14:11) is used of "lovers" at Jer 3:1, etc.; only so does the rhyming verse Judg 14:18 make sense, "If you had not plowed with my heifer, you would not have found out my riddle." If the verse riddles preceded their prose context, no more than the companions could we guess "honey in the lion's body." Their supposed answer (Judg 14:18), "What is sweeter than honey? What is stronger than a lion?" in itself is not an answer but a double riddle, two questions with a single answer, namely, "Love." Both comparisons are proverbial. What, then, about the original riddle? What is its answer? Judg 14:14: "Out of the eater came food, and out of the strong came sweetness." It can be illustrated by folktale, where the vagina "eats up" the penis: "Out of the vagina came secretions, out of the penis came semen." What could only have been discovered by "plowing with my heifer" was that the Philistine woman had brought in some non-Canaanite sexual novelty: intercourse that was oral or in which the woman also became aroused. Thus

19. F. J. H. Letters, *The Life and Works of Sophocles* (London: Sheed and Ward, 1953), 224, quoting De Quincey.

20. Kock iii.591 Adespota no. 1111 (no context).

riddles may be double or triple, with a hidden sexual orientation underneath the ostensible one.

The Foreign Princess

When a woman remains matrilocally in the city of her parents, her power needs no guarantee.[21] When she acts as agent of their house in her husband's city, an agreement or treaty guaranteeing her status is required. In the Hittite vassal treaties the final paragraph may enforce the vassal's fidelity to his wife, "the daughter of the Great King of the Hatti land."[22] Powerful rulers might marry out many daughters born from their harem to bind subordinates to them; the woman served as the overlord's ambassador in residence. In yet a third sense she is an honest woman "sent to *lie* abroad" for the good of her country. Jezebel's privileged status in Jerusalem, holding Ahab's seal (1 Kgs 21:8) and promoting Sidonian religion, is naturally explained if Ethbaal has some guaranteed lordship over Israel. (But also she was a stronger personality than Ahab.) So in the agreement between Laban and Jacob: Laban says, "If you ill-treat my daughters, or if you take wives beside my daughters, although no man is with us, remember that Elohim is witness between you and me" (Gen 31:50). Here God takes the place of the Great King as enforcer of the treaty, as generally treaty language is adapted for the covenant between Israel and its God.

Helen, in accounts other than Homer's, had so many suitors not just because of her beauty, but also because of the power of Sparta that passed through her. Tyndareus, in the oath he imposed on the suitors (Apollodorus 3.10.9), followed the Greek treaties with their pledges to "assist": "[Odysseus] told [Tyndareus] to exact an oath from all the suitors that they would assist [the chosen bridegroom]."[23] After Helen's abduction her status shifts from matrilocal to foreign princess. A new compact and oath are required. And so at *Iliad* 3.253–57 (cf. 3.69–75) Alexander (Paris) and Menelaus are to fight with long swords "over the woman": "the woman and her property are to fall into the hands of the winner; all the others, cutting friendship and faithful oaths," are to inhabit Troy, Argos, and Achaia as before.

Weinfeld[24] points out how treaty formulas parallel marriage contracts; in fact, they are the original marriage contracts. The foreign princess, with her

21. Saul Levin notes that Megacles' daughter complained effectively when Pisistratus mistreated her sexually (Herodotus 1.61.1–2).

22. *ANET*[3] 206b: Suppiluliuma and Kurtiwaza.

23. Thucydides 1.9.1 misreads the situation when he opposes Agamemnon's power to the oaths of the suitors as causes of the war.

24. M. Weinfeld, "Covenant Terminology in the Ancient Near East and Its Influence on the West," *JAOS* 93 (1973) 196.

status as representing the Great King's overlordship, creates a new role available to other women carrying the prestige of their houses. To define the treaty as "friendship" marks its role as regulating sexual intercourse, denoted by the same word *philotēs*; after Paris is defeated by Menelaus, he says to Helen (*Iliad* 3.441), "Come, let us go to bed and turn to making love." So at Deut 7:9 the "treaty" between God and Israel has the double title "covenant and kindness." "Kindness" may have a sexual connotation; at Jer 2:2 Yahweh says to Jerusalem, "I remember the devotion ['kindness'] of your youth, the love of your betrothals." So *rḥm* is used of Yahweh's favor: Exod 33:19, etc.: "I will be gracious to whom I will be gracious, and show compassion on whom I show compassion." Its physical sense (cf. *reḥem*, "womb") is at Isa 49:15, "Can a woman forget her suckling child, that she should have no love for the son of her womb?" The two words come together in a context both of covenant and of marriage at Hos 2:20-21: Yahweh will "cut a covenant" with the creation and goes on: "I will betroth you to me . . . in love and compassion."

In Athens, restrictions on women are partly compensated for in drama. In tragedy, feminine strength is projected onto the past; in comedy, onto the utopian future. Two of Aristophanes' plays deal with the bases of male power: landowning with voting rights, military service. In the *Ecclesiazusae* the women take over the assembly; in the *Lysistrata* they take over the military, and will come back to their men only under a treaty (*Lys.* 1185): "There give oaths and good faith to each other." The women, whose rights were originally defined by the vassal treaty, in the poet's vision take the treaty power back into their own hands.

The Concubine

When the Great King (Hittite or other) disappears, his former vassals continue the honorific practice of taking foreign women, but now in the lesser status of concubine. The concubine retains, though not in her own name, the political role of the matrilocal princess as the key to the succession. She is the perquisite of the former king, like his throne and scepter, and whoever claims her claims his office. The Levite divides the body of his concubine and sends it to the twelve tribes (Judg 19:29) as if she were the divided animal (1 Sam 11:7). No foreign man could achieve social status in a state; David's foreign mercenaries, like the Cretans (2 Sam 8:18; 20:23), are under a native Israelite, Benaiah. It is through foreign women, particularly the concubine, that foreign customs and words enter a society. In her baggage, like the foreign princess, she brings fine linens, spices and ointments, jewels, cosmetics; in her new home she calls each item by its name, and reinforces with her handmaidens the linguistic borrowing mediated in a different context by traders.

A formula of praise for a woman seems an international word. "Faultless" (*amumōn*) is often said of men in Homer and occasionally of a woman, thus *Iliad* 14.444, "the faultless naiad nymph." Rarer *amōmos* applies only to women; thus among the daughters of Nereus is "Euarne lovely in shape and without blemish of form" (Hesiod *Theog.* 259). Both are related to *mōmos* "blame": *Odyssey* 2.86, "you would like to attach blame to us." Hebrew *mūm* "flaw" is used in identical contexts. Thus, of a man, Absalom, 2 Sam 14:25, "there was no flaw in him"; the LXX translates with the Greek word of nearly identical sound and meaning, *mōmos*. And so of the woman of Song 4:7 "there is no flaw {*mūm*} in you" (LXX *mōmos*). Only as applied to women, with their greater mobility, can the word's traveling be explained.

The Hebrew word is also used in the sacrificial cult: Lev 22:20, etc., "whatever has a flaw {*mūm*} in it," where the LXX again has *mōmon*. (Thus, as applied to women these words would denote the absence of any merely physical defect.) Hence Gordon thinks it was carried by the cult.[25] But neither *mōmos* nor its derivatives are attested as a sacrificial term before the LXX; the "inspectors of blemishes" (*mōmoskopous*) of Philo is surely derived from the LXX,[26] as is *mōmoi* (2 Peter 2:13). The form of *-mum-* seems more Semitic than Indo-European, but the original source is not easy to locate.

Housewife and Harlot in the Autonomous City-State

The Split in Women's Roles

In the first period the roles of women are all of a piece: moving between households, between societies, they have elements both of foreignness and of domesticity. Helen at home, abroad, and home again remains the same person. The exotic foreigner may be praiseworthy like the queen of Sheba, or a despot like Jezebel. But under the independent city-state the domestic and alien traits are firmly divided between two categories, in principle always separated; housewife and harlot. Most remarkably, in both societies the new dichotomy is reflected in *allegories* of the choice between Virtue and Vice. Prodicus (Xenophon *Mem.* 2.1.21–28) describes Heracles' choice between two women, modest and immodest. In Proverbs 7–9 right and wrong conduct for men are allegorized as two women, Wisdom and her opposite, the foreigner (7:5) and the harlot (7:10).

25. Cyrus Gordon, "Homer and Bible: The Origin and Character of the East Mediterranean Literature," *HUCA* 26 (1955; rept. 1967) sect. 36.
26. Philo, *de agric.* 130 (LCL ed. iii. 174).

When the allegories are demythologized, a man's choice of women in the actual social world is described in exactly the same terms: "We have *hetaerae* for pleasure, concubines for the daily care of our body, wives to beget legitimate children and to have a faithful guardian of our domestic affairs" (Ps.-Demosthenes 59.122). The anonymous orator emphasizes the differences because he is out to get Neaera and Stephanus for palming off their alleged daughter as an eligible bride;[27] still, he must be appealing to perceptions generally held by his (male) audience. (Menander [*Dyskolos* 842 and elsewhere] uses the loaded phrase "for the *plowing* of legitimate children," which may come from Attic law.) The gulf is between wives and the other two. The *hetaera* differs from the concubine by being independent and often available to other men (at a price); both are non-Athenians and defined solely in their sexual capacity. Neaera, in the same oration ([Demosthenes] 59.49), is characterized as originally a slave, twice sold, "making her living by her body as a *hetaera*," and now an alien. See Prov 23:27 with blatant imagery, "For a harlot is a deep pit, a foreign woman a narrow well." Wisdom demythologized is the "woman of worth" of the acrostic poem Prov 31:10-31. The good woman is carefully regulated: Gen 3:16, "Your desire shall be for your husband, and he will rule over you."

Athenian wives were under many restrictions. Women were not the only restricted group in Hellas; they were invisible to Rostovtzeff, who, as Pomeroy[28] points out, noticed "only two unenfranchised classes in Greece: the resident aliens and the slaves." Aristotle (*Pol.* 1.5.8 = 1260a 10) says that by nature there are several categories of rulers and ruled. "For in a different way [in each case] the free rules the slave, the male the female, and the man the child." The differences (he goes on) are because "the slave lacks the deliberative part [of the soul] altogether; the female has it, but inconclusively;[29] the child has it, but in an undeveloped form."[30] The Hebrew Bible is in general agreement, though not so programmatically. Mal 1:6, "Son honors father and slave his master."

27. Perhaps Apollodorus son of Pasion, who appears in the suit. See the commentary by Christopher Carey, ed. and trans., *Apollodoros against Neaira: {Demosthenes} 59* (Warminster, Eng.: Aris & Phillips, 1992).

28. Pomeroy, *Goddesses,* xii.

29. This is why (Aristotle implies) she needs a *kyrios* in law.

30. On this passage see Just, *Women in Athenian Law and Life,* 188. Raphael Sealey, *Women and Law in Classical Greece* (Chapel Hill: Univ. of North Carolina Press, 1990), 1, on the basis of the word order in passages like Herodotus 8.40.1: "to evacuate *children and wives* from Attica" suggests that "Greek men valued their children for their own sake and valued their wives for supplying them with children"; but this goes beyond the evidence.

The church after Paul in its household code of subordination settled on precisely Aristotle's three categories. "Wives, be subject[31] to your own husbands as to the Lord" (Eph 5:22);[32] "Children, obey your parents" (Eph 6:1); "Slaves, obey your masters after the flesh" (Eph 6:5).

For Aristotle, everybody outside Hellas is on one level. At *Pol.* 1.1.5 (= 1252b5) he states that "among the barbarians the female and the slave have the same rank"; and, in fact, since barbarians lack any natural ruling class (by virtue of its deliberative or rational powers), "barbarian [men evidently included] and slave are the same by nature." So he approves the words that Euripides (*Iph. Aul.* 1400–1401) puts in the mouth of Iphigeneia: "It is proper for Hellenes to rule over barbarians, but not, mother, barbarians over Hellenes; for one party is slave, but the others free." However, there has been a change in the New Testament, for Paul himself rejects any subordination for precisely this variant set of three categories: "In [Christ] there is neither Jew nor Hellene, slave or free, male or female" (Gal 3:28).[33]

Thus, for Aristotle, as man rules over woman in the family, so the state rules over noncitizens and "barbarians"; for the state is a family writ large. "The primary partnership made out of several households for more than daily needs is the village" (*Pol.* 1.1.7 = 1252b16). And in turn (*Pol.* 1.1.8 = 1252b29) "the perfect partnership made out of several villages is the Polis"; it exists by nature, and hence (*Pol.* 1.1.9 = 1253a3) "man is by nature a political animal." At another place (*Pol.* 3.5.14 = 1281a1) he puts clans practicing intermarriage between the family and the village. Likewise, Josh 7:14 puts two levels between the whole state and the household: the tribe broken down into clans, and clans broken down into households.

The Status of Men

In contrast I outline the status of men in the autonomous city-state. It was (from a long-term viewpoint) an ephemeral social form threatened on land or sea by neighbors of its size, and by bigger but distant empires. Its only defense was a militia, and in some cases a navy, composed of the entire free male adult population. Aristotle (*Pol.* 4.10.10 = 1297b16ff.):[34] "The first

---

31. The verb is lacking in P[46] "B," but in any case is implied from the preceding verse.

32. Note the echo of Attic legal language that would imply "as to your lawful *kyrios.*"

33. Similar, but lacking "male/female," are Rom 10:12 and 1 Cor 12:13: inferior manuscripts of Col 3:11 add "male and female" from Gal 3:28.

34. Aristotle wrongly thought that the dominance of small cavalry forces in the earliest period was due to lack of tactical science (rather than to lack of iron weapons), but states the facts correctly.

form of constitution among the Hellenes after kingships was drawn from those who were actually fighting, originally from the cavalry; . . . but as the Poleis grew and those in heavy armor got more power, more men came to have a share in the *politeia.*" Under Draco (*Ath. Pol.* 4.2) "the state [citizenship?] had been entrusted to those who provided themselves with arms."[35] So in Num 1:3, etc. Israel consists of males twenty years and over (up to some unspecified age) "who go forth to the army." Deuteronomy 20:5-8 in principle exempts those who have built a house, planted a vineyard, betrothed a wife; and the "fearful and fainthearted." Tribal males in Israel, though not voting, had a monopoly on the privileges of law, cult, and economy; they are close to the Greek idea of a citizen.

A poem of Simonides quoted by Plato (*Protag.* 339A–346D) begins: "It is hard for a man to become truly good, foursquare in his hands and feet and mind, constructed without fault."[36] The poet probably had in mind a parallel between man and the ideal square city, as Plato sees a parallel between man and the state. Plato (*Rep.* 427E) uses the poem to ask about the relation among the four virtues Wisdom, Courage, Temperance, Justice.[37] Wisdom is the virtue of the statesman (his "guardian," *Rep.* 428D), and courage of the soldier (430A). Plato is unhappy when the same person is "trader, fighter and legislator"; justice exists when each "does his own business" (*Rep.* 434). The situation he criticizes was that of the polis as correctly seen by Simonides: the men entitled to vote and run for office are precisely those who own real estate, and therefore can afford to buy armor and fight in the militia. Plato wants to move from democracy toward a smaller, highly trained standing army and an aristocratic ruling class. As "a member of the ruling and landed class in a slave-owning society, his passion for unity, therefore, . . . took the reactionary form of a demand for subordination."[38] Ellen and Neal Wood summarize a long discussion: "For all its philosophical complexity, Plato's is at bottom the ethic of an urbane leisure class whose fundamental moral distinctions correspond to the contrast between aristocratic style and common vulgarity."[39]

---

35. Draco's supposed constitution is thought by many scholars a piece of oligarchic propaganda from the late fifth century B.C.E., which imposed on Aristotle; but the general principle stated here was widespread.

36. Simonides frag. 37. *PMG* 282.

37. At *Protag.* 349B Plato adds a fifth, Holiness.

38. Alban Dewes Winspear, *The Genesis of Plato's Thought,* 2d ed. (New York: Russel, 1956), 214. But Saul Levin reminds me that Plato was disgusted with what he saw as rule by the mob and stayed out of Athenian politics.

39. Ellen M. Wood and Neal Wood, *Class Ideology and Ancient Political Theory: Socrates, Plato, and Aristotle in Social Context* (New York: Oxford Univ. Press, 1978), 155.

But beyond Plato's critique of the existing order, his quadrangle of virtues opens a window on the reality of power in the polis; each free adult male, as claimed, mirrors the whole state. Of the two remaining virtues, temperance is "the agreement of the naturally superior and inferior which of them should rule" (*Rep.* 432A); against his better judgment he (*Rep.* book 5) elevates some women to the rank of guardians, but only reinforces the rule that *some* majority should be ruled rather than rule. Justice finally he declares to consist in "having and doing what is one's own and belongs to one" (*Rep.* 433E); it does not directly challenge the current distribution of landed property. Thus the ideal Greek man is courageous as a soldier; wise in his participation in the political process; prudent in his rule over his natural inferiors (including women); and just in maintaining the reciprocal rights (including his own) of landowners.

The basis for participation in Israel also is hereditary possession of landed property, with its accompanying obligation of military duty. The king, though not absolute, was an idealized model; and so when Judaism came under Platonic influence, the four virtues were ascribed to Solomon: "[Wisdom] teaches temperance and prudence, justice and courage" (Wis 8:7).

In both societies the democratization of power was regressive for women. The privileged female roles created by matrilocal houses and the vassal treaty were lost along with the institutions. Subordination of women was inevitable since the new autonomous city-state rested on two types of power, of which one, landowning, was on the whole (with some variations, as in Sparta) a male monopoly; and the other, the citizen militia, was necessarily, in the conditions of ancient warfare, a male monopoly.

Status of the Housewife

The upper-class woman supervises servants or slaves in a domestic mode of production: storing and cooking food, stockpiling and repairing equipment, spinning wool. Women in Homer and vase painting are "white-armed," *leukolenos*; the indoor organizational role of the housewife of Proverbs 31 is parallel to the instruction that Ischomachus gives his fifteen-year-old wife.[40] She grasps her job so quickly that Socrates exclaims, "By Hera, you testify that your wife has a masculine intelligence" (Xenophon, *Econ.* 10.1). The housewife "puts her hands to the distaff and her palms hold the spindle" (Prov 31:19). Andromache drops the shuttle only when she hears the outcry that announces Hector's death (*Iliad* 22.448). Calypso is con-

---

40. But further she "considers a field and buys it" (Prov 31:16); in this case she acts as steward of the estate.

stantly plying hers (*Odyssey* 5.62). Even an unusual queen, Pheretima of Cyrene, is refused the armies she asked for and given a "golden spindle and distaff" (Herodotus 4.162.5). Peace is apparently when a woman can walk along the highway spinning (*KAI* 26.II.6). A Paeonian girl could simultaneously carry water on her head, draw a horse with a bridle on her arm, and turn the spindle (Herodotus 5.12.4). It is treated as a release when Dionysus frees women from looms and shuttles (Euripides, *Bacchae* 118).

In Hellas "the ceaseless weaving acquires a magical quality, as though the women were designing the fate of men";[41] the lives of human beings are spun on the "spindle of Necessity" (Plato *Rep.* 616C). Odysseus "will suffer whatever Fate and the weighty Spinners wove in his thread at birth, when his mother bore him" (*Odyssey* 7.197–98). Here we have remnants of a cosmology modeled on a female spinning divinity of Germanic style.[42]

The manageress of such a domestic textile factory is under many restrictions, particularly on her ownership of real estate. Athens had complex legislation to keep land with the original family. Although a woman never owned her property "in the sense of being able to dispose of it, it could never be alienated from her at all, or from her paternal family except through her children; so far as we can see it was always able to return to her family unless she had adult descendants."[43] A girl with no brother, an *epinlēros,* had an absolute right to inherit her father's property, but must marry her next of kin on the male side to keep it in the family. Just summarizes:

> the only women who benefited by the archon's oversight [namely, widows claiming to be pregnant and *epikleroi*] were those through whom a male heir could be supplied for an *oikos* [household] which was temporarily bereft. The concern of the law in this respect was to ensure the correct transmission of property and, importantly, of religious rights and duties via direct *male* descent. . . .[44]

So in Israel if a man dies without a son, his property passes to his daughter, and only if he is childless to his brother or nearest male kinsman (Num 27:8-11); the daughter is under a special obligation to marry within the tribe

---

41. Pomeroy, *Goddesses,* 30.

42. Levin wonders if rather the classical theme of a spinning deity has influenced Germanic mythology.

43. W. K. Lacey, *The Family in Classical Greece* (Ithaca, N.Y.: Cornell Univ. Press, 1968), 139.

44. Just, *Women in Athenian Law and Life,* 32.

(Num 36:3-9).[45] But if such a man has been living beside his brother on ancestral property, his brother must take his widow as wife, and the first son she bears is reckoned the offspring of the original brother (the levirate, Deut 25:5-10). As in the vassal treaties, the woman acts as representative of her own family in her husband's house; the difference is that her family, being close at hand, does not need to delegate any personal powers to her.

Sealey, almost in parentheses, explains why a woman's property had to be managed for her by her *kyrios*.[46] Not because women were perpetual children:

> Judicial legislation among the Greeks had originated from self-help. Public authority intervened to interrupt the pursuer's act of self-help and entrust the issue to a court for decision. Fossilized relics of self-help persisted, for example in the designation of the plaintiff as "the pursuer." People who have recourse to self-help usually bear arms. Greek women, including Athenian women, were excluded from armed and organized fighting. That exclusion may explain why an Athenian woman could not protect property by self-help or later by litigation.

The Heightening of Sexuality: The Harlot and Her Cosmetics

Hebrew locates human likeness to the divine in bisexuality: "And God created humanity in his own image . . . male and female created he them" (Gen 1:27). Aristophanes, in the myth of Plato's *Symposium* (189–93), sees each of us as only a half-person, and our couplings as efforts to restore an original unity. Exotic trade goods brought by merchants and foreign women—jewels, diaphanous linen garments, perfumes—produced a heightened sexuality and the new genre of the epithalamium. When this sexuality collided with military-based male domination, in Athens male erotic sentiment was partially transferred to boys or other men, especially in the military and in what amounted to the reserve training of the gymnasium. More broadly, Just observes:[47]

> Homosexual relationships were the sole form of sexual relationship which could, outside the bonds of legitimate marriage, be entered into by partners who were both of the same social status. Furthermore, they were the sole form of sexual relationship in which an element of mutual admiration and respect might be considered fundamental . . .

---

45. R. de Vaux, *Ancient Israel,* 2 vols. (New York: McGraw-Hill, 1965), 1:166.
46. Sealey, *Women and Law,* 152.
47. Just, *Women in Athenian Law and Life,* 147.

Although for Homer the love of Achilles and Patroclus hardly has sexual overtones, Phaedrus in Plato's *Symposium* (179E) takes it for granted that one must be lover (Patroclus) and one beloved (Achilles).[48] The love of David and Jonathan comes closer, 2 Sam 1:26, "Your love to me was more wonderful than the love of women." The Sacred Band of Three Hundred at Thebes was supposed to consist of pairs of lovers, and Plutarch says of it (*Pelopidas* 18) that "a military corps composed by erotic love is indissoluble and unbreakable."

The need to keep real estate in the family imposed a double standard, so that respectable women in general had to be ever more secluded and circumspect in view of the sexual license in Attic comedy and the Song of Songs—and in Athens the ever-present representations of the phallus.[49] The new sexuality demanded nonrespectable female roles. For a while Athens maintained the marginally respectable role of the educated *hetaera* like Pericles' Milesian mistress Aspasia, who "brought up girls to be *hetaerae*" (Plutarch, *Pericles* 24.3, who strongly disapproves of the whole enterprise).[50] But more and more, female roles were polarized into the alternatives of housewife and harlot. Herodotus (1.2–4) initially proposed to motivate foreign wars through the mutual capture of princesses: Phoenicians took Io to Egypt; Hellenes carried Europa to Crete and Medea from Colchis; Paris took Helen to Troy—violent counterparts of the vassal-treaty arrangement. Aristophanes (*Acharn.* 524–28) in parody motivates the Peloponnesian War by the mutual seizing of harlots, *pornai*. Drunken Athenians had stolen from Megara a harlot Simaetha; the Megarians in turn had stolen two harlots from the whorehouse managed by Aspasia. The harlot's name comes from *pernēmi*, "sell"; she is a purchased woman.

The identity of prostitution in Israel and Hellas, and of the fashions for which it set the tone, is illustrated in shared cosmetics, perceived no less than in later centuries as exotic: thus Pope, *Rape of the Lock* 1.133–34:

> This casket India's glowing gems unlocks,
> And all Arabia breathes from yonder box.

---

48. The relations between Achilles and Patroclus have been much discussed; see B. Effe, "Der griechische Liebesroman und die Homoerotik," *Philologus* 131 (1987) 103.

49. See Eva C. Keuls, *The Reign of the Phallus: Sexual Politics in Ancient Athens*, 2d ed. (New York: Harper & Row, 1993).

50. If Pericles really said, as Thucydides (2.45.2) quotes him, that "great credit is also due the woman of whom there is least talk among men whether in praise or blame," his words do not reflect very favorably on Aspasia.

The Roman matron's *ornatrix* (Ovid *Ars Am.* 3.239) painted her out of the various jars "which contained her daytime face,"[51] white, red, and black. For her face did not sleep with her (Martial 9.37.6). Our Hebrew sources only mention the darkening of the eyes with mascara. Jezebel in her last hour "set off her eyes with stibium" (2 Kgs 9:30). *Stimmi* is an Egyptian word[52] and appears in various spellings, for example, in Antiphanes;[53] Strabo 16.4.17 of the Trogodyte women.

Hebrew *puk* suggests Greek *phykos,* which in addition to "seaweed" (*Iliad* 9.7) meant some kind of cosmetic. At Theocritus 15.16, Praxinoa sends her husband to the grocery store: "Daddy, get some soap *{nitron}* and *phykos* from the shop." Both words have Hebrew counterparts that appear in Jeremiah's theme of Israel as harlot. At Jer 2:22, "though you wash yourself with soap *{nether}*." Again at Jer 4:30 (cf. Ezek 23:40), "that you enlarge your eyes with *puk.*" Nitron in the form *litron* is the principal element in embalming (Herodotus 2.86.4–6) and is also from Egyptian.[54]

LSJ identified *phykos* with the word meaning "seaweed" and implausibly explains it as orchil dye from lichens used as rouge. At *Anth. Pal.* 9.415 (Antiphilus) the two senses are felt different enough to create a pun: the speaker is alternatively a ship and a prostitute: "My rig befits a lady of pleasure; my *carpasa* (both 'sails' and 'dress') are light, there is light *phykos* on my timbers." Frisk derives *phykos* in both senses from the Hebrew and thinks that the cosmetic is primary.

What kind of cosmetic were *phykos* and Latin *fūcus*? In Greek it mostly appears to be one particular kind, which can only be rouge. Thus in Pseudo-Lucian *Amores* 41, "loose women redden their cheeks with *phykos* in ointment, so that the crimson color may empurple their pale skin"; Wis 13:14 of the manufacturer of idols, "smearing it with ochre and reddening its skin with *phykos.*" Latin *fūcus* mostly designated "cosmetic, artifice" in the abstract. But in Propertius 2.18C.31–32 it must mean "eye shadow": "Or if some girl paints her eye-sockets with steel-blue *fūcus,* on that account is a blue complexion fine?" Both the Latin and Greek must come from the Orient: Latin, as it seems independently of the Greek, retains the original sense "mascara," while Greek transfers the meaning to "rouge."

51. J. Carcopino, *Daily Life in Ancient Rome* (London: Routledge, 1960), 169.

52. Egyptian *mśdm.t* (Erman-Grapow ii.153); "stibium," from the verb *śdm* (iv. 370), "paint the eyes"; J.-L. Fournet, "Les emprunts du grec à l'égyptien," *Bulletin de la Société de Linguistique de Paris* 84 (1989) 65.

53. Antiphanes frag. 189, Kock ii.88.

54. Egyptian *ntr* (Erman-Grapow ii.366); Fournet 64.

The local men of a small ancient city could not support substantial prostitution by themselves. The prostitutes of Aphrodite Ourania at Corinth, increased at a stroke by a hundred through the munificence of Xenophon of Corinth, and celebrated with embarrassment by Pindar,[55] serviced the seaport trade. The proverb "not every man has the luck to sail to Corinth"[56] indicates that they provided offices elsewhere unavailable. An alert city, recognizing the value of having a foreign trader in residence, gave him quasi-civic status through a local sponsor, a *xenos*. Earlier the stranger was given quasi-religious status by attaching guest houses to a temple, where he had the divine protection resting on a stranger. Aristophanes (*Ranae* 112–16) lists the needs of a traveler: "harbors, bakeries, whorehouses, rest-stops, turn-offs, springs, roads, cities, guest-suites, women innkeepers and as few bedbugs as possible." Some of what is called "sacred prostitution" simply provided for the needs of travelers under protection of a sanctuary. At Babylon it must be with a stranger (Herodotus 1.199.1), and so at Byblos (Lucian, *de dea Syria* 6). The places where Aphrodite was called Hetaera (Tmolos, Samos, Ephesus, Athens south of the Acropolis [Athenaeus 569–73]) were commercial centers. By the Roman period inns were desacralized; Casson[57] cannot clearly determine whether establishments at Rome and Pompeii with erotic frescoes were inns, brothels, or bars.

As foreign residents, prostitutes formed a potentially disloyal enclave; hence parallels between classical and Hebrew stories.[58] When Capua was taken by the Romans in 210 B.C.E. (Livy 26.33.8), a certain Cluvia, who "made her living by her body," had secretly brought food to needy captives; she was one of two women restored their property and freedom by the Senate. Another text[59] explains why there was a temple of Aphrodite Porne at Abydos:

> When the city [Abydos] was reduced to slavery, the soldiers garrisoned in it once conducted a sacrifice, and after drinking took several harlots. One of them, after she saw that the soldiers were asleep, took their keys, climbed over the wall, and told the men of Abydos [who were outside]. They immediately came under arms, killed the guards, took the walls,

55. Fragment of Pindar at Athenaeus 13.573E.
56. Aristophanes frag. 902a, Kock i.591.
57. Lionel Casson, *Travel in the Ancient World* (London: Allen & Unwin, 1974), 197–218.
58. H. Windisch, "Zur Rahabgeschichte (Zwei Parallelen aus der klassischen Literatur)," *ZAW* 37 (1917/18) 188–98; W. Baumgartner, "Israelitisch-griechische Sagenbeziehungen," in idem, *Zum Alten Testament und seiner Umwelt* (Leiden: Brill, 1959), 147–78.
59. Neanthes, Jacoby *FGH* 84 F 9 = Athenaeus 13.572.

and regained control; they gave the harlot the gift of freedom and built a temple of Aphrodite Porne.

Similarly, Rahab the harlot of Jericho (Josh 6:22-25) alone is saved with her household for having befriended the Israelite spies in her *philoxenia* (*1 Clement* 12). Her house was built into the city wall (Josh 2:15), so that it was easy for her to get them out—her status was less sacral than extraterritorial. That Paul was let down from Damascus in a basket (Acts 9:25; 2 Cor 11:33)[60] suggests that he was staying at the inn by the gate like any out-of-town stranger. His stiffness against *porneia* is motivated when we realize that he was constantly working in close quarters with *pornai*.

The Breakdown of Distinctions

Nothing so unsettled men as the breakdown of clear distinctions between respectable and nonrespectable women. Elsewhere I discuss women able to raise the dead, Sibyls and the witch of En-Dor, and the connection of Gergithes and Girgashites.[61] Euripides' *Bacchae* reveals the (male) fear that city women under the influence of Dionysus can become homicidal fanatics. In Rome, the fear of a slave uprising was tempered by the annual temporary reversal of roles at the Saturnalia; and so by tradition or prudence, women were allowed tasks and festivals where their restrictions were temporarily removed. In Hellas the women alone celebrated the Thesmophoria, the most widespread of all Greek festivals.[62] In Attica (Isaeus 8.19) the wives of the demesmen elected women from their number to preside at the annual festival; rotten pork drawn up from pits *(megara)* was mixed with grain on the altars.[63]

Women had a special expertise in mourning; in Israel, for four days annually in memory of Jephthah's daughter (Judg 11:40). And in rejoicing too. David's lament calls on the "daughters of Israel to weep" and for all to "tell it not in Gath . . . lest the daughters of the Philistines rejoice" (2 Sam 1:19-24). The daughters of Judah are to rejoice over the justice of Yahweh and the fortification of Zion (Ps 48:11). The daughters of Jerusalem have the task of

60. Curiously, it is Paul himself, the participant, who at 2 Cor 11:33 cites the LXX of Josh 2:15 "through a window"; Luke, the secondhand narrator at Acts 9:25, expresses himself differently.

61. See chap. 3.

62. The festival is described by the scholiast on Lucian *Dial. Mer.* 2.1, conveniently reprinted by Ludwig Deubner, *Attische Feste* (Darmstadt: Wissenschaftliche Buchgesellschaft, 1932), 40. See Saul Levin, *"Thesmophoros = legifera:* The Import of the Primeval Thesmophoria," *General Linguistics* 31 (1991) 1–12.

63. There is a possible Semitic connection for the festival in that this word for "pit" is often compared with Hebrew *me'arah* "cave," in particular as place of burial (Gen 23:9).

locating lovers for each other (Song 5:8), and are not to weep for Jesus but for themselves and their children (Luke 23:28).

In the *Iliad* it is more often women who "wail" (19.301, etc.), although the same verb is applied to old men (19.338) and citizens generally (22.429). At the wake for Hector there is a differentiation of function, 24.722: "The men [skilled at singing] sang the lament, and the women wailed [nonverbally]." A fable of Aesop[64] describes how at the death of a daughter a rich man "hired mourning women," evidently professionals.

In Israel and Hellas, the most prominent cult in which women could exercise their specialty of mourning was the same. Ezekiel (8:14) in the Temple found "women sitting and lamenting for Tammuz." Lucian *de dea Syria* 8 describes the cult of Adonis at Byblos, and Milton (*Par. Lost* i.446–53) sumptuously versifies both texts:

> . . . *Thammuz* came next behind,
> Whose annual wound in *Lebanon* allur'd
> The *Syrian* damsels to lament his fate
> In amorous dittyes all a Summers day,
> While smooth *Adonis* from his native Rock
> Ran purple to the Sea, suppos'd with blood
> Of *Thammuz* yearly wounded; the Love-tale
> Infected *Sions* daughters with like heat . . .

The Akkadian god Dumuzi mostly appears in the form Du'uzi (*Gilgamesh* VI.46). A Syriac text ascribed to Melito bishop of Sardes tells the story in a Hellenized form.[65]

The people of Phoenicia worshiped Balthi, queen of Cyprus, because she fell in love with Tamuz, son of Cuthar, king of the Phoenicians, and left her own kingdom, and came and dwelt in Gebal, a fortress of the Phoenicians, and at that time she made all the Cyprians subject to the king Cuthar: for before Tamuz she was in love with Ares, and committed adultery with him, and Hephaestus her husband caught her, and was jealous over her, and came and slew Tamuz in Mount Lebanon, while he was hunting the wild boar; and from that time Balthi remained in Gebal, and died in the city Aphaca where Tamuz was buried.[66]

64. Aesop 310, "The rich man and the mourning women," ed. E. Chambry.

65. W. Cureton, *Spicilegium Syriacum* (1855) 25 top (tr. p. 44).

66. The cult of Aphrodite at Aphaka, the great spring at the source of the Adonis river, is well known from Zosimus 1.58, etc. Josh 13:4, '*Apheqah* shows the same name and perhaps the same site; see my *The Lebanon and Phoenicia: Ancient Texts Illustrating Their Physical Geography and Native Industries* (Beirut: American Univ. of Beirut, 1969), 67–69.

Greeks had a distant reflection of the deity's original name. Plutarch tells how a supposed Egyptian pilot Thamous hears his name called from on shore and is asked to convey the message "Great Pan is dead."[67] Salomon Reinach plausibly conjectured that the story rationalized a ritual cry, "Thamous all-great is dead."[68] Jerome on Ezek 8:14[69] connects the god with the Hebrew month *Thamuz* of sowing (*m. Taan.* 4.5) and refers to the "seeds which die in the earth." Elsewhere (*Epist.* 58.3) he identifies Tammuz with Adonis, "Bethleem where I now live was once overshadowed by a grove of Thammuz, that is of Adonis." Sappho tells the votaries of Adonis to tear their tunics; Aristophanes describes the *tympanismos* of tambourines at her rites. Theocritus 15 describes the Syracusan ladies Gorgo and Praxinoa at the ceremony for Adonis in the palace of Ptolemy II. Jerome is referring to the intentionally short-lived "gardens of Adonis" (Plato *Phaedr.* 276B); they seem to appear at Isa 17:10, "therefore you plant pleasant(?) plants, and set out slips of a strange god."[70]

Women under the Universalizing of Restrictions

Women in Relation to Slaves and Criminals

As women had a kind of alternative society with their own cults, so did the poor and slaves: their spokesman had a sacral immunity. So in Hellas did the youth or ephebes. Jason, when he built the gymnasium in Jerusalem (2 Macc 4:12), for a brief time "organized the noblest of the ephebes and made them wear the Greek hat." Thus women, youths, and slaves each formed a kind of city within the city.

The kinship of women with slaves shows up in the foundation legends of our societies. The ancestors of Israelites had been slaves in Egypt, with their liberation begun by women—the midwives and Miriam. So the ancestors of all Romans were the fugitive slaves under Romulus and the respectable

---

67. Plutarch, *de defectu orac.* 17 = *Mor.* 419B.

68. Salomon Reinach, "La mort du grand Pan," *BCH* 31 (1907) 5–19 = his *Cultes, mythes et religions,* 2d ed. (Paris: Leroux, 1913), 2:1–15. The Egyptian name *Thamous* (Plato, *Phaedrus* 274D) made the story possible.

69. Hieronymus *In Hiezechielem* 8, 14; Corp. Christ. 75.99.

70. Lewy *Fremdwörter* 49 thinks *na'aman* a title of Adonis and compares the flower-name "anemone" with a folk-etymology "windflower." Ovid (*Metam.* 10.737–39), while suppressing its name, has it come up from the blood of Adonis. See in general the article "Adonies" DCPP 6–7; Marcel Detienne, *Les Jardins d'Adonis* (Paris: Gallimard, 1972); Sergio Ribichini, *Adonis: Aspetti "orientali" di un mito Greco* (1981).

Sabine women whom they abducted—as the Benjaminites took the "daughters of Shiloh" (Judg 21:21). According to Polybius (12.5.6), Locri of Italy was founded from its mother city in Greece by the union of women with slaves; and so the aristocracy of the Italian city traced descent from the mother, "all ancestral nobility among them is reckoned from the women." Strabo 6.3.3 explained the founding of Tarentum by the "Partheniai" through the oath of Spartan men not to return to their wives until they had captured Messene.[71] As the war dragged on, the younger men, who had not taken the oath, returned to Sparta and lay with as many women as they could.

Persia and its successor empires (the Hellenistic kingdoms, Carthage, Macedon, Rome) took over the previously independent city-states and introduced new sanctions, in particular crucifixion. As rebels were crucified, their women were prostituted, and a new solidarity between the two groups appeared. Sennacherib, after he killed the leaders of Ekron and hung their bodies on "poles surrounding the city," seized the daughters and concubines of besieged Hezekiah.[72] At the capture of Jerusalem (Lam 5:11-12) "women are ravished in Zion . . . princes are hung up by their hands." Pheretima queen of Cyrene crucified the leading rebels of Barca, and cut off their wives' breasts and nailed them to the city walls (Herodotus 4.202). Alexander Jannaeus crucified captives while drinking and reclining with his concubines (Josephus, *BJ* 1.97). And legend gives each crucified rebel a female companion, as those executed found a woman, a Rizpah or Aphrodite, to keep the dogs and vultures off their bodies by day and night.

So the companion of Prometheus is Io, once a princess with the misfortune to captivate Zeus (Aeschylus *Prometheus Bound* 560ff.), now a heifer stung by the *oistros* of sexual heat (567, 675); she is pursued over land and sea by the fly, and by thousand-eyed Argos, seen alternately as her cattleherd and as an unsleeping secret police. Their fates are interwoven: Prometheus declares what her future will be; a descendant of hers (Heracles) is to release him. As the "cow-horned maid" (v. 588) she resembles the moon; perhaps, then, her name is Egyptian, compare the Bohairic of Matt 24:29 *pi-ioh* "the moon."

The empathy for women of Second Isaiah is sometimes missed. Israel is doubly represented in the Servant of Yahweh and in the "captive daughter of Zion" (Isa 52:2). She has been sold into slavery, in effect prostitution, the "shame of your youth" (54:4); now the "time of her service" (40:2) is ended

---

71. See Aristotle *Pol.* 5.6.1 = 1306b30.

72. D. D. Luckenbill, *The Annals of Sennacherib* (Chicago: Univ. of Chicago Press, 1924), 32–34 (3.10,46); also translated in *ANET*[3] 288a.

and, like Hosea's woman, she is remarried to Yahweh in a "covenant of peace" (54:10). Future roles will be reversed and the "daughter of the Chaldaeans" will be sold into prostitution (47:1-3) and set to work at the mill. Job 31:10 wishes the same for his wife if *he* has been unfaithful, although "grind for another" may also have a sexual connotation. At Lysias 1.18, another's slave girl is threatened to be "whipped and thrown into the mill."

"Publicans and Harlots"

Jesus ironically accepts the hostile designation of his followers, Matt 21:31, "Verily I say to you that the publicans and harlots enter the kingdom of God before you." The harlot of Prov 7:19-20 lives with one who has a "bag of silver," perhaps himself a tax collector. Even more so the parallelism is classical. Theophrastus (*Char.* 6) says that the Shameless one is "a great one to manage an inn and to be a brothel-keeper and to bid on tax-contracts." In fact, Athens had a prostitution tax (Aeschines 1.119). In Latin "harlot" can be *publica*; Didymus the grammarian (Seneca *Ep.* 88.37) asked "whether Sappho was a prostitute." Cicero, withdrawing from his praise of the *publicanorum ordo,* alleges (*Ver.* II.3.78) that Verres in Sicily had a mistress Pipa who also worked as tax collector, whom he styles in a nice pun as *mulierculae publicanae.* The rabbis criticized the Romans in the same terms: "Rabbi Yehuda said, 'How splendid are the works of this people! They build markets, they build bridges, they build baths.' . . . R. Simeon b. Yohai answered and said, 'All that they build, they build only for their own needs: they build markets to set harlots in them, baths for their own pleasure, bridges to collect toll on them'" (*b. Shabb.* 33b).

The Gospels skate on the thin ice of giving Jesus a romantic connection with one such woman. It is said ambiguously of that nameless one of the city who kisses his feet that she has "loved much" (Luke 7:47). The life-of-Jesus industry has gingerly circled around an affair with Mary Magdalene, "from whom seven demons had gone out" (Luke 8:2)—colored by other women of the story. Rembrandt makes the woman taken in adultery the representative of all such. His painting of 1644 (now in London) sets the woman, at once harlot and princess, in a temple of soaring architecture never seen on land or sea, where incalculable treasures of gold appear out of the darkness.

Ernest Renan in his *Life of Jesus* says of Mary Magdalene: "Elle avait été affectée de maladies nerveuses en apparence inexplicables. Jésus, par sa beauté pure et douce, calma cette organisation troublée. La Magdaléenne lui fut fidèle jusqu'au Golgotha" (She had been wracked by seemingly inexplicable nerve disorders. Jesus, with his pure and sweet beauty, would calm her troubled body. The Magdalene was faithful to him until Golgotha). And so in his description of the Easter event:

> Mais telle était la trace qu'il avait laissée dans le cœur de ses disciples et de quelques amies dévouées que, durant des semaines encore, il fut pour eux vivant et consolateur. . . . Disons cependant que la forte imagination de Marie de Magdala joua dans cette circonstance un rôle capital. Pouvoir divin de l'amour! moments sacrés ou la passion d'une hallucinée donne au monde un Dieu ressuscité![73]

> But such was the mark he had left in the hearts of his disciples and some devoted women friends that in the ensuing weeks he was a living presence consoling them. . . . But let us say that the strong imagination of Mary Magdalene played a crucial role in this event. O the divine power of love—the sacred moments in which the passion of a hallucinating woman gives the world a resurrected God!

So a popular identification of one of the women at the cross and empty tomb as a harlot was inevitable, though John 19:25 thought it more suitable for Jesus' mother to occupy first place. Toynbee compares the Passion narrative with Plutarch's accounts of the proletarian reformers Agis and Cleomenes of Sparta, Tiberius and Gaius Gracchus of Rome.[74] Cornelia the mother of the Gracchi is a figure somewhat like Jesus' mother; the wives of the Spartans were executed with them. Vogt attaches importance to the fact that both Jesus and his mother define themselves as slaves (Mark 10:44; Luke 1:38);[75] in the church the Saturnalia in principle become permanent, the first is slave of all (Mark 10:44).

The Universality of Debt

The loss of male autonomy with the fall of the city-state can be seen in the all-embracing category of the debtor. As Carthage, Greece, and the Hellenistic empires were taken over by Rome, every independent ruling class was absorbed. As the distinction between citizen and foreigner became blurred, slavery was subsumed under debt. Even under the polis a foreigner was in

73. Ernest Renan, *Vie de Jésus* (Paris: Levy, 1864), chaps. 9 and 26.

74. Arnold Toynbee, *A Study of History* (London: Oxford Univ. Press, 1939), vol. 6, annex 2: 478–91.

75. Joseph Vogt, *Ancient Slavery and the Ideal of Man,* trans. T. Wiedemann (Oxford: Blackwell, 1974), 152.

danger of enslavement, and debt looked much like slavery. So Prov 22:7, "the debtor is slave to the creditor." Likewise Deut 28:12, "You will lend to many nations and you will not borrow." The LXX follows classical usage: Demosthenes 35.11, "the debtors will pay the money due the creditors."

Pericles says that Athens, far from owing money herself, took pains to do benefits gratis, "since the person bound is more lukewarm, knowing that he is destined to demonstrate fidelity, not as a favor, but as a debt" (Thucydides 2.40.4). The promise of the Israelite covenant was freedom from debt (Deut 28:12, 44), or equivalently, freedom from slavery (Deut 28:68). But under the empire the old pattern of obligation represented by the vassal treaty was privatized into a universal pecking order of debt. The situation was grasped clearly by Jesus, who presumes that everybody is simultaneously, in different relationships, both debtor and creditor. In the most familiar text of the ancient world, he asks "and forgive us our debts as we forgive our debtors" (Matt 6:12). The language is that of the late Roman republic. Thus Appian *Ital.* 9, "[Manlius] forgave all those who owed to him their debts"; Cicero *Att.* 13.23, "and don't expect that those who normally try to claim what is not owed them, will forgive what is really owed them."

Even if Jesus' prayer includes the notion of debt as sin against God, we cannot ignore its surface meaning. Social unrest brings a demand to destroy the records of debt. When the wicked "covet fields and seize them" (Micah 2:2) and "add field to field" (Isa 5:8), there will be a warm welcome for a remission of land leases every fifty years (Lev 25:8-17) or of debt every seven years (Deut 15:1-6). Did it really happen? Moneylenders and the poor in need of loans at least thought it might, and Hillel devised the *prozbul* to cancel the cancellation of loans in the Sabbatical year (*m. Sheb.* 10.3–4).[76] Solon says, "I removed the markers everywhere fixed" in black earth.[77] Under Agis of Sparta Agesilaus had mortgages burned (Plutarch *Agis* 13.3, cf. *Cleomenes* 10.6). In 86 B.C.E., a law of Valerius Flaccus at Rome had debts contracted in silver paid off in copper at 75 percent loss.[78] In 66 C.E., the Jewish rebels burned the archives of debt (Josephus *BJ* 2.427).

In late republican Rome the old language of treaty making was transferred, under the symbolism of debt or obligation, to the place of real politics—namely, to the party politics of aristocratic families. Thus Cicero *de*

---

76. Surely a Greek word, but distorted beyond recognition; see Daniel Sperber, *A Dictionary of Greek and Latin Legal Terms in Rabbinic Literature* (Ramat-Gan: Bar-Ilan Univ. Press, 1984), 154–56.

77. M. L. West, *Iambi et Elegi Graeci,* 2 vols. (Oxford: Clarendon, 1971), frag. 36.5–7 = Aristotle *Ath. Pol.* 12.3.

78. Sallust *Cat.* 33, cf. Velleius 2.23.

domo sua 66, in reference to an agreement between Clodius and the two consuls, "Gabinius broke the agreement, while Piso remained in good faith." But even the aristocrats no longer possessed the autonomy of the ruling class of the polis, since power had moved over to what were essentially private armies. Hence roles previously subordinate came into their own, since now they were no more subordinate than any other. Women and slaves achieved equality, not on the level of public institutions, but in alternative cultures inside imperial society. And the wheel comes full circle in that the bond of that equality is expressed in the archaic treaty language.

Roman Elegiac Poets and Their Mistresses

Within the city of Rome, a new role is given the mistress by the elegiac poets of the late Republic—along with rejection of traditional career goals and inversion of the language in which they were expressed. Hallett[79] shows how the language of party politics is turned upside down. Thus Catullus 109.6 asks the great gods that his relationship with Lesbia may endure throughout their lives; but he calls it "this eternal treaty of our sacred friendship." This is treaty language as in Livy 23.33.9, "[Philip] made a treaty and friendship with [Hannibal]." Catullus loves Lesbia (72.4) "as a father loves his sons and sons-in-law"—sons-in-law especially, since he picked them out with utmost care to create alliances that will further his position and his family's. So Propertius 3.20.15–16: "first I must make a treaty, decree rights, and sign a law in my new love." Cicero (*pro Archia* 4.6) speaks of the relation between Heraclea and Rome "with a most well balanced law and treaty." The lover is slave of his mistress (Propertius 2.13.36).

In particular, while the elegiac poets express toward literal war an ostentatious and un-Roman pacifism, they turn military imagery upside down to express their relations with their beloved, in language strangely reminiscent of the New Testament. Tibullus (1.10.1–2)[80] asks with a weak pun: "Who was it that first brought out horrible swords? How savage he was, and literally iron!" Then at 1.1.75: "Here I am a general and a good soldier" (cf. 2 Tim 2:3). Propertius 1.6.30–31: "I was not born fit for praise or arms; this is the campaigning which the fates wish me to undertake" (cf. 2 Cor 10:4).

It seems wildly paradoxical to compare the relationship of Propertius and Cynthia with that of Jesus and Magdalene (even as inflated by Renan). But the literary subculture of Rome and the new community of Jesus share

---

79. Judith P. Hallett, "The Role of Women in Roman Elegy: Counter-Cultural Feminism," *Arethusa* 6 (1973) 103–23.

80. Compare the pacifism of Propertius at 2.7.14; 2.15.43ff.

several features. (1) They use treaty or covenant language to express a separation from that imperial society that claims all legitimacy. (2) The mistress (at
Rome upper-class, of course) or harlot is the point of breakthrough for
increased equality of women. (3) Symbolically with the poets (in the theme of
the lover as the mistress's slave), sociologically in the church, an area is found
for increased equality of slaves. (4) Their equalizing the role of the woman
and the slave is associated with an explicit nonviolence.

The last point is illustrated by Ephesians 5–6, whose version of the household code was discussed earlier. In spite of its subordination ethic, the mutu-
ality that it sees in the relation of husband and wife, master and slave, parent
and child is so big a step from paganism that it can only be taken through
putting on "the whole armor of God," which in the end involves the renunciation of any other kind of militarism. The connection is emphatic in the six
antitheses of Matt 5:21-48. Trible claims inaccurately, and with (misdirected)
disapproval, that "the laws of Israel address only men,"[81] but the commands
in Matthew really are all addressed to men. For they deal, on the one hand,
with the sexual exploitation (seduction and divorce) of women by men; on the
other hand, with aggression, revenge, and self-defense, in the context of violence by men against men. The conclusion is inescapable that for the New
Testament, violence against women is part and parcel of violence against
men, so that they must be dealt with together or not at all; its feminism and
nonviolence are inseparable.

---

81. Phyllis Trible, "Woman in the OT," in *IDBS* (1976) 964.

CHAPTER 5

Paradise and the Forest of Lebanon

Columbus and the Earthly Paradise

On October 18, 1498 (Old Style of course), Columbus wrote to Ferdinand and Isabel(la) from Hispaniola an account of his third voyage, expressing his conviction that he had found the Earthly Paradise, *el parayso terrenal*. We do not have his letter, but a hand copy by Bartolomé de Las Casas with the heading:

> Account of the voyage which the Admiral Don Christóval Colón made the third time that he came to the Indies, when he discovered mainland [the South American continent], as he sent it to the Sovereigns from the island Española.[1]

This is the document in which he expresses his conviction that the Western Hemisphere, unlike the Eastern, was not truly spherical:

> But I say that this [hemisphere] is as it were the half of a very round pear which has a raised stalk, as I have said [above, same page], or like a woman's nipple on a round ball.[2]

---

1. *Select Documents Illustrating the Four Voyages of Columbus,* vol. 2, ed. and trans. Cecil Jane (Hakluyt Society second series no. 70, 1933; repr. Millwood: Kraus, 1967), 3. The Admiral appears to have been born in Genoa as Christoforo Colombo, but all his letters are in Castilian like this one, and his name in Spanish Christóval (as here) or Christóbal. I do not know on what authority the date of the letter rests. These passages are discussed by Kirkpatrick Sale (*The Conquest of Paradise: Christopher Columbus and the Columbian Legacy* [New York: Knopf; 1990], 174–77)—a work very harsh on Columbus and the whole enterprise of European colonization.

2. Jane, ibid., 31.

The Admiral reached this surprising result partly by observations misunderstood (he felt that he was sailing uphill), partly by theory (the Earthly Paradise would have had to be on a raised mountain to survive the Flood). His further indications that he was in the vicinity of the paradise were the mildness of the climate, *la suavíssima temperancia,* and the outflow of fresh water (the mouths of the Orinoco river in the bay of Paria) (p. 39); for Paradise, he knew, was the source of four great rivers. He realizes that the summit on which the paradise lies, and from which the water comes, could not be reached; but, he says, "I am firmly convinced in my own mind that the Earthly Paradise is there, where I have said" (p. 43).

Amerigo Vespucci and his successors in Brazil make the same judgment.[3] Likewise in North America:

> George Alsop advertised Maryland as the only "Terrestrial Paradice." Its very trees, plants, fruits, flowers and roots spoke in "Hieroglyphicks of our Adamitical or Primitive situation," and their general effects and properties still bore "the Effigies of Innocency according to their original Grafts."[4]

All these travelers are drawing from a long tradition of speculation around the biblical data of "paradise." The word is Iranian, entering Greek and Hebrew at the same time to designate the same thing—the hunting parks and timber preserves of the Old Persian satraps. How did it come to have all the resonances that Dante, Shakespeare, Milton, Goethe, and so many others have exploited? Here is a word and concept that has infiltrated from Iran through classical Greek and Hebrew into the Septuagint, the New Testament, Jewish apocrypha, the Qur'an, and the church fathers—Greek, Syriac, and Latin—and so on to the Renaissance and Reformation. It gathers up what Greeks said about the Islands of the Blessed and the Elysian Fields; and both the Hebrew and Phoenician versions of the Garden of Eden. No other single word creates anything like such unity among all these seemingly disparate cultures. What can we learn from its history?

We begin with the point at which "paradise" enters Greek and Hebrew history, the enclosures of the Persian king and satraps. The usage is verified

3. Jean Delumeau, *History of Paradise: The Garden of Eden in Myth and Tradition,* trans. Matthew O'Connell (New York: Continuum, 1995), translation of *Une Histoire du Paradis: Le Jardin des délices* (Paris: Fayard, 1992), 109–15.

4. C. L. Sanford, *The Quest for Paradise* (Urbana: Univ. of Illinois Press, 1961), 84, citing George Alsop, *A Character of the Province of Maryland, 1666,* reprinted in *Publications of the Maryland Historical Society* no. 15 (Baltimore, 1880), 37 (not seen by me).

by two original Iranian texts. The status of the Lebanese forest as timber preserve was anticipated long before by the expeditions of Sumerian and Akkadian kings and the myth of Gilgamesh. Before extensive naval warfare, the
original forests of the Mediterranean were most impressive; logging on the
Lebanon was controlled by bureaucratic officials. After the word *paradise*
entered Greek and Hebrew it was diminished to denote any garden. But in
later Judaism and the New Testament it is supernaturalized to denote the
restoration of Eden. Ephrem of Nisibis in the Syriac church retains a lively
sense of the symbolism. This religious usage went side by side with the deforestation of the actual Lebanese "paradise" and other Mediterranean woodlands. I end this chapter with a few excerpts from the enormous patristic,
medieval, and later literature.

And we start with the Greek Xenophon, like Columbus an explorer of new
realms, but on land, and initially as attached to a ragtag army, of which he
later became the general.

The Satrapal Hunting Parks

In 401 B.C.E. Cyrus, younger son of Darius II of Persia, led an army of Greek
mercenaries from Sardes to overthrow, if possible, his elder brother Artaxerxes
II, who had just succeeded to the throne. After seven days' march they reached
Kelainai, a large and prosperous city of Phrygia (Xenophon *Anab.* 1.2.7–9):

> There Cyrus had a palace and a large *paradeisos* full of wild beasts, which
> he used to hunt from horseback whenever he wanted to give himself and
> his horses exercise. The river Maeander flows through the middle of the
> *paradeisos,* and its springs are from the palace. . . . The Great King also
> has a fortified palace in Kelainai at the springs of the Marsyas river, at
> the foot of the acropolis. . . . Here Xerxes, when he retreated from Hel-
> las after his defeat, is said to have built the [royal] palace and the acrop-
> olis of Kelainai.

When they reached Syria they encamped at the river Dardas (1.4.10):

> Here was the palace of Belesus governor of Syria, and a very large and
> beautiful *paradeisos,* with all the fruits that the seasons produce; but
> Cyrus cut it down and burned the palace.

After Cyrus's death in battle the Hellenes encamped at Sittake on the Tigris
(2.4.14) "near a large beautiful *paradeisos* thick with all kinds of trees."

The *paradeisoi* that Xenophon saw were at once hunting parks for the king and his satraps; timber reserves; and sites for fortified "palaces" or glorified hunting lodges built over self-contained water supplies. The orchard on the Dardas is probable but not certain. Meiggs[5] sees them more as parks strictly speaking, "trees for pleasure," with their function as "hunting reserves" secondary. Briant emphasizes their symbolic role in investing the satrap with derivative attributes of the king; along with their ancillary villages he sees them as ideal agricultural models of land development, *vitrines idéologiques*;[6] he proposes further that each satrapy in principle had one or more, and draws up a list of those known.[7] Fauth focuses on the cultic and propagandistic role of the king and satraps in planting the park, and stocking and then hunting the animals.[8]

In the twentieth year of some Artaxerxes, Nehemiah the Jew, the king's cupbearer, asked for permission to rebuild the walls of Jerusalem. The books of Ezra and Nehemiah are in some confusion: if the monarch was Artaxerxes I, the date would be 445/4 B.C.E.; if Artaxerxes II, 385/4 B.C.E. In either case, the events are within a generation of Xenophon one way or the other. Nehemiah asks (Neh 2:8) for "a letter to Asaph, keeper of the king's *pardes,* that he should give me timber." On the parallel of the rebuilding done by Ezra under Cyrus (Ezra 3:7), the "king's *pardes*" can only be the forest of Lebanon. Here alone do we have testimony to the Persian bureaucracy, in which an official (with a West Semitic name) must grant permission for all logging in the *pardes*. In another place[9] from my seven years in Beirut I have chronicled the exploitation of the Lebanese cedar forest from earliest contacts with Egypt to the time of Justinian, 527 C.E.

Two mutually contradictory themes run through the descriptions of the forest *paradeisoi*. On the one hand, their great age and the size of the trees is emphasized. A century after Xenophon, Theophrastus had apparently been on the Lebanon:

> In Syria in the mountains the cedar-trees reach an exceptional height and thickness; some are so large that three men cannot join hands around

5. Russell Meiggs, *Trees and Timber in the Ancient Mediterranean World* (Oxford: Clarendon, 1982), 270–72.

6. Pierre Briant, *Rois, Tributs et Paysans: Études sur les formations tributaires du Moyen-Orient ancien* (Annales littéraires de l'Univ. de Besançon, 269; Paris: Belles-Lettres, 1982), 451–56. This is the best account of the Persian "paradises" known to me.

7. Ibid., 451, n. 109.

8. Wolfgang Fauth, "Der königliche Gärtner und Jäger im Paradeisos: Beobachtungen zur Rolle des Herrschers in der vorderasiatischen Hortikultur," *Persica* 8 (1979) 1–53.

9. John Pairman Brown, *The Lebanon and Phoenicia: Ancient Texts Illustrating Their Physical Geography and Native Industries* (Beirut: American Univ. of Beirut, 1969), 175–212. The mate-

them; and in the *paradeisoi* they are even larger and finer. (*Hist. Plant.* 5.8.1)

Quintus Curtius 8.1.12 affirms that a forest in "Bazaira" (somewhere in Bactriana) had been "intact from cutting for four consecutive generations." In the poem of Ezek 31:3-9 the cedar of Lebanon has become the world-tree: its head is in the clouds, its roots go down to the subterranean Deep (*tehom,* v. 4), all birds nest in its branches, all animals give birth underneath it, all nations live under its branches; the place where it grows is in the "garden of Elohim," and since all the "trees of Eden" envy it, it appears that the Lebanon is an alternative placement in Phoenician myth (as at Ezek 28:13) of the Garden of Eden. The forest *paradeisoi* could not possibly have been created by the Persians de novo. Rather, the Great King annexed the principal existing forest lands, some like the Lebanon still holding the climax vegetation from after the last glacial period or before (for the Lebanon, it seems, was never glaciated). Many no doubt were already held as the property of native kings, perhaps principally as timber preserves. The king and his satraps threw some kind of boundary around them, further stocked them with game, built hunting lodges or "palaces" for king or satrap (or both as at Kelainai), provided them with supervisors (perhaps disposing troops), and gave them a uniform legal status.

But, on the other hand, the hoary antiquity of the forest was tempered by the doctrine that the king or satrap himself must have planted it. Xenophon (*Oecon.* 4.20–24) has Cyrus the younger, at that time satrap of Lydia, show Lysander the Spartan his "paradise at Sardes," and pride himself that some of the trees "I even planted myself." Berossos describes the "hanging *paradeisos*" of Babylon built by Nebuchadrezzar,[10] in fact a whole novel creation. In a new palace he built high stone terraces imitating mountain scenery:

> he planted them with trees of every sort, and so worked up and completed the so-called "hanging *paradeisos,*" because his wife, who had been brought up in Media, had a longing for mountain scenery.[11]

rials have been worked over again by Meiggs (note 5 above), chapter 3, "The Cedars of Lebanon," 49–87, with generous acknowledgments to myself.

10. Josephus, *con. Ap.* 1.141 = Berossos *FGH* 680 F8.141. Cf Diodorus 2.10.2.

11. The "hanging garden" cannot long have outlived the Chaldaean kings of Babylon. But it was quickly invested by the Greeks with a dreamlike Orientalism and appears throughout the Middle Ages in the lists of the "seven wonders," beginning with the first, *Anth. Pal.* 9.58 by an Antipater, perhaps of Sidon. Antipater's list also included Pheidias's statue of Zeus at Olympia; the Colossus of the Sun at Rhodes; the Pyramids of Egypt; the Mausoleum of Halicarnassus; the temple of Artemis at Ephesus; and the walls of Babylon. Gradually the Pharos of Alexandria (which remained standing until the fifteenth century) displaced the walls of Babylon. The Seven Wonders are mentioned by Strabo 17.1.33 and Pliny 36.30 *(septem miracula)* but not listed by either author. See now the *OCD* 1397.

Only the king who in theory planted the trees may cut them; Artaxerxes II (Plutarch, *Art.* 25.2) must set an example to his own soldiers of cutting down a tree for firewood by "taking an axe." It was an act of war when Cyrus cut down the paradise of Dardas (Xenophon, *Anab.* 1.4.10 above); or when Agesilaus in 396 B.C.E. (Diodorus 14.80.2) "destroyed the *paradeisos* of Tissaphernes" at Sardes. In 350 B.C.E. (Diodorus 16.41.5), when the Sidonians at Tripolis of Phoenicia "destroyed the royal *paradeisos*, in which the Persian kings had been accustomed to take their recreation, by cutting down the trees," it was plainly a declaration of war that served the further purpose of getting timber for their new fleet of triremes.

The logic behind this apparently contradictory belief is to assimilate the king to the divinity who (with more antecedent time at his disposal) was credited with having planted the forest in the beginning. The principal documentation is Hebrew.[12] The vine from Egypt overshadowed even the "cedars of El" (Ps 80:11; but RSV "mighty cedars"). We may compare the "oak" of Zeus (*Iliad* 5.693, 7.60). Ps 104:16: "The trees of Yahweh are watered abundantly, the cedars of Lebanon which he planted."

The God of Israel as planter is, of course, primarily recorded at Gen 2:8, "And Yahweh the God planted a garden in Eden, in the East." It will be worthwhile to survey the Versions to see the changes that the verse undergoes. It is essentially unchanged in *Targum Onqelos*. The Septuagint makes the momentous innovation of replacing the "garden" by a "paradise"; it also renders *miqqedem* unambiguous "in the East." The Peshitto Syriac follows either the Hebrew or Targum in reading *mn qdym* but knows the LXX also, from which it draws "paradise." The Old Latin follows the Septuagint, *et plantauit Deus paradisum in Eden contra orientem.*[13] Only at this date (to our knowledge) does *paradisus* enter Latin; Gellius 2.20.4 cites it as Greek. The Vulgate, where we must see Jerome's own hand, treats "Eden" as a common noun, "pleasure," and reinterprets *miqqedem* as "in the beginning," *plantauerat autem Dominus Deus paradisum uoluptatis a principio.* The first of these changes follows the LXX of Gen 3:23 where for "And Yahweh the God sent him out of the garden of Eden" the LXX has "from the garden of delight."

But the word *paradise* was extended to rather different kinds of enclosures with different functions. We have seen that some contained "palaces," perhaps grander than hunting lodges, in some cases fortified. Greek *basileia* may represent Old Persian *apadana* in the inscriptions of Artaxerxes II: thus (Kent

---

12. See further the extensive documentation of Fauth, note 8 above.

13. Attested in this wording in the Latin of Irenaeus *con. Haer.* 5.5.1, ed. A. Rousseau et al., Livre V (Sources chrétiennes 153; Paris: Cerf, 1969), 64.

155) "[this] palace of stone in its columns." The Iranian went into Hebrew at Dan 11:45, "And he shall pitch the tents of his palace" (Vg *Apedno* as if a proper noun), thought to refer to Antiochus IV Epiphanes; hence, in more secular usage to rabbinic *'pdnw,* "country place" (e.g., *b. Keth.* 62a). The tomb of Cyrus the elder was at Pasargadae "in the royal enclosure" (Arrian *Anab.* 6.29.4). East of Syrian Apamea stood the "fortified town Caphrena" (Pliny 6.119); it was "called Palace of the Satraps where tribute was brought." Here only do we read of a centralized site for the satraps generally, though no paradise is there mentioned. But not far off was the site near the springs of the Orontes seemingly called "Paradise" as a proper noun (Strabo 16.2.19; Pliny 5.82); it may be identical with the "Triple Paradise" of Diodorus 18.39.1, and perhaps is still marked by the pyramid of Hermel with its reliefs of hunting scenes.[14]

Perhaps the original function of the paradises was as hunting parks; this is attested by Xenophon for Media in his fictional biography of Cyrus the elder.[15] The paradises that were simply maintained in the wild state must have served above all as timber preserves; this is the case without doubt for the paradise of Mount Lebanon, where, further, it is hard to imagine wild game having been released, or extensive hunting from horseback on the steep slopes. Alexander built part of his Red Sea fleet in Babylon from "the cypresses in the groves and paradises" (Strabo 16.1.11).[16] Others, like the paradise of Cyrus the younger and that of Tissaphernes at Sardes, may have in fact been like modern parks with only moderate-sized trees and created from the ground up by the satrap. The language that Xenophon (*Anab.* 1.4.10) uses of the paradise of the satrap Belesus on the Dardas river suggests that it contained fruiting trees and perhaps was primarily an orchard. The text on which Briant relies for his idea of the paradise as a center of agricultural development is Xenophon, *Hell.* 4.1.15. In 395 B.C.E. Agesilaus goes to Dascyleium of Lesser Phrygia,

> where lay the palace of Pharnabazus, and around it many large villages with abundant provisions, and fine areas for hunting, some in enclosed paradises, others in open spaces. Beside it flowed a river full of all kinds of fish; and there were abundant birds for skilled fowlers.

14. D. Krencker and W. Zschietzschmann, *Römische Tempel in Syrien,* 2 vols. (Arch. Inst. des Deutschen Reiches; Band 5; Berlin: Denkmäler antikes Architektur, 1938), 161.

15. Xenophon, *Cyr.* 1.3.14; 1.4.5; 8.1.38; 8.6.12.

16. Other ships were built in segments in Cyprus and Phoenicia and dragged overland to Thapsacus!

So *paradeisos* covered a wide variety of environments from wild mountainous forests to artificial parklike gardens to whole village complexes.

Original Iranian Texts

One feature common to all these types of "paradise" must have been the fact of their enclosure, as we just saw at Dascyleium. Forests, whether natural or artificial, which served mainly as the home of wild animals to be hunted must have been walled around, both to keep the animals (just indigenous or also imported?) in and to keep poachers out. Hadrian surrounded the remnants of the Lebanese cedar forest with hundreds of inscriptions to forbid unauthorized logging; no signs of walls are reported by Breton, but there may have been some fencing in antiquity. The more artificial paradises were not intended as leisure playgrounds for citizens of nearby towns (if any) or inhabitants of villages, but for the Great King, the satrap, and their entourages; for this there must at least have been a fence clearly marking its boundary. Quintus Curtius 8.1.11–13 describes the eastern district that he calls Bazaira:

> There is no greater sign of barbarian opulence in those parts than the herds of noble wild beasts, penned in great woods and parks.[17] To this end they select extensive forests made pleasant by numerous perennial springs; the woods are surrounded with walls and have towers as blinds for the hunters. It is known that the forest had been untouched for four successive generations when Alexander entered with his whole army and ordered the beasts to be beaten up on every side.

The parallel usage of Nehemiah and Xenophon (with his successors) shows that the word is Iranian. There can be no doubt that in Old Persian and Median it named the satrapal hunting parks and gardens. The constant statement or implication that the paradise must be an enclosure in fact springs from the word's etymology. It appears once (only) in Avestan at *Videvdat* 3.18 where its form and etymology are believed clear.[18] It is used of the "enclosure" to be built around a man who has perpetually defiled himself by carrying a corpse single-handed: *pairi.dae-zan pairi.dae-zayan* (with cognate accusative masculine plural of the noun preceding the verb), "they shall heap up a sur-

---

17. Greek *paradeisos* never went into Latin *paradisus* until the Old Latin versions of the Bible, so Curtius uses what vocabulary he has.

18. C. Bartholomae, *Altiranisches Wörterbuch* (Strasbourg: Trübner, 1904), 865; translation of this text in Fritz Wolff, *Avesta, die heiligen Bücher der Parsen* (Strasbourg: Trübner, 1910), 328.

rounding wall."[19] The noun (Frisk s.v.) would be exactly cognate with Greek masc. *peritoichos, nearly attested in the neuter in different grade periteichos (LXX 2 Kgs 25:1) for Hebrew dayeq "siege-wall."

It is remarkable that in this unique Avestan usage the word is used in a highly pejorative context. It may also appear in nearly the honorific sense of the Greek and Hebrew in an Old Persian text of Artaxerxes II at Susa in four copies (Kent 154–55), where the key words are of uncertain meaning. Kent prefers "By the favor of Ahuramazda this is the palace (hadiš = hedos) which I built in my lifetime as a pleasant retreat (paradayadam)," but notes (p. 195) the version of Emil Benveniste "paradis de vie." The Old Persian word can be identified with the Avestan form under plausible assumptions. And since paradeisoi are attested at Susa (Aelian, Hist. Anim. 7.1 in fantastic context), likely "paradise" is intended in the Susa Old Persian texts also.

Gilgamesh and the Forest of Lebanon

What became the "paradise" of the Lebanon was from the beginning of history an object of aggression from the East. Rowton, going as far as possible behind the historical cuneiform sources, concludes:

> Now the Gilgamesh epic probably originated, at least in oral form, . . . not much later than the middle of the third millennium B.C. And if we go back that far in time there is no difficulty in believing that this valley [between Mt. Hermon and the Lebanon] was a scene of surpassing sylvan beauty, with the two great mountains, deep in forest, soaring on either side.[20]

Moderns, relying on modern translations of the Gilgamesh epic, see its hero as the first representative of Western humanism—perhaps the only such in Mesopotamian literature. What is he about? He is assigned or undertakes the task of overcoming Huwawa (Old Babylonian version) or Humbaba (Assyrian) the guardian[21] of the Cedar Forest:

---

19. The i in Avestan pai- is a regular phonetic phenomenon by which the i following the r is anticipated.

20. M. B. Rowton, "The Woodlands of Ancient Western Asia," JNES 26 (1967) 267. In general see Horst Klengel, "Der Libanon und seine Zedern in der Geschichte des Alten Vorderen Orients," Das Altertum [Berlin] 13 (1967) Heft 2, 68–76.

21. In the translations available I do not find that Huwawa is anywhere given this exact description, but his role seems clear enough.

> At whose name the lands are ever in terror
> I will conquer him in the Cedar Forest! . . .
> My hand I will poise and will fell the cedars,
> A name that endures I will make for me! . . .
> Huwawa—his roaring is the storm-flood,
> His mouth is fire, his breath is death![22]

Originally the Cedar Forest was surely in the West, not very closely located in real geography, perhaps on the Amanus or the Lebanon. Humbaba is a formidable adversary, though not clearly defined. In a new fragment of the Old Babylonian the scene becomes precise:

> E[nkidu] killed [the *watchman*] of the forest,
> At whose word Saria[23] and Lebanon [*trembled*].[24]

There is no extended account of felling the cedars; in the Hittite version[25] it appears that Gilgamesh has cut down a single cedar (standing for the whole forest? or a world-tree?) before he and Enkidu dispatch Humbaba.

We are obviously meant to identify sympathetically with Gilgamesh in his contest with the fearsome Humbaba, and in his failure (Tablet XI end) to grasp the plant of rejuvenation. The serpent that eats the plant of youth in his place and sheds its slough made its way as far as Greece. But how does he look in the light of history? The epic suggests no motivation for felling the cedar except that it is there. Historic rulers cut cedar for the practical purpose of building temples: thus first the Sumerian Gudea (c. 2000 B.C.E.).[26] Ashur-Nasir-Pal (883–859 B.C.E.) cut cedar on the Amanus; Tiglath-Pileser III (744–727) built his palace at Calah with Lebanese cedar; Sennacherib (705–681) cut very large cedar logs in Sirara (Hermon) and used them to build his palace; similarly Esarhaddon (680–669) and Ashurbanipal (668–633).[27] There is a beautiful agreement with the Akkadian texts in the words that Isa 37:24 (= 2 Kgs 19:23) puts in Sennacherib's mouth: "I went up to the height of the mountains, the slopes of Lebanon; again and again I cut the highest of its cedars, the most choice of its junipers, and ascended to its farthest height, the forest of its plantation." It would almost seem that the

22. Old Babylonian Version III.v.2-3; *ANET*³ 80a.

23. Mt Hermon, Bib. Hebr. *Shiryon* Deut 3:9; Ps 29:6.

24. New fragment, *ANET*³ 504b.

25. *ANET*³ 82a.

26. *ANET*³ 268–69; Brown, *The Lebanon and Phoenicia,* 176–77.

27. Texts and references in ibid., 179–95.

prophet had some idea of Sennacherib's actual words (on the "Bull Inscription") "Asshur and Ishtar . . . showed me how to bring out the mighty cedar (GIŠ *eri-ni*), logs which had grown large in the days gone by, and had become enormously tall as they stood concealed in the mountains of Sirara."

In the texts of the (Sumerian and) Akkadian rulers, the obstacle to timber cutting is the kings whose territory they had to pass through; Humbaba has disappeared. While the use of the cedar logs to build palaces is emphasized, the exploit is not merely practical; perhaps even the reverse, the palaces are proof of the king's symbolic prowess as shown in entering the forest. Solomon's palace, "the House of the Forest of Lebanon" (1 Kgs 7:2), unlike the Akkadian ones, had not merely cedar beams but cedar pillars; it reproduces the forest. The motive of the Akkadian rulers is then similar to that of Gilgamesh: a heroic accomplishment. Is the obstacle that Gilgamesh had to meet merely mythological? If Humbaba corresponds to a reality, it would have to be a forest predator; since the lion was familiar to Mesopotamian heroes, the predator would have to be the *bear*. To a symbolic mind, the bear would be the agent or representative of the guardian deity of the forest. Both Yahweh of Israel and Melkarth of Tyre have ursine characteristics. Perhaps once the god of the cedar forest was Shadday, although in Psalm 29 it is Yahweh: it seems he has replaced a Phoenician deity.[28] As the Mesopotamian kings made claim to the coastland and its tutelary deities, to cut its timber is their right and their boast; they carry out in reality what the epic projects in myth.

Likewise, the Phoenician monarchs considered the forest was theirs by right; Hiram of Tyre sends wood and carpenters to David (2 Sam 5:11); Hiram sends Solomon timber for his palace and temple, but Solomon must provide the labor, and in addition cede cities (1 Kgs 5:15-32; 9:10-14). Josephus cites the Hellenistic writers Menander of Ephesus and Dios to the same effect (*Ap.* 1.106–20).[29] Still, the Israelite kings regard the Assyrian kings not merely as invaders but as usurpers of the forest claimed for their own God. Isaiah goes on to say (37:26-29) that it had been Yahweh's purpose all along that Sennacherib should rage against him, and therefore that "I will put my hook in your nose and my bit in your mouth." Thus what seems humanistic to us in Gilgamesh seems both imperialist and blasphemous to the Hebrew prophet in Sennacherib. The ironical lament of Isaiah 14 over the "king of Babylon," where the junipers and cedar say "since you were laid low,

---

28. See Fritz Stolz, "Die Bäume des Gottesgartens auf dem Libanon," *ZAW* 84 (1972) 141–56.

29. *FGH* 783, 785.

no hewer has come up against us" (14:8), may be a later addition to the book, looking at Nebuchadrezzar's logging on the eastern Lebanon.[30] Thus we possess recorded contrasting views of the same transaction as they appeared to the two opposing parties.

Original Forests of the Mediterranean[31]

At the end of the last glacial age, a remarkable climax vegetation grew up around the Mediterranean in spite of its moderate and erratic rainfall. Although many mountains, including the Lebanon, were not glaciated, the rising sea level created a new regime of temperature and rainfall. Theophrastus, in a passage we quoted in part above (*Hist. Plant.* 5.8.1,3), further observes:

> . . . Any tree, if it is let alone and not cut, left in its natural position, becomes remarkable in height and thickness. In Cyprus the kings did not cut the trees, both because they took good care of them and husbanded them, and also because it was difficult to get the timber out. The timber cut for the eleven-oar ship of Demetrius [Poliorcetes] was 13 spans long [about 25 m.], and besides being of marvelous length was without knots and smooth. But they say that the trees of Corsica are much the largest of all; for while both the fir and pine in Latium are very handsome, being bigger and finer than those of [southern] Italy, they are puny compared with the trees of Corsica. . . . The country of the Latins is well watered. The coastal plain bears laurel, myrtle, and wonderful beech; of the last they cut timbers big enough to run the whole length of the keel of an Etruscan ship. The hill-country bears pine and fir.

Theophrastus, born in barren Lesbos and settling in barren Athens, must have traveled to some extent in order to have discovered the wealth of an actual forest; evidently not to Corsica (where he quotes others), but perhaps to Italy and the Lebanon. Plato in the unfinished myth of the *Critias* imagines that once the sea level of Attica had been lower before the present mere skele-

---

30. Brown, *The Lebanon and Phoenicia*, 195–99.

31. Generally for this section see Meiggs *Trees and Timber* (note 5 above) passim; Olli Makkonen, *Ancient Forestry: An Historical Study*, 2 parts, *Acta Forestalia Fennica* 82 (1967) and 95 (1969), Helsinki; Ellen Churchill Semple, "Climatic and Geographic Influences on Ancient Mediterranean Forests and the Lumber Trade," *Annals of the Association of American Geographers* 9 (1919) 13–37 (= pp. 261–96 of her *The Geography of the Mediterranean Region: Its Relation to Ancient History* [New York: Holt, 1931]).

ton of the land was left—nine thousand years before his time (just right for the last glaciation!):

> It had much timber in the mountains, of which clear evidence still remains. For there are mountains today which can only produce nourishment for bees [from the scrub-flora of the maquis]; but it is not long since that trees for roofing the largest buildings were cut from them, and the roofs are still intact. There were also other tall cultivated trees which provided a great deal of pasturage for flocks. Likewise the country turned to good use the yearly rain from Zeus, not as now wasting what flows from the bare ground to the sea; but since it had deep earth and received the rain into it, it stored up the water from the heights behind impervious clay such as potters use.[32]

Thucydides 1.2.5 says that "Attica because of its mostly thin soil did not attract invaders" like other parts of Greece; but this may reflect conditions after deforestation rather than before.

Theophrastus's testimony about the old forests in Cyprus is brought forward by Strabo 14.6.5:

> Eratosthenes says that in ancient times the plains [of Cyprus] had gone to wood, so that they were covered with thickets and were not farmed. He goes on to say that the mines helped somewhat in this situation, since men cut down the trees for the smelting of copper and silver; the building of fleets was of further assistance, since the sea was now sailed without fear [of pirates] and [was patrolled] by naval forces. Even so they were not able to stem [the growth of timber], and so they permitted those able and willing to cut it out and hold the cleared land as their own property, free from taxes.

Rostovtzeff[33] thinks that the period of protection attested by Theophrastus was by the autonomous city-kings of the fourth century B.C.E., the period of exploitation by the fleets of Antigonus and Demetrius, and adds a probable period of management of the forests by the Ptolemies. Thirgood, who had been a forester in Cyprus, chronicles its ongoing deforestation, climaxed by Turkish "aerial incendiary bombing" of the forests in July 1974.[34] By the

32. *Critias* 111C–D.

33. M. Rostovtzeff, *Social and Economic History of the Hellenistic World,* 3 vols. (Oxford: Clarendon, 1953), 3:1612, n. 113.

34. J. V. Thirgood, *Man and the Mediterranean Forest: A History of Resource Depletion* (London: Academic Press, 1981), 148.

Roman period the greatest natural resource of the Mediterranean was regarded as a nuisance and obstacle to agriculture; and its wasteful utilization in metallurgy, naval building, and indiscriminate clearing was seen as the greatest of benefits to the state.[35]

In ancient Lebanon, which I know best, the perennial springs were fuller and more constant throughout the year from retention of water by the soil. The most conspicuous example of many is the river that bursts out from an underground limestone cavern (flowing over impenetrable clay) at Afqa; "You who make springs break out in the valleys; they run between the hills" (Ps 104:10). And further, the water received on the land was actually greater, from the dripping of fog off needles onto the ground, and from greater rainfall than now through the transpiration of water vapor from the forests. The coastal redwood forests of California show the same pattern. Vaumas[36] believes (like Rowton) that the entire Lebanon and Antilebanon were originally forested, with hardwoods and pine on the western slope of Lebanon up to about 1,300 meters; cedar (*Cedrus Libani*) and Cilician fir (*Abies cilicica*) up to 2,000 meters; and juniper (*Juniperus excelsa*) on both slopes of both mountains above 2,000 meters. The ARBORVM GENERA IV of Hadrian can mostly be identified. Mouterde[37] is certain that they included the cedar, the Cilician fir, and the *Juniperus excelsa*; for the fourth, ancient species identifications need not have exactly corresponded with ours. In the north there are small remnant forests of cedar today on the eastern slopes of Lebanon, and Nebuchadrezzar (we saw) logged them about 587 B.C.E. The Cilician fir, better preserved today in Turkey, must have produced on the Lebanon long trunks suitable for masts, but was cut back early and scarcely shows in the Akkadian records. The *Juniperus excelsa,* today very much degraded, once also was a great forest tree. Even the picturesque cedars of Bsharre, preserved in the sacred enclosure of a Maronite monastery, show a low branched habit from dysgenic selection by centuries of grazing goats; the ancient cedar was a *tall* forest tree (see Theophrastus).

Not long before Hadrian, Tacitus in his famous phrase (*Hist* 5.6) is struck above all with the shade of the forest in its semitropical environment: "among such heats, Lebanon is dark with shade and constant with snows; it generates

35. See Julia E. Burnet, "Sowing the Four Winds: Targeting the Cypriote Forest Resource in Antiquity," 59–69, in S. Swiny et al., eds., *Res Maritimae: Cyprus and the Eastern Mediterranean from Prehistory to Late Antiquity* (Atlanta: Scholars, 1997).

36. Étienne de Vaumas, *Le Liban: Étude de géographie physique,* 3 vols. (Paris: Firmin-Didot, 1954), 1:286.

37. Paul Mouterde, "Note sur les essences forestières du Liban," *Mélanges de l'Univ.-Saint Joseph* 25.3 (1942/3) 48–49.

and fills the Jordan river." The sacred wild place of the Hebrew Bible is the slope of Lebanon—very likely adapting Phoenician literary motifs now lost. Here from Psalm 104, besides the streams breaking out in the ravines between the hills with the sea broad beneath, are the ibex and coney, the wild asses and lions, the stork building her nest in the junipers above the cedar line. What is most impressive in the California forests of the coastal redwood (*Sequoia sempervirens*) is not even the height and shade of the trees, but their enormous vegetative power in springing up from the roots of the cut or fallen, and the energy in the twisted buttresses that they throw out on whatever side their stability is threatened.

Bureaucratic Control of Logging

After the liquidation of the Persian empire by Alexander, in some places the former paradises were kept up, but not under that name. Thus the forest of Lebanon was controlled or exploited by successor monarchs: by Antigonus in 315 B.C.E. (Diodorus 19.58.1–5); by Antiochus III of Syria after 200 B.C.E. (Josephus *AJ* 12.141); by Agrippa II of Judaea in 50–68 CE (Josephus *BJ* 5.36–38).[38] But the old name "paradise" does not reappear. The Hellenistic monarchs who controlled the forest of Lebanon must have done so through a bureaucracy more or less patterned on the Persian as recorded in Neh 2:8, for it reappears in the Roman period under Hadrian.

Aristotle (*Pol.* 6.5.4 = 1321b31, 7.11.4 = 1331b15) records "forest keepers" but does not specify the area or their duties. When Pharnabazus promises the Spartans timber for ships (Xenophon *Hell.* 1.124–25) at Mt. Ida in Phrygia (410 B.C.E.), the forest, though in his satrapy, was at least nominally held by the Great King. Latin inscriptions in the Roman world have been thoroughly enough investigated that we can say with some confidence: only on the Lebanon did Romans record systematic forest management. Hadrian put up boundary markers on the living rock at what must have been the perimeter of the Lebanese forest in his own day; the extent of deforestation is indicated when we discover that today without exception they stand in the midst of treeless rocky shale. They were restudied under dangerous political conditions by Jean-François Breton,[39] who was unable to enter the northern Lebanon at all. Still, he saw or republished a total of 187 inscriptions.

38. See Brown, *The Lebanon and Phoenicia,* 206–10.

39. Jean-François Breton, *Les Inscriptions forestières d'Hadrien dans le mont Liban* (IGLS 8,3; BAH 104; Paris: Geuthner, 1980). In the *Barrington Atlas of the Greek and Roman World,* ed. Richard J. A. Talbert (Princeton: Princeton Univ. Press, 2000), I sketch the forest as it existed under Hadrian on the basis of Breton's maps.

The key to their abbreviations is his IGLS 5001, now on the campus of the American University of Beirut:

IMP(eratoris) HAD(riani) AVG(usti) DEFINITIO SILVARVM

"Boundary of the forests of the Emperor Hadrian Augustus." Many of them further read, mostly in abbreviations (IGLS 5124):

ARBORVM GENERA IV CETERA PRIVATA

"Four species of trees [are forbidden]; others are private." Above we discuss likely identifications of the four species. Two inscriptions show procurators of Augustus who have inherited the task of Asaph. IGLS 5096:

IMP(eratoris) HAD(riani) AVG(usti) VIG(ilis?) C(aius) VMBRIVS PROC(urator) AVG(usti) IMP(eratoris) I(terum) S(alutati) P(osuit)

"Of the Emperor Hadrian Augustus. Gaius Umbrius, guard(?), procurator of Augustus when saluted for the second time as Emperor, placed it." And finally (IGLS 5186, cf. 5185) on the eastern slope of the Lebanon, where Nebuchadrezzar cut timber:

IMP(eratoris) H[AD](riani) AVG(usti) D(e)F(initio) S(iluarum) XII P(er) PR(ocuratorem) Q(uintum) VET(ium) RUF[u]M

"Boundary [marker] no. 12 of the forests of the Emperor Hadrian Augustus, by the procurator Quintus Vetius Rufus."

The Garden as Private Paradise

In the Hellenistic period Xenophon's word *paradeisos* is privatized to mean "garden" simply. Hebrew offers a transitional usage at Eccl 2:5, where the supposed Solomon says, "I made myself gardens and paradises, and planted in them trees bearing every kind of fruit." The date of Qoheleth must be late Persian or early Hellenistic; the ostensible author is given the style of an ancient Near Eastern monarch or divinity, setting out trees in a grand enclosure; but the reality is of a rich man planting a garden. The usage is clear in rabbinic, *m. Arakh.* 3.2 "in the gardens of Sebaste." An inscription from

Sardes of about 305 B.C.E.,[40] where the *paradeisos* of Tissaphernes was perhaps still remembered, uses *paradeisoi* as "gardens" only. In Egypt, Nicias gives Zeno's agent Apollonius fruit trees from his "paradises" and so reports on January 19, 257 B.C.E.[41] The citizens of Itanos on Crete about 246 B.C.E. dedicate "the garden by the gate" as a sacred precinct to Ptolemy III Euergetes and queen Berenice.[42] Antiochus IV Epiphanes set out vast parks (Josephus *AJ* 12.233) on his country estates. In the Greek of the "Rosetta stone" (*OGIS* 90.15, 196 B.C.E.) the "paradises" (the Demotic version otherwise) are plantations of palms and other fruiting trees taxable for the benefit of the "gods," Ptolemy V and his sister-wife. An Egyptian Jew fancifully imagines himself as an irrigation canal leading from the Nile (Sirach 24,30) "And I was like a canal from a river, like a watercourse I entered a paradise." Josephus like Theophrastus *Hist. Plant.* 9.6.1 names as "paradises" the plantations of Jericho (*BJ* 4.467) and Judaea (6.6); when he describes the "paradises" of Solomon (*AJ* 8.186, cf. 7.347), he may have Jerusalem gardens in mind.

The usage of the Septuagint partly (and perhaps always in original intent) follows the same pattern, translating Hebrew *gan* by *paradeisos*. Thus at Num 24:6 for "gardens *(ganoth)* beside a river" it has "like paradises beside rivers"; at Jer 29:5, where the prophet addresses the exiles in Babylon, he says "Plant gardens and eat their produce" (LXX 36:5). The "garden" of *Susanna* is a "paradise" throughout. But where the LXX likewise makes the Garden of Eden a "paradise" (perhaps anticipated by the usage of Song 4:13) it creates a new concept.

The Restoration of Eden

The LXX of Gen 2:8 and 3:23 translates the "garden" as "Paradise." Likewise, in most of the prophetic passages referring to Eden (Isa 51:3; Ezek 28:13; 31:8-9; Joel 2:3) for *gan* the LXX has *paradeisos* with variations. At Ezek 31:3-9 the cedar of Lebanon is envied by the cedars in the "garden of God" and the

40. W. H. Buckler and D. M. Robinson, "Greek Inscriptions from Sardes I," *AJA* 16 (1912) 1–82; no. I col. 1 line 15.

41. C. C. Edgar, Zenon Papyri vol. 1, *Catalogue général des antiquités égyptiennes du Musée du Caire* 79.1 (Le Caire 1925), no. 59033, p. 54. The Zeno papyri contain at least seventeen references to a *paradeisos:* P. W. Pestman, ed., *A Guide to the Zenon Archive,* 2 vols. (P. L. Bat. 21; Leiden: Brill, 1981), 2:696.

42. *Sylloge inscriptionum graecarum,* ed. W. Dittenberger, 4 vols., 3d ed. (Leipzig: Hirzel, 1915–1924), 463.

"trees of Eden"; this strongly suggests that in the Phoenician myth of Ezek 28:13 Eden is on Lebanon. In the erotic symbolism of Canticles the body of the beloved is assimilated to the landscape of Lebanon. In her virginity she is like the satrapal forest (Song 4:12-13), "a garden locked . . . a fountain sealed." Thus she herself becomes a "paradise of pomegranates." To that extent Song of Songs anticipates the LXX in seeing Eden as the satrapal paradise.

Rabbinic is hesitant about making the connection; in its thought Paradise becomes a place of danger.

> Four men entered Paradise: Ben 'Azzai, Ben Zoma, the Other (Elisha b. Abuyah), and R. 'Aqiba. [In the same sequence] One gazed and perished; one gazed and was smitten; one gazed and 'cut down sprouts' [apostatized];[43] one went up whole and came down whole. (t. Hag. 2.3)[44]

The verbs associated with 'Aqiba indicate that this Paradise is *above* the earth. The Targums do not recognize this special usage; Aramaic *prdys'* appears in the *Targum Jonathan* of Jud 4:5 as "garden"; in Targum Pseudo-Jonathan of Gen 14:3, etc., for "valley"; but never for "Eden." Thus the Talmudic text rests on the LXX naming of the Garden of Eden as "paradise," while shifting the site.

Non-canonical Judaism continues more boldly along the same line. The Aramaic original of *1 Enoch* 32 from Qumran[45] has "And I passed on to the Paradise of Righteousness." *Sibylline Oracles* 1.24-25 with a Homeric reminiscence "in ambrosial Paradise." The *Testament of Levi* 18:10,[46] perhaps here with a Christian overlay, says that "one will open the gates of Paradise." The concept is that Eden, long ago debarred from humanity by cherubim and the fiery sword, has again become accessible. Latin *4 Esdras* 8:52 has God say to Ezra: "because it is for you that paradise is opened, that the tree of life is planted."

---

43. Jastrow 1407 explains this idiom (which is said to continue into modern Hebrew also) as "corrupting the youth," i.e., the "new shoots" in the garden of society.

44. Ed. Saul Lieberman (Philadelphia: Jewish Theol. Sem. of America, 5722/1962), 381. A different version of this passage at *b. Hag.* 14b.

45. J. T. Milik and M. Black, *The Books of Enoch: Aramaic Fragments of Qumran Cave 4* (Oxford: Clarendon, 1976), 232. Translation in Charlesworth 1.28. How did the Aramaic come to be lost? The Vulgate explains! Enoch "was translated" (Heb 11:5 *translatus est*)—evidently into Ethiopic—and thereafter the original "was no more to be found" (*non inueniebatur*).

46. Ed. M. de Jonge (Leiden: Brill, 1978). Translation in Charlesworth 1:795. See *Psalms of Solomon* 14.3.

A possible pagan echo of the LXX usage appears in Aristides, *To Rome* 99: among the benefits brought by Rome: "And the whole earth has been beautified like a *paradeisos*." If this reflects solely Hellenistic usage, the rhetorician is comparing the earth to a garden. But the scope of the comparison, anticipating medieval thought, suggests that some resonance of Eden has come to his ears. Thus Aristides can be added to the authors who may have had knowledge of the Greek Bible: Ovid, Vergil, Horace, Lucan, Athenaeus, Diodorus, "Longinus," and Plutarch and Lucian.

The Apocalypse of John reverses the expulsion of humankind from Eden but otherwise does not conceptually go beyond the Septuagint: "To him that conquers I shall grant to eat of the tree of life which is in the paradise of God" (Rev 2:7). At Gen 3:22 this is precisely the outcome feared by God, as a result of which humankind must leave the garden; John says that the judgment has now been reversed. The expression could not possibly be derived from working over the language of the Hebrew Bible or the Targum; like much in this book it presupposes the LXX.

At 2 Cor 12:2-4 Paul speaks of a man in Christ fourteen years ago, whom most commentators consider to be Paul himself. Paul says two things about him: that "such a one was seized to the third heaven" and "that he was seized to paradise and heard unspeakable words." Commentators ancient and modern differ about the relation between the "third heaven" and "paradise," and whether the third heaven was the highest to which one could attain or an intermediate state. The parallelism of the two clauses suggests that the two were more or less identified; but we need not assume that in Paul's thought the topography of either was precisely located. Since here, if anywhere, we have the exact language of the historical Paul, we must conclude that he has taken a step beyond the usage of the Septuagint; for there is nothing in the passage to suggest that "paradise" is the Garden of Eden. Rather, it is a special realm or place of revelation, which it is more natural to locate in the heavens than anywhere else. Paul here as elsewhere anticipates the experience and language of 'Aqiba; both locate Paradise above rather than on the earth, both visit it unscathed.

The dialogue that Luke (23:42-43) gives to the good bandit and Jesus suggests a different equivalence: "Jesus, remember me when you come into your kingdom"; "Verily I say to you, today you will be with me in paradise." The historical Jesus normally speaks of "the kingdom of God" or equivalently "of heaven"; "your kingdom" reminds us of Luke 22:28 "so that you may eat and drink at my table in my kingdom." We cannot be certain, then, at 23:42-43 of piercing behind Luke's language to anything earlier. The fathers are divided whether "paradise" here is identified with "heaven" or distinct from it. But the dialogue suggests that "Jesus' kingdom" and "paradise" are treated as alternative symbols. It is more natural here than in Paul to take "paradise" as the restored Garden of Eden, which the Apocalypse presumes has been reopened by the work of Christ. Luke (intentionally or by good luck) has here contrasted two Persian themes. For crucifixion was the preferred punishment meted out by the Great King to rebels or pretenders. Thus Jesus, while being put to death as a pretender, is represented as making an audacious claim to future presence in the satrapal or regal *paradeisos*. And that means that correspondingly he is making the claim for himself as its rightful regal or divine proprietor.

The Vision of Ephrem Syrus

The novel concept of Paradise in the New Testament as the place forbidden to Adam and reopened by Christ is variously interpreted by the fathers, especially the Greek, who work hard to fit it in to the categories of their thought. But in the Semitic world it is understood in a more comprehensive manner in the fifteen *Hymns of Paradise* by Ephrem of Nisibis (306 [?] to 373 C.E.). These Syriac hymns are all written in six-line syllabic stanzas with the syllables arranged in the pattern: 5+5, 5+5, 5+5, 5+2, 5+5, 5+5. There is much rhyming and assonance. It is unclear whether Ephrem may have known some Greek. But, except for loanwords from Greek, most or all of which can be attested from elsewhere in Syriac, neither his syllabic metric, nor verse-forms, nor thought can plausibly be derived from any Greek original. But there are remarkable continuations of rabbinic thought.

For Ephrem, "paradise" is not one state of affairs contrasted with "heaven" or the "kingdom," but the unique scene, both of creation, where Adam and Eve were placed and then expelled, and of the consummation when it was reopened by Christ. (It was precisely when Jesus' side was pierced by the lance [John 19:34] that the fiery sword was removed.)[47] Paradise is envisaged as a mountain, for otherwise it would have been destroyed by the Flood (*Hymn* 1.4.1–3):

With the eye of my mind	I gazed upon Paradise;
the summit of all mountains	is lower than its summit,
the Crest of the Flood	reached only its foothills.

---

47. *Hymn* 2.1 refrain with Graffin's note.

This mountain encircles the whole earth, beyond the sea in every direction (*Hymn* 2.6.4–5): "[Paradise] girds the loins of the world; encircling the great sea, neighbor to the beings on high."

As we know, God planted it in the beginning (*Hymn* 6.10.1–2):

The effortless power,	the arm which never tires,
planted the Paradise,	adorned it without effort.

After Adam's departure it had a "fence" put around it—namely, a *syg'*, the word that the rabbis used for the "fence around the Torah" (*m. Ab.* 1.1): "The cherub and the sharp sword were the fence of Paradise" (*Hymn* 4.1.6). At Mark 12:1 when one puts a fence around his vineyard the Peshitta has *syg'*.

To accommodate different categories of people, both in the beginning and in the end, Paradise has several regions. Simple-minded people, Syriac *hdywt'* (Greek *idiōtai*), who sinned out of ignorance, after expiation are established by the Good One at the "border of Paradise" (*Hymn* 1.16). In the center of the garden was the Tree of Knowledge (3.3). At the summit is the Tree of Life, "the sun of Paradise" (3.2.2). The levels are summarized at 2.11.5–6:

Its ground level for the penitent,	its middle for the just,
its top for the victorious,	its summit for the *Shekinah*.

In the Syriac realm the rabbinic concept of the *shekinah* or tabernacling presence of God is continued in the Christian church. And it reappears further at Qur'an 9.26, "Then Allah sent down his *Sakinah* on his Messenger."

The reopening of Paradise was due to Christ, seen under many images, in particular as the "athlete" (12.6.1).[48] But we have our own part to play (2.2.1):

Forge here and take with you	the key of Paradise.

That would be in identical Greek "the key of Paradise." For (15.6.1–3) our intelligence is like a treasurer who can fit a key to each locked door. Paradise would be defiled by the presence of chalcedony or beryl, 7.4—this text goes beyond Plato (*Phaedo* 110D) and Ezek 28:13, in both of which our jewels are good enough to belong to the better land.

---

48. The true Christian is seen as an athlete at Ignatius *Polycarp* 1.3; see rabbinic *Gen. Rabbah* 77.3. Athletes were introduced into Jerusalem by Herod the Great (Josephus *AJ* 15.269) and brought their name into the language. Similar metaphorical use in Latin, Varro *Res Rust.* 3.5.18, *nos athletae comitiorum* "we old hands at politics."

In the restored Paradise human beings are marked above all by the "robe of glory,"[49] which they were given and lost at the beginning, but now get back in even finer fashion, the "robe of the house of Adam" (6.9.3) with the Greek loanword *stolē*. Here several themes come together. The "tunics of skin (*'owr*)" of Gen 3:21, it appears, were reinterpreted as "garments of light (*'owr*)"—perhaps an original, more ethereal bodily substance. But they also are parallel (in whichever direction the influence ran) to the supernatural garment or toga that the Zoroastrian awaits after death, in some sense his alter ego in heaven, and that comes to meet the hero in the Syriac *Hymn of the Pearl*. And Paul says (2 Cor 5:4), "we do not wish to be unclothed but to be clothed upon." The early church, much as it strives to overcome gnostic or Neoplatonic dualism, remains uneasy about sexuality and cannot abide nakedness. Especially in the Syriac realm, profoundly influenced by Iran, its ideal humanity is clothed from head to foot in iridescent garments like Sasanid nobles.

Deforestation in the Lebanon and the Mediterranean[50]

The forests described by the ancient sources are today reduced to scattered groves, degraded stands, or nothing. A survey of deforestation begins thus:

> There is a close interconnection between ruined cities and ruined land. The fact that the broken statues and scattered column drums of the centers of ancient civilization have deforested and eroded landscapes as their settings does not seem to be an accident. The general impression of synchronicity, the contemporaneous ruin of ancient societies and ancient environments, has been inescapable.[51]

49. Ephrem *Hymnen de ieiunio* 3.2.6, ed. E. Beck CSCO 246-7 = Scriptores Syri 106-7 (Louvain 1964); discussion Brock, 66–72.

50. See E. W. Beals, "The Remnant Cedar Forests of Lebanon," *Journal of Ecology* 53 (1965) 679–94; Marvin W. Mikesell, "The Deforestation of Mount Lebanon," *Geographical Review* 59 (1969) 1–28. More generally: John D. Currid, "The Deforestation of the Foothills of Palestine," *Palestine Exploration Quarterly* 116 (1984) 1–11; William C. Brice, "The Desiccation of Anatolia," 141–47, in idem, ed., *The Environmental History of the Near and Middle East since the Last Ice Age* (London: Academic Press, 1978); Marvin W. Mikesell, "Deforestation in Northern Morocco," *Science* 132:3425 (August 19, 1960) 441–48.

51. J. Donald Hughes and J. V. Thirgood, "Deforestation, Erosion and Forest Management in Ancient Greece and Rome," *Journal of Forest History* 26 (April 1982) 60–75. This thought is expanded in Hughes's chapter "Deforestation, Overgrazing, and Erosion," in his *Pan's Travail: Environmental Problems of the Ancient Greeks and Romans* (Ancient Society and History; Baltimore: Johns Hopkins Univ. Press, 1994), 73–90.

The authors quote the intuitive judgment of Thoreau:

> The civilized nations—Greece, Rome, England—have been sustained by the primitive forests which anciently rotted where they stand. They survive as long as the soil is not exhausted. Alas for human culture! Little is to be expected of a nation, when the vegetable mould is exhausted, and it is compelled to make manure of the bones of its fathers.

The authors feel that 90 percent of the wood used in the ancient world (in the natural form or as charcoal) was as fuel. Strabo 5.2.6 found Italian Populonia nearly deserted apart from some reworking of the ore from Elba (Aithaleia), while Diodorus 5.13 (following Poseidonius about 90 B.C.E.) describes the furnaces of Aithaleia itself as in full operation. The decline was probably less due to depletion of the ore than to exhaustion of the mainland forests by which it was smelted. On the Lebanon, the damage done in the ancient and medieval world was much extended by the wood-burning Turkish railroad engines in World War I, which Hitti estimates took 60 percent of the remaining forest.[52] When the forests had been reduced to stumps, new shoots, and scrub, the omnipresent goat finishes off the damage by constantly grazing off the sprouts before they can grow beyond its height. Eupolis the comic poet (Macrobius 7.5.9 = Kock i.269 frag. 14, cf. Hughes 78) has a chorus of goats in five elegant lines list the plants they graze—a catalog of the *maquis* flora. On the Lebanon, where our documentation is best and which I tried to study exhaustively, the documented timber use in the ancient world was for two main purposes: building of temples and of naval fleets. Of the two, shipbuilding appears to have been by far the more destructive.

The ancient world saw two great periods of naval shipbuilding: the naval arms race of 315–250 B.C.E. and the civil wars of the generals of the Roman republic. Our best figures for Lebanon are from 315 B.C.E. (Diodorus 19.58) when Antigonus had 8,000 men logging and sawing and 1,000 yoke of oxen dragging the timber down—perhaps for one full summer season. A temple took something like the same labor as one of these fleets: Solomon had labor conscription of 30,000 men to cut the Lebanese timber for his temple, but used only 10,000 at a time on the mountain (1 Kgs 5:27). However, temples lasted for hundreds of years; Solomon's timbers presumably endured with some replacements until Nechuchadrezzar burned the temple to the ground in 586 B.C.E. (2 Kgs 25:9). The longest-lived Athenian trireme was in use

---

52. Philip K. Hitti, *Lebanon in History from the Earliest Times to the Present* (London: Macmillan, 1957), 34.

twenty-six years; at the outbreak of the Second Punic War in 218 B.C.E., Rome had 200 quinqueremes, which were almost certainly those built or captured from Carthage in 242 B.C.E.[53] In periods of action their life-expectancy was much shorter; many no doubt were sunk or scrapped in the month they were commissioned. Thus, besides the fifteen or so temples in the ancient world known or conjectured to have been roofed with Lebanese cedar, the maintenance of the fleets controlling (among other things) the Phoenician cities was a far greater burden. The systematic Romans, locking the barn door after the horse had been stolen, put men who were probably procurators of the treasury, C. Umbrius and Q. Vettius Rufus, over the remains of the forest.

In the same way, the destruction of the great pine trees of New England was due to the insatiable demand of the British navy for masts. Malone[54] shows how the New England forests were a key element in colonial relations, and discusses two English policies:

> The first visualized New England as a more useful unit of the colonial system through realizing its potential as a producer of naval stores [pitch and tar]. The second sought to safeguard the supply of masts for the Royal Navy, the most important sources of masts being the stands of tall *Pinus strobus,* or white pine, in New England. Both of these policies were expressions of the mercantilistic viewpoint.

The death of a hero on the battlefield is compared by the *Iliad* (13.389–91 = 16.483–85) to the cutting of a great tree by woodworkers on the mountains with their sharp axes for ship timber. When Vergil (*Aeneid* 2.624–31) adapts the old simile to describe the fall of *Neptunia Troia,* in principle he has the understanding of modern historical ecologists: when the forest that was the wealth of a city falls, the city falls. So far as the Germanic motif of a world-tree has entered here, it testifies to the same insight, that the life of civiliza-tion as a whole is dependent on the forest under which it grew and which nurtured it. Solomon's palace, we saw, with its cedar beams, was a literal reconstruction of the forest; the temple on every Greek acropolis replants the forest in stone, though it might be roofed with timber. The makers attest to the interconnection of the forest and the temple, but are insufficiently aware that the temple can in no manner serve as substitute.

53. Lionel Casson, *Ships and Seamanship in the Ancient World* (Princeton: Princeton Univ. Press, 1971), 90, 120.

54. Joseph J. Malone, *Pine Trees and Politics: The Naval Stores and Forest Policy in Colonial New England, 1691–1775* (New York: Longmans, 1964), ix.

Later History of Paradise

In a few places Christian commentators, looking back to the Greek world, see it as a distorted version of the biblical witness. So Tertullian (*Apol.* 11–13) rebuts critiques of Christian doctrine by pointing out that Greek paganism had comparable doctrines—which could only be inaccurate echoes of biblical truth:

> All things against the truth were fabricated from the truth itself. . . . And if we speak of paradise, a place of divine pleasantness destined to receive the spirits of the saints, separated from the knowledge of the world at large by a wall composed of a certain fiery zone—the Elysian fields previously captured belief [for a comparable tale]. From what source, I inquire, did philosophers and poets acquire notions so similar [to ours]? It could only have been from our mysteries.

Again, an apparently Christian scholiast on Hesiod, *Opera* 171, "in the islands of the blessed": "By 'islands of the blessed' [Hesiod] hints at Paradise, which is what they called the Elysian field—either because it keeps bodies free of decay *(alyta)* and immortal, or from the dispersal *(lysis)* of ills"; the text then goes on to cite *Odyssey* 4.563–64.[55]

From some Jewish-Christian or Jewish source, the name and concept went into Islam.[56] Twice only *firdaws(un)* appears in the Qur'an. At 18.107 "Lo, those who believe and do good works, theirs are the *gardens of Paradise* for welcome." At 23.10–11: "Those are the heirs who *will inherit Paradise.*" In this manner Islam was preformed at its very beginning for its fateful acceptance in Iran. The national poet of Persia, author of the *Shahnameh*, took the pen name Firdawsi (941–1020 CE), an Iranian word, but in its Arabic form. In the Moslem world it entered folklore.

The Venetian Marco Polo, after decades of travels, by all appearances real, was imprisoned at Genoa in 1298–99; he told his experiences to his fellow prisoner Rustichello of Pisa, who wrote them down in (Old) French.[57] Chapters

55. A. Pertusi, *Scholia Vetera in Hesiodi Opera et Dies; Pubb. dell' Univ. catt. del S. Cuore n.s.*, vol. 53 (Milan: Vita e Pensiero, 1955), 66–67.

56. An attempt has been made to derive the description of the doe-eyed houris of the Moslem Firdaws from Ephrem *Hymns on Paradise* 7.18; it is refuted by Graffin *ad loc.* (103).

57. Luigi Foscolo Benedetto, *Marco Polo: Il Milione* (Comitato geographico nazionale italiano Pubb. N. 3; Firenze: Leo S. Olschki, 1928). Levin tells me that *Il Milione* was in origin a nickname of Marco's, *(E)milio*, later misunderstood as a title of his book. The Tuscan and Venetian versions must all be secondary or tertiary translations from the French. It is said that no two manuscripts have the same contents, and it seems that a big task of textual criticism remains, both of the French and of its relation to the other versions.

41–43 describe what Marco learned about the Old Man of the Mountain *(le Viel de la montagne)* and his Assassins *(asciscins)*. The English Mandeville,[58] drawing (it appears) mostly from Marco, tells the story of Gatholonabes the proprietor of the castle with its wondrous garden and "welles faire and noble and alle envyround with ston of iaspre, of cristalle, dyapred with gold and sett with precious stones and grete orient perles." To his hired murderers he makes this promise:

> For after hire deth he wolde putten hem into another paradys that was
> an c. fold fairere than ony of the tothere, and there scholde thei dwellen
> with the most fairest damyselles that myghte be and pley with hem
> eueremore.

The Latin and especially the Greek fathers of the church did their best to organize what the two Greek Testaments say about Paradise into a consistent topography and history. But since the texts reflect floating symbolic concepts, their best efforts could only result in irreconcilable contradictions.[59] Was the paradise of Eden the same as the "paradise of God" (Ezek 28:13 LXX)? Was the "third heaven" into which Paul was caught up the same, or higher, or even lower, than the paradise of which he says the same (2 Cor 12:2-3)? Was paradise an intermediate state, where the souls of the just await the general resurrection?[60] A text cited by Lampe[61] asks, "where do you think Paradise is?" and answers, "Some say it is heavenly and perceptible by the intellect; some earthly and perceptible by the senses." The language of Columbus and his contemporaries about "the earthly Paradise" would suggest that it was contrasted with a distinct heavenly Paradise; but in fact I do not find that any patristic or medieval author clearly affirms the existence of two concurrent paradises.

In Dante, *Paradiso* becomes the preferred name of the true heavens, and the earthly paradise appears at the summit of Mount Purgatory, but not under that name, nor even under the name of Eden. But further, in what C. S. Lewis calls the invention of romantic love, Paradise is internalized: Dante first knew it in Beatrice, and she needs to tell him *(Paradiso* 18.21), "Paradise is not in

---

58. Ed. M. C. Seymour (Oxford: Clarendon, 1967), 202.

59. The patristic discussions are conveniently summarized in the extensive citations of Lampe, 1010–13, and Delumeau's *History of Paradise* (note 3 above).

60. Texts for this Lampe, 1011b C.2, especially Irenaeus *Haer.* 5.5.1 (PG 7.1135AB). Ephrem includes this as one of the zones of a stratified Paradise.

61. Ps. Caesarius of Nazianzen, *Dial.* 141 (PG 38.1089).

my eyes alone." This leads naturally to the usage of Shakespeare, where *paradise* is mostly a stock concept with sexual overtones; most intensely at *Romeo and Juliet* III.ii.82, where Juliet marvels that Romeo can have so murderous an impulse: "In mortall paradise of such sweet flesh."

The process becomes complete in Milton, where ostensibly Paradise at first is the name of the earthly paradise alone.[62] At the end of the sequel (*Paradise Regain'd* 4.612–13) the Angelic Quires celebrate Christ's victory over temptation:

> For though that seat of earthly bliss be fail'd
> A fairer Paradise is founded now.

Here almost uniquely we have the concept of two consecutive realms of paradise, on earth and in heaven. But in *Paradise Lost* the commentators Michael and Satan, in different ways speaking for the poet, explicitly subordinate the Garden of Eden to internal spiritual states. Where the Angel recommends to Adam the cultivation of the virtues, they become a "happier" substitute for the garden (*Par. Lost* 12.583–87):

> . . . add Love,
> By name to come call'd Charitie, the soul
> Of all the rest: then wilt thou not be loath
> To leave this Paradise, but shalt possess
> A paradise within thee, happier farr.

When the fallen angel voyeur sees the conjugal delights of the first human beings, he says (*Par. Lost* 4.505–8):

> Sight hateful, sight tormenting! thus these two
> Imparadis't in one anothers arms
> The happier *Eden,* shall enjoy their fill
> Of bliss on bliss, while I to Hell am thrust

Here Satan professes what Milton cannot, that sexual love has taken precedence over any other realm of fulfillment, it is "the happier *Eden.*" And since the authors of Genesis and Canticles were poets, Ephrem and Milton (and

---

62. The centuries of speculation that lie behind Milton have been excellently studied by Joseph E. Duncan, *Milton's Earthly Paradise: A Historical Study of Eden* (Minneapolis: Univ. of Minnesota Press, 1972)—the most helpful work on the topic I have found.

Dante also, in spite of his greater reworking of the tradition) grasp their thought better than all the theologians who came in between.

Philologists too have their own thoughts, and perhaps some final paragraphs on the understanding of paradise will be permissible. That Median princess, homesick for her native hills and forests, had the "hanging paradise" of Babylon built for her. Whenever the Persian Great King, coming from barren, dry, and treeless Iran (Herodotus 9.122 has it called "rough" and "miserable"), in his conquest of the West found running streams and forests, he enclosed them and claimed them as his own *paradeisos*. Near Eastern rulers, though they had in mind building temples and fleets, perhaps obscurely realized that their "enclosures" represented the world at its best, and that it stood or fell with them.

One secret current of patristic or medieval thought affirmed that the whole earth was intended as Paradise.[63] Thus Hugh of St. Victor: "So some affirm that the whole earth was to become paradise, if man had not sinned, and that the whole earth became exile through sin."[64] So Luther tentatively in his *Table Talk* in the winter of 1542–43:[65]

> *Genesis* is a lofty book; it is never read all the way through. The first five chapters are fundamentally not understood. *Totus mundus* became *paradisus*, or [it] came to be very broadly encompassed, round about Jerusalem; for the four rivers all belong around there. But the Deluge quite destroyed it afterward.[66]

Similarly Sir Thomas Browne, *The Garden of Cyrus*, dedication: "But the Earth is the Garden of Nature, and each fruitful Country a Paradise."

The Old Persian kings, then (we may say), had a true sense of what the earth was meant to be. The environmental catastrophe of the ancient Mediterranean world has become a prototype and warning of the current environmental crisis of the whole planet. Robert Pogue Harrison sees that crisis running parallel to a psychic crisis:[67] "Because we exist first and fore-

63. Delumeau, 150–51, documents it from several authors seemingly not reprinted since the sixteenth century.

64. Hugo de S. Victore, *in S. Scripturam* on Gen 2:10 (Patrologia latina, ed. J.-P. Migne, 217 vols. [Paris, 1844–64], 175.39D).

65. *D. Martin Luthers Werke: Kritische Gesamtausgabe,* Tischreden 5. Band (Weimar: Böhlaus, 1919), 199–200, no. 5505. But I understand that elsewhere he rejects this opinion.

66. I thank Levin for this translation.

67. Robert Pogue Harrison, *Forests: The Shadow of Civilization* (Chicago: Univ. of Chicago Press, 1992), 201.

most *outside of ourselves,* forests become something like an ancient and endur-
ing correlate of our transcendence. And because our imagination is a measure
of our ecstasis, the history of forests in the Western imagination turns into
the story of our self-dispossession." And further: part of our mind knows that
the earth, even under the best ecological management, can survive for many
millions of years, yet not forever. If that prospect is unacceptable to us (perhaps it is unacceptable to all), and if still we do not give up hope, we are driven like the ancients to affirm an eternal paradise—every minute and acre of
the planet taken up constantly into eternity. But that eternity, like the corresponding resurrection of the body, can contain forever only what once existed
on earth. Our cue, then, when we pass from scholarship to activism is to re-
create the paradise wherever we are. The whole planet is to become Lebanon.
And, of course, as Ephrem and Milton remind us, that presupposes wholly
new levels of justice and charity throughout the global society.

So we may strongly affirm the horticulturists who ship seedlings of
Lebanese cedar (or of California redwoods, or the *Metasequoia* of China) to gardens and forests around the globe. The tomb of George and Martha Washington at Mount Vernon, not built until thirty years after his death in 1799,
is today shaded by a fine Lebanese cedar with its resinous fruiting cones like
striated green apples. The custodians, like Xenophon, solemnly affirm to
tourists that it was planted by none other than the president himself. It is a
handsome tree surely over a century old; I am unclear whether seedlings had
gotten to England or France in his time. Still, the guides are correct in principle when they insist that none but the proprietor may plant paradise. When
not just every botanical garden in the world, but every street and backyard,
holds (along with native plants) green and growing trees of Lebanese cedar,
we may affirm that Paradise has begun to reconquer the planet.[68]

---

68. See the collective volume edited by G. P. Luttikhuizen, *Paradise Interpreted: Representations of Biblical Paradise in Judaism and Christianity* (Themes in Biblical Narrative 2; Leiden:
Brill, 1999). Those essays and my chapter supplement each other extensively.

CHAPTER 6

From Particularity to Universalism

This final chapter is a historical summary intended as an overview of the work as a whole.

We presuppose the emergence of a new genus, and several species, of free societies at the fringe of the absolutist ancient Near Eastern empires. Here we review that history from perspectives in part already introduced.

(1) We include the *complementarity* of Israel and Hellas worked out in chapter 1, without compromising the new beginning that they jointly represent.

(2) At each stage of the historical development, we note the *guarantee* for its continuance represented in the symbolism of the High God and his equivalents. And we ask, How far can that guarantee be translated into terms generally acceptable today?

(3) So far as Israel and Greece run parallel, the evidence for all these themes is their shared invention of the *book,* both as record of their historical novelty and its main product. Not so much the book in the sense of a physical object, the fourth-century codices of Latin Vergil and the Greek Bible, or the ninth-century codices of the Hebrew Bible; but the book as a living tradition, whose text, pronunciation, and meaning are handed down from one generation to another. (Ancient Greece provides a second body of evidence, its art and architecture, which both illustrate its books and are illustrated by them.)

(4) After the novelty represented by Israel and Greece is fully developed, we chronicle a fundamental change in both from *particularity* to *universalism* (or perhaps better *cosmopolitanism*), correlated with a basic *shift* from autonomy to incorporation into new empires. Each society moves from saying "We

are different from all the others" to saying "We have something of infinite value that should be made available to all the others."

(5) This universalism has an opposite side with two features. The reality that the walled city-state was not eternal but transitory brings the *fragility* of the natural created order also into new awareness. Above all, there emerges a new *individualism* replacing family solidarity and requiring a victory over death.

(6) When warring empires are replaced by Rome, and the church begins to represent a new worldwide community, to some degree in a *second shift* the old particularity is restored. The walls of the city-state are replaced by the frontier armies of the Roman Empire; and a new set of outsiders is recognized. The lost solidarity of the genetic family is replaced by the universal brotherhood of the church. Still, the new individualism with its demand for a life beyond death, once generated, is never lost; likewise, the expectation of an end to the natural order remains—although with a more hopeful coloration. But the full story and documentation of this second shift lies beyond the limits of this volume.

Underlying everything is the concept of *emergence*. Here my thought rests on several readings of Bernard Lonergan's *Insight*. Emergence is the link that unites cosmic expansion, biological evolution, and historical development. It says that galactic and stellar formation cannot be fully explained from particle physics, though depending on it and presupposing it, but represents a higher level of organization; that chemistry cannot be fully explained from physics, nor living organisms from inorganic, nor animals from plants, nor human beings from (other) animals. The present work carries the logic a step further. It maintains that, while the new free societies presuppose the ancient Near Eastern empires and rest on them, they cannot be fully understood from the inner life of those empires, but represent a higher level of organization.

A level far from predetermined: the new thing being born had (as always) an even broader range of potentialities than previous ones. The very differences among Israel, Hellas, and Rome too show this. In the Greek sculpture of the youth or *kouros* we see a permanently valid image of the new humanity, which could have been (we may imagine) very different, but, once it came into being, imposes itself thereafter on our imaginations. The pressure for emergence reflects the undetermined character of the novelties—which, however, once realized, constitute the necessary framework for any further emergences in the following two millennia up to the present. Still, some or all of the characteristics of the new Mediterranean world already in principle were available in the Near Eastern empires of Egypt, Mesopotamia, Anatolia; but blocked, stunted, enslaved. It goes without saying that the novelties of Israel and Hellas were all along possible, since at the right time they became actual. Can we say that they existed potentially in the ancient Near East?

That question suggests a search for antecedents of the new free societies in the empires—a search that I do not here carry out, in my ignorance of cuneiform and hieroglyphic. It would be worthwhile for somebody with other skills to ask: How far does the simple phonetic script of the alphabet rest on previous scripts? Do the decrees of Assyrian kings embody a true idea of justice going beyond their ruling interests? Does the infantry of Near Eastern empires ever express itself (as in the new societies) through the demand or reality of political power? Do any Near Eastern texts represent an internal critique of ruling monarchs or entrenched priesthoods? Can we properly speak of a Near Eastern humanism?

Cosmic emergence is slow, taking billions of years, because each stage represents the appearance of events with low probability. Historical emergence operates much faster, because to an ever-increasing degree it springs from conscious human planning. Any doctrine of emergence presupposes that it never stops, but is ongoing. That raises the question for us: Has the novelty of the Hebrew and Greek societies been, in part or in whole, superseded by subsequent emergences; or does it still hold the field? The point of view here adopted is that the insights of Hebrew and Greek texts, far from being rendered obsolete by the progress of technology or anything else, remain a standard for us to rise up to, rather than an accomplishment on which we can build new structures. They were such a big step that assimilation takes a long time.

The one novelty *of the same kind* as their innovations that I can see is the musical notation permitting the conception and record of large-scale compositions. Of course, we know a lot of new things—cosmic history, planetary evolution, calculus, quantum mechanics, molecular biology. Even more remarkable: we behave the same old way and understand our behavior the same old way. Harold Bloom credits Shakespeare with the "invention of the human," characters capable of change; but a greater step was the emergence, in both literature and real life, of creatures possessing character in the first place. Surely a new emergence is in the cards: but to identify it with the

Internet or anything else would not merely usurp the role of prophet, but affirm that it was already in our midst. Each emergence remains as a substructure for what follows. Far from being replaced, it achieves its true meaning by the revelation of what can be built on it—and on its successors. A true novel emergence is literally unimaginable; for if we could imagine it, it would already be upon us. Opinions differ whether nonviolent direct action is a step beyond the New Testament or simply a contemporary application of it. Still, the prospect of the new emergence should not trouble Christian theologians who see the New Testament as not to be superseded; for it itself contains the promise, "And greater works than these shall he do" (John 14:12).

In the sections of this chapter we survey in sequence the phases that Israel and Hellas jointly passed through, striving to do justice to both their shared novelty and their differences. In each section we cite a few texts that define the phase most exactly.

First I discuss the *physical environment* of Israel and Hellas so far as shared: hills and valleys, the defensible citadel; farming with the staples of wheat and barley, raising the noble fruits of fig and olive, grazing of sheep and goats; the technology of iron and lime; ambivalence about the forest cover of the land with its predators; the *rain* (with other "elements") from the High God that makes all possible; the interpenetrating sea and a first cosmology.

Second, I survey the *external human environment:* the complementary relation of both peoples to the ancient Near Eastern empires and to the maritime palace societies; seafaring and land trade; warfare and the treaty; the foreign woman and exotic imports; the ethnic paradigm naming foreign peoples, and their interchange between societies.

Next I lay out the *internal organization* of the new societies, with rings of agriculture and grazing around the central citadel: kingship and its successors the magistrates, council of elders, and assembly of the people; larger structures in which they are included; the sacrificial cult of the bull and the seer; the central role of ecstasy from the fruit of the vine; the myth of dragon combat (with the tuna fishery).

I then summarize the *primary discoveries* of the two societies: the objective depiction of heroic *honor and shame*; the critique of sacral institutions; the discovery of *humanism,* along with family solidarity. Above all, the idea of *justice* and the possibility of its historic realization, attributed to the High God but announced by people's spokesmen with sacral immunity, initially as validating land-tenure, and carried by land trade. The record of all this in the invention of the *book*; the inturning of the new societies on themselves in *particularity,* "We have a unique treasure."

I further chronicle the *loss of independence to new empires:* the destruction of the city *wall*; the function of imperial *sanctions* and *legitimation*; discovery of world citizenship or membership in the entire human race as outsiders pass from presumed enemy to potential friend; the ladder of debt; the saving role of the rebel victim. The concept of war as spiritualized. Increased awareness of the world's likely end. As a result the societies pass from particularity to *universalism:* "We are custodians of a treasure for all"—in particular, of the old texts. The appearance of a near-universal church and empire as a *second historical shift.*

Finally, I look at a new *individualism* facing the enigma of death. As historical continuance of the state, the family, even the natural order becomes problematical, all hope is laid on the *continuance of the individual beyond death.* I survey each principal type of symbolism and ask: How far does this rely on previous hopes? How far is it demonstrable in the sense of previous novelties?

The Physical Environment

All the features we discuss here are shared by much of the Mediterranean: the Levant, Anatolia, the Balkans, Italy, Spain. Only the Mediterranean itself plays a different role in Greek and Hebrew symbolism. Thus the reason why the new step was taken in Palestine and Greece rather than elsewhere is more due to the human environment than the physical, which imposes necessary but far from sufficient conditions.

The Geographical Setting

The earth. Semitic and Germanic share a name for the land, Arabic *'arḍa* (accusative) and German *Erde,* modified by regular rules in Hebrew *'ereṣ* and English *earth*. Levin compares Akkadian *ina er-ce-tim* with English *in earth*. The agreement seems an old one, perhaps denoting the earth as female deity, preceding Greek, where only scholars know a noun *eras* (Strabo 16.4.27). But poets know a derivative *eraze,* that is, **eras-de,* which appears in particular with the element *snow* (Russian *sneg,* Hebrew verb *tašleg*), perhaps then as a Northern word: Job 37:6 "For he says to the *snow,* Fall to the *earth*"; *Iliad* 12.156 "[the missiles] fell like *snow*flakes to *earth.*"

Mountains. In contrast to the alluvial valleys of Mesopotamia and Egypt, Mediterranean lands are marked by hills and mountains. Hebrew *har* and Greek *oros* "mountain" are surely related; they appear as quasideterminatives in names of mountains, for example, Lebanon (Judg 3:3; Strabo 16.2.15).[1] The mountain is the property of the High God, Sinai of Yahweh (Num 10:33) and Kithairon of Zeus (Pausanias 9.2.4). In the Near East the mountains *are* gods (Lebanon and Carmel). Each people knows a mountain to the north, not strictly speaking part of its territory, where the gods assemble and death is overcome, mounts Kasios and Olympus. The Aramaeans (though unaware of Hebrew monotheism) correctly observed, "their gods are gods of the hills but not of the valleys" (1 Kgs 20:28). No invader will follow the locals up into their mountain fastnesses: *montani semper liberi.* Especially as snowcapped and forested, the mountain provides permanent streams during the long dry summer: Amos 5:24, "But let justice roll down like waters, and righteousness as an ever-flowing stream"; Yahweh "makes springs break out in the valleys; they run between the hills" (Ps 104:10) as at Afqa of Lebanon. The flow of water is described in detail by Plato *Laws* 761A. The role of the mountain backdrop in maintaining independent life is expressed by assigning the mountain to the High God or gods who watch over the people.

The defensible citadel. Again in contrast to flat and arid Egypt and Mesopotamia, where the only water supply comes from the river, the new societies build a city around a fortified citadel with a natural spring inside the city wall. It is surrounded with a magic circle. Somewhere nearby is the "navel of the land," perhaps thought of as united by an umbilical cord to heaven: Ezek 38:12; Aeschylus *Eum.* 166 (Delphi); Cicero *Verr.* 2.4.106 (Enna of Sicily). The Siloam inscription (*KAI* 189, ab. 700 B.C.E.) tells how the two parties of diggers in the Jerusalem tunnel met. Limestone karst is "the hydrogeological basis of civilization" (Dora P. Crouch). The citadel may be called a "high place," Heb. *Ramah* (Neh 11:33); perhaps *Roma* (not the true Latin name of the city!) was so named by Phoenicians in residence. As the High God has his own proper house on a mountain (*Iliad* 8.442–43, Exod 15:17), a grateful people sets up a temple to him (or one of his associates) on their citadel. He can be identified with it as a *feste Burg.* Beside it is the palace of the king, a Priam or Solomon or Agamemnon or Tarquin. As the spiritual center of the people's continuity, the god is naturally established at the site that is the physical center of their continuity.

1. This was seen by A. Cuny, "Les mots du fonds préhellénique en grec, latin et sémitique occidental," *Revue des Études Anciennes* 12 (1910) 161.

Farming and Grazing

Wheat and barley. In the rain-watered fields around the citadel are grown the two long-domesticated grains. There is a possible link in a subordinate name of the grain: Latin *far* "spelt," Greek *pyros,* and Hebrew *bar* "grain" generically. Besides the physical conditions for their flourishing, the texts add a social one: disguised Odysseus compares Penelope (*Odyssey* 19.111–12) to a king (!) whose judgments ensure the growth of wheat and barley; Job (31:40) wagers his crops on his own justice, and so with the Davidic king (Ps 72:16). In further ways the crops are compared to humanity. The death of soldiers in an infantry battle (*Iliad* 11.67–69) is compared to the falling of wheat and barley at the hands of mowers; Eliphaz tells Job (5:26) that "you shall come to your grave in ripe old age, as a shock of grain [to the threshing floor] in its season." In those texts there is no thought of human beings living as individuals beyond the grave: the Homeric hero looks forward to permanent renown through poetic remembrance; Job's vindication (Job 42:13) comes from restoration of his family as before. But in the New Testament the death and life of the seed signifies the death and life of the individual: John 12:24, "if it dies, it bears much fruit"; 1 Cor 15:36, "That which you sow is not quickened unless it dies."

The noble trees. Jotham (Judg 9:7-15) thinks of three "noble trees" fit to rule over the others: fig, olive, and vine. We treat the vine below and add the pomegranate here. Each of the trees symbiotically joins the human family. The fig in both lands stands for a woman's sexual maturity. Its lengthy maturation makes a fully grown fig tree a living witness of peace: when swords have been beaten into plowshares, every man may sit unafraid under his vine and fig tree (Micah 4:4, etc.); Athenians carrying sacred things from Eleusis to the city rested under the sacred fig, given by Demeter (Pausanias 1.37.2). Gautama became the Buddha sitting under the royal fig; Adam and Eve achieved enlightenment near a fig tree (perhaps parodistically *under* it), for they straightway made aprons of its leaves, Gen 3:3-6; Jesus so saw Nathanael (John 1:48); Augustine was converted lying under a fig tree (*Conf.* 8.28). For it is *the* fruit tree *par excellence*. The bride of Cant 4:13 is a "paradise of pomegranates," and Hades wed Persephone by making her eat the pomegranate seeds (*Hom. Hymn* 2.412–13). The marriage bed of Odysseus and Penelope is built into a living olive tree (*Odyssey* 23.190); children are olive shoots (Ps 128:3). Israel *is* an olive tree (Jer 11:16; Hos 14:6); Athens is identified with the olive planted by Athena (Herodotus 8.55), which sent up a fresh shoot the day after Xerxes burned it.

All the trees are old in the Mediterranean and their names have at best distant connections. The words for "fig" are closest: Heb. *paggah,* Greek *sykon* with dialect *tykon,* Latin *ficus.* In contrast, the close relation among words for the "vine" and "wine" suggests a later entry into the languages. Americans and North Europeans must make an effort to realize how intrinsic these fruits are to Mediterranean life; Deissmann called Paul's world the world of the olive tree.

Legumes. It took centuries of experiment and failure to discover the necessities of agriculture in fields not fertilized by a rising Nile or Euphrates: fallow periods, mulch and manure, rotation with legumes. The humble bean made its way across the Mediterranean: Hebrew *powl* "beans," Greek *pyanios poltos,* and Latin *puls fabata* "pease porridge." The Sabbatical year "so that the poor of your people may eat" (Exod 23:11) perhaps originally was for the land to recover; Greeks understood fallow time and manuring.

Sheep and goats. The two animals were early domesticated and usually grazed in mixed herds; the adult names are distinct except for the doubtful comparison of Greek *oïs* with Egyptian *ʿwt* "sheep and goats, flocks."[2] But names for "lambs" and "kids" can plausibly be compared. While bovines are, of course, known, and the bull is the noblest animal for sacrifice, the grazers are much better suited to the hilly and infertile Mediterranean. The docile and unenterprising lamb is everywhere known as the natural prey of the wolf; and even in the shepherd's family it plays an ambivalent role, a favorite of father and children, but in the end to be slaughtered. In the landscape the herds of goats play a clearly destructive role. After the native forest and second growth have been cut down for temples and ships, the goats graze the former forest floor, nibbling off each shoot before it can grow above the animal's height. On the mountain of Lebanon today the writ of no government has force, and the Bedouin goatherds roam freely, their flocks annually cropping off the new growth of the cedar; only in the precincts of Maronite chapels and a few farsighted villages is it protected.

Technology: Iron and Lime

Metallurgy of iron. As long as copper was the only metal available, and the process of its alloying with scarce tin to make bronze remained a trade secret, there was no possibility of arming whole populations, or giving them metal tools to cut down brush, plow the fields, and dig cisterns. Iron ore, once identified, was common: Canaan is a land whose "stones are iron" (Deut 8:9) and the Caucasus is the "mother of iron" (Aeschylus *Prometheus Bound* 301). Just

2. Allan R. Bomhard and John C. Kerns, *The Nostratic Macrofamily: A Study in Distant Linguistic Relationships* (Trends in Linguistics 74; Berlin: de Gruyter, 1994), 521.

possibly Latin *ferrum* reflects Hebrew *barzel*. Iron was thought regenerated in the mines of Elba (Strabo 5.2.6), and so perhaps Job 28:1, "There is a spring of silver." The Philistines at first tried to keep the monopoly of iron farm tools "lest the Hebrews make themselves sword or spear" (1 Sam 13:19-20); Porsenna in the vassal treaty he imposed on the Roman people forbade it "to use iron except in agriculture" (Pliny 34.139). The high temperatures required for smelting iron were at first seen as magical, "tempering" iron is called *pharmassōn* (*Odyssey* 9.391–93). But rapidly the secret got out and the new polis found its whole citizenry under iron arms—if necessary by beating them out of plowshares and pruning hooks (Joel 4:10; Vergil *Aeneid* 7.635–36). Only so could it defend itself against another such city, and war became a regular occurrence. So the Delphic oracle was vindicated, and "iron was discovered to the hurt of man" (Herodotus 1.68.4), "created to shorten man's days" (*m. Middoth* III.4). But only so, it seems, could the assembly of citizen soldiers achieve their own share of political power.

Plastered cisterns. In neither Palestine nor Greece was any territory distant from permanent streams truly habitable unless it could store water over the long dry summer for human beings, animals, and crops. Cisterns could be dug with the new iron tools; the technology of lime was necessary to make them watertight. The Hebrew Bible understands whitewashing, and Theophrastus (*de lap.* 64–69) describes the burning of limestone to lime in Phoenicia for cement; the precise use of lime in cisterns is attested at *m. Avoth* II.8, where a retentive student is a "plastered cistern that does not lose a drop."

The Wild and Its Animals
The forest. From the beginning, written record shows progressive deforestation in Mediterranean lands. Already in the time of classical Israel, Palestine was not heavily forested, to judge by the reverence paid to certain individual trees like the terebinths of Mamre (Gen 13:18). Shepherds and farmers had been going over it for many centuries, and in well-populated areas the only trees or groves remaining were those with sacral protection. In Greece, the Mycenaeans did less damage to the countryside, but their successors more; Plato (*Critias* 111C) knew large buildings in Attica with roofs of wood cut from mountains "which can only produce nourishment for bees today." Shortsighted Eratosthenes (Strabo 14.6.5) saw the forests of Cyprus (even though reduced by smelting the local copper) mainly as an impediment to farming. Ecologists today correlate "ruined cities and ruined land."

Most tree names like themselves were local; but shipbuilding timber might be international, for cypress (Latin *cupressus,* Vegetius 3.34) is used to build a galley as Hebrew *goper* the Ark (Gen 6:14). Only special sites such as the cedar forest of Lebanon attracted the admiration alike of Hebrews and of Greeks such as Theophrastus (*Hist. Plant.* 5.8.1). Persian kings and satraps planted forests afresh and walled in the ancient ones they found as "enclosures," Greek *paradeisoi*—Lebanon was already one such in the time of Theophrastus. No doubt it was in large part for hunting preserves, but coming as they did from desolate Iran, it seems they were also touched by the reality of the forest, as Nebuchadrezzar built the "hanging gardens" (Berossos) for his homesick Median wife.

Gilgamesh/Gilgamos, who gets such a fine press as a proto-humanist today, seemingly went and cut cedars in the West, against the opposition of their guardian Humbaba, because they were there. While Lebanon naturally attracted the attention of kings building palaces or temples, far more devastating was the Hellenistic and Roman push for naval fleets. Israel, in spite of perplexing texts that show Yahweh as logger (Isa 10:33-34), sees the Assyrian successors of Gilgamesh as impious. The axe is the token of the woodsman-God as of magistrates who represent him. For it was Yahweh who planted the cedars of Lebanon (Ps 104:16), as originally he planted the Garden of Eden (Gen 2:8). The trees belong to the High God, the "cedars of El" (Ps 80:11); at Troy a special oak was the property of Zeus (*Iliad* 5.693).

A few texts record a dawning realization that the life of a city is bound up with its forest, as in Germanic mythology the whole human race is bound up with the health of the world-tree. The Egypt of Pharaoh (Ezekiel 31) is compared to a world-cedar. At *Iliad* 13.389–91 (= 16.483–85) the death of a hero on the battlefield is compared with the cutting down of a mountain tree for ship timber. Vergil (*Aeneid* 2.626–31), enlarging the Homeric passage, compares the fall of Troy to the logging of a mountain ash.

Lion and bear. The other side of the forest, and the wild generally, is the shelter it gives to the great enemies of the shepherd and his flock, the lion and bear. (The wolf can live anywhere and is more nearly taken for granted in the texts.) A lion or bear is equally probable (1 Sam 17:34; Amos 5:19; Lam 3:10); in Greek art they appear together (*Odyssey* 11.611). The names of the lion in Mediterranean languages are related. Although Herodotus (7.126) confidently affirms the presence of lions in Thrace in his own day, it seems that no firsthand knowledge of them underlies the Homeric tradition: T. J. Dunbabin points out that the Homeric lion "is never heard to roar," although its roar would be very suitable in comparison with roaring heroes.[3] Contrast

---

3. T. J. Dunbabin, *The Greeks and Their Eastern Neighbors: Studies in the Relations between Greece and the Countries of the Near East in the 8th and 7th Centuries B.C.* (Journal of Hellenic

Amos 3:8, "The lion has roared; who will not fear? Lord Yahweh has spoken; who will not prophesy?" The king like the High God may appear as a lion or (in Israel) a bear; the shamanistic seer has a deep connection with the bear. Odysseus has a she-bear among his ancestors, and Elisha calls out she-bears against his tormentors (2 Kgs 2:24). Nowhere does the terrible demonic force of the god or his human agents come out more clearly than in these comparisons.

Rain from the High God

Both Deut 11:10-12 and Herodotus 2.13.3 contrast irrigated Egypt with their own land watered by the rain of the High God. The rain was unreliable, and urged on by various forms of rainmaking. We find two parallel names for the rain: words meaning "water" (Greek *hydōr,* Heb. *maṭar*); and meaning a "blessed rain" *(brochē, berakah)*. The "water" of rain is said specifically to be of the High God, Zech 10:1 and Plato *Laws* 761A. Of all the geographical features we discuss, rain is the most absolutely necessary for an autonomous society independent of any authority opening and shutting a river's sluice gates. Here and there a brook will spread out into a "soft meadow" full of lilies with their several Mediterranean names: Persephone (*Hom. Hymn* 2.427) and Europa (Moschus 2.32) were abducted while picking lilies in such a meadow, and the Shulamite (Song 2:1) is a "lily of the valleys"; Jesus (Matt 6:28) sees the lilies as evidence of God's universal care. Somehow two sets of river names spread across the Mediterranean: Hebrew Jordan (*Yarden*) and Homeric *Iardanos* with "Scythian" *dan* "river"; Hebrew Arnon, Greek Orontes, Etruscan Arnus, Hurrian *arinni* "well, spring." The High God is the name given by the two societies for the agency that guarantees the rain. He may be thought of in physical terms as urinating through the rain (Aristophanes *Clouds* 373); or as the artisan who perforates the sky (Mal 3:10; Herodotus 4.158.3). Once in Greek and regularly in Latin the "rainbow" (Gen 9:13; Ezek 1:28) is described as the bow of warfare.

The Sea and Cosmology

All the symbolism of irresistible power that we associate with the ocean, the ancients invested in the Mediterranean (which can get very rough at times, as Odysseus, Paul, and Aeneas can testify); Mark (4:35-41; 6:45-52) transfers it down yet further to the Sea of Galilee! Israel, effectively landlocked, knows storms at sea mostly by rumor (Jonah; Ps 107:23-30). Here complementarity

Studies Supplementary Papers 8; London: Society for the Promotion of Hellenic Studies, 1957; rept. 1979), 46, cited by Hainsworth in the Cambridge *Iliad* on 10.485 (3:200).

separates them from Hellenes. But both see the plane of land and sea as circular: Yahweh inscribes a circle on the face of the Deep (Prov 8:27; Job 26:10) as Earth is wheel-shaped (Herodotus 4.36.2). The sky overhead is bronze (*Iliad* 5.504, etc.; Deut 28:23; later iron), and held up by pillars (*Odyssey* 1.52–54; Ps 75:4 and frequently). Where Hephaestus hammers out sky and earth on Achilles' shield (*Iliad* 18) he parallels the action of God in Genesis 1. Human beings "live around the Sea like ants or frogs around a marsh" (Plato, *Phaedo* 110C); Yahweh "sits on the circle of the earth, and its inhabitants are as grasshoppers" (Isa 40:22). Later the heavens become an imperial star-spangled cope.

Our difference from the ancients lies in a more developed science; we may translate their "High God" as the mysterious synchronization of planetary conditions with the evolution of a species ready to take advantage of it. Thus the confluence of elements that came together to make independent societies possible is named by them as the work of a High God: the Mediterranean hilly terrain blocking movements of imperial armies; the defensible citadel with its providential limestone strata channeling water to a spring; the wheat and barley that must die to be quickened; the sacred fig and olive; the inherited domestication of sheep and goats; the forest planted in the beginning by the god; the emblematic violence of lion and bear; the indispensable and unpredictable rain. It is not easy for the historian of planetary evolution to explain how all came together at the right time to make the first free societies possible; the High God is *their* name for it.

The External Human Environment

The presence of other human societies determined both the time and the place where free societies emerged. We saw the *differences* between Israel and Hellas, especially with relation to the ancient Near Eastern empires: the new pattern arose in Israel just *inside* the realm of the empires, in Hellas just *outside*. Here as in the previous section we mostly return to features that the two societies exhibit in common—except again in their relation to the sea and seafaring. Those features do not yet define the special novelty represented by Israel and Hellas, but are shared by a broader circle of states. Still, they are best attested in Hebrew and Greek; and each cultural item jointly borrowed acquires in its new setting a halo of symbolic meaning unattested in the empires or elsewhere in their fringe of lands. Exotic products from far-off places are felt suitable as images of the High God, distant and inscrutable. Both war and its resolution, the treaty, are carried out in his name. The special roles of women mediate a unique relationship to the unseen world.

The Ancient Near Eastern Empires

From the empires, the peoples at their periphery received the novelties of city life, commerce, and organized warfare, with all their features of central administration, technology, a formalized cult, and writing. But the city lived under absolutist regimes, relied on irrigation by rivers rather than rainfall (except in Anatolia), and kept writing as a difficult scribal monopoly. The imperial reality both fostered the new free states and in the end swept over them—but not until they had rendered their innovation independent of its civic birthplace. The texts and arts of both Israel and Hellas witness their close relations to the empires: some vocabulary items that they share show a cross-section of cultural influence.

(1) *Assyria and Babylonia*. Some Greeks by the fourth century B.C.E. knew the actual beginning of *Enuma Elish,* and both peoples the figure of Gilgamesh. From Mesopotamia, Hebrews and Greeks received the linen garment of the tunic (Heb. *kuttonet,* Greek *chiton,* Latin *tunica*), both outer and inner, more for leisure than for work. It came to be seen as a second skin standing for the private matters of birth, sexuality, mourning, and death. The stratum of Hebrew recorded in the book of Proverbs got from Akkadian a name of gold (*ḥarūṣ*) universally adopted in Hellas *(chrysos),* along with its measure of a kilo or so, the mina (Heb. *maneh,* Greek *mnā,* Latin *mina*). As a special feature of Babylonian building, both societies noted the brick (Hebrew *levēnah,* Greek *plinthos*). A spectacular example is the Ishtar gate, now in the Pergamon Museum, Berlin. Greeks for their temples borrowed the feature and name of the precinct (*temenos,* Akkadian *temennu*), which Hebrews also used as the first word of a city name *(Timnath);* it is taken over further in Latin *templum,* a "space for augury" before it became a building.

(2) *Egypt*. The Hebrew Bible, with all its knowledge of Egypt, says nothing of the pyramids or Sphinx; Jeremiah (43:13) does mention the obelisks and temples of Heliopolis; possibly the mythical phoenix bird appears; the hippopotamus and crocodile, which so struck Herodotus, show up as the Behemoth and Leviathan of Job. In contrast, both peoples note and adopt the cosmetics used in Egypt to enhance the living and the dead. Egyptians discovered and exported to Lydia (the inventor of coinage) the touchstone for assessing the purity of gold (Hebrew *bohan,* Greek *basanos*). Two precious materials, ivory and ebony, were always thought of as Egyptian, though imported from farther south.

Egypt was the land of the ancient Near East the most accessible to both Hebrews and Greeks. As a result, they are most aware of their differences from it rather than from the other empires. (1) Both noted their own rain-watered fields as over against its irrigation. (2) Romans especially noted the merits of the phonetic alphabet over against awkward hieroglyphics, a system both defective and redundant. (3) Both were struck by the obsession of the Egyptians with the preservation of the dead. (4) The Greek naked *kouros* is an Egyptian pharaoh striding into life.

(3) *Anatolia*. The Hittite empire was known to Israel and Hellas only by remote tradition, for the "Hittites" of the Hebrew Bible, though carrying the old name, are hardly closer related to the kingdom than the Lydians and Lycians. From the Anatolian world both peoples remembered an old name for the helmet (Hebrew *qoba*, Greek *kymbachos*), and a designation of oppressive rulers (Philistine *sarney* and Greek *tyrannoi*). Almost certainly from the same land came the name of the torch as a designation of lightning (*lappiyd*, *lampas*) and the woman's tambourine (below).

The culture of the empires was less well known to Hebrews and Greeks at first hand than at one remove through the palace societies of the Mediterranean coasts: Ugarit and the Phoenician cities, the cities of Cyprus and Cretan Cnossos, Mycenae and Pylos. While the alphabetic scripts of Ugarit and later Phoenicia are well understood, they were preceded by syllabic scripts—pseudo-hieroglyphic at Byblos and Linear A of Crete for unknown languages, syllabic Cypriote and Linear B for Greek—which present many problems. Relations among all these peoples are best understood through the remains of their arts and industries, and through such shipwrecks as those of Cape Gelidonya[4] with its cargo of "ox-hide" copper ingots and of Ulu Burun.[5]

Seafaring

Although certain concepts were carried mainly by overland trade (in particular the full notion of justice), diffusion of imperial civilization and interchange of novelties happened more readily by sea. Inland sites like Jerusalem, Boeotian Thebes, and the Etruscan cities had connections with nearby seaports: much to Nehemiah's displeasure, in the fifth century B.C.E. resident Tyrians sold marine fish in Jerusalem on the Sabbath with their indispensable

4. George F. Bass et al., *Cape Gelidonya: A Bronze Age Shipwreck* (Transactions of the American Philosophical Society n.s. 57.8; Philadelphia: American Philosophical Society, 1967).

5. George F. Bass, "A Bronze Age Shipwreck at Ulu Burun (Kas): 1984 Campaign," *AJA* 90 (1986) 269–305, etc. Two Phoenician wine ships were recently found off Tyre by Robert Ballard (*New York Times,* June 24, 1999).

iodine (Neh 13:16). That does not reduce the dangers of the sea, as in Odysseus's shipwreck; "it is a fearful thing to die among the waves," says Hesiod (*Opera* 687); "they went up to heaven, they went down to the depths" (Ps 107:26). Not to mention pirates: one who got safely to land like Damon of Ascalon would set up a stele, or a votive anchor like Sostratus at Graviscae and nameless dedicants at Byblos. The later flood legends as of Noah and Deucalion surely rest in part on the great tsunami of (perhaps) 1628 B.C.E.; folk memory may have retained some relic of the great cataract when the level of the Black Sea was raised 350 feet about 5600 B.C.E.

Since Greek *gaulos* with different accents can mean both a table "vessel" and a ship, Heb. *gullah* ("bowl") surely also meant "round (Phoenician) ship." The earliest anchors, Greek *eunai,* may be just Semitic "stones." Archilochus testifies that sailors were accustomed to sample the wine cargo held in big pottery amphoras (Heb. *kad,* Greek *kados,* Latin *cadus*). (That may account for some of the shipwrecks!) Both by sea and by land prudent buyers insisted on "*full*" containers with a worldwide adjective. Another fleet went out after the enormous annual run of tuna (Hebrew *tanniyn,* Greek *thynnos*), today reduced to a small fraction of what it was even in the 1500s. The catch was assimilated to the aboriginal battle of the god against the great sea monster.

Caravans and Traders

As the wine-trade at sea has the common vocabulary of the carrier and container, so on land the ass (Heb. *'athon,* Latin *asinus*) with its twin pannier sacks (*śaq,* Greek *sakkos,* Latin *saccus*). The crafty Gibeonites put "wornout sacks on their asses" (Josh 9:4); the parvenu Trimalchio serves olives in an *asellus . . . Corinthius cum bisaccio* "an ass of Corinthian silver with twin pannier sacks" (Petronius 31.9). The caravans are an extension of the upland farmer bringing his produce in to the city market. The wool-trade brought the international name *śēs* of the clothes-moth between lands. By land or sea, the merchant-banker is the most familiar representative of a neighboring culture. The down-payment he asks for his goods is a Phoenician term (Heb. *'erabown,* Greek *arrhabōn*). He is the custodian of the touchstone. And since that test is the primary metaphor for human excellence in the proverb-books of Solomon and Theognis, he must be the carrier of the equally international proverbs—embodying an international practical wisdom, with a marked upper-class bias.

Warfare

Trade and warfare are the two occupations whereby men of neighboring peoples learn to know each other. In war, as enemies, allies, mercenaries. In the

Bronze Age, when only affluent heroes could afford weapons and armor, the panoplies got so heavy that the combatants must be carried to and from the fight in chariots; and the horse with its old international name acquired an honorific character that it never lost even when iron weapons brought in the clash of infantry lines. It was the light weapons whose names were carried back and forth between languages as the weapons changed sides: lances (Heb. *romḥey,* Greek *longchai,* Latin *lanceae*); arrows *(ḥiṣṣey, oistoi, sagittae).* With ambivalence of life and death, the bow is assimilated to the lyre: David, Odysseus, and Apollo are equally skilled at handling each. The military tent (Greek *skēnē*) was probably named after an unattested Phoenician word, adapted as rabbinic *šekiynah* "'tabernacling' Presence of God," which continues in Syriac Christian verse and Qur'anic *sakinah.*

Hebrews and Romans professed that victories were won by the military *numen* of the state, sent out to battle from a box or building—the Ark of the Covenant, the Temple of Janus. A prominent part of sacral theory was the effort to win over the opposing deity by *evocatio.* Ceremonially, the fighting was ended by the "triumphal" return of one claiming to be victor, legally, by a treaty, which, as an international document, achieved a nearly fixed format throughout the Near East and Mediterranean world. The earliest attestations are the vassal treaties of the Hittite Great King. In Israel his role is taken by Yahweh, and the formularies of the covenant follow the vassal treaty, but now given by a benevolent deity to his people. When it is laid by a superior on an inferior, it always has the provision "to have the same enemies and friends" as the giver. The cosmic elements—Earth and Sky, sea and winds and rivers—appear as witnesses in the Hittite treaties and in literary adaptations: "Listen, heavens, and hear, earth" (Isa 1:2); Prometheus's complaint about the injustice done him by a fellow god (Aeschylus, *Prom.* V. 88–92). The anthology of curses that the weaker party must lay on himself is current throughout the Mediterranean.

Foreign Women and Imports
Hebrews and Greeks both had a taste for the exotic, above all in the foreign woman and the enticing items she brought in her trousseau. She came on three levels. Topmost is the foreign queen or princess. The lowest level is the harlot, who (we boldly proposed) is known in Hebrew as a Greek "woman." It was the middle level of the concubine who became the international figure with her (seemingly Indo-European) name, Hebrew *pilegesh,* Greek *pallakis,* Latin *paelex.* For a prince to take his father's concubine is the most radical claim to the throne; so with Amyntor (*Iliad* 9.452) as with Reuben, Abner, Absalom, Adonijah. It is her qualifications that are closest scrutinized: Cant

4:7, "There is no flaw *(mūm)* in you"; a girl in Hesiod *Theog.* 259 is "without flaw," *amōmos*.

Probably it was the foreign woman who first brought in the cosmetics taken for granted by the matrons of Alexandria: Praxinoa sends her husband off to the store for soap *(nitron)* and rouge *(phykos)*, Theocritus 15.16. Perhaps both were originally Egyptian, but Greek "rouge" usurped the proper name of "mascara." Israel as harlot washes with soap *(nether,* Jer 2:22) and sets off her eyes with mascara *(pūk,* Jer 4:30) like Jezebel (2 Kgs 9:30); in Propertius 2.18C.31–32 *caeruleo . . . fuco* is "steel-blue eye shadow."

It was surely also the concubine or harlot who brought in the diaphanous tunic worn only to be taken off (Herodotus 1.8.3, Cant 5:3). Her exotic scents, each with its proper international name, are imagined as growing on Lebanon (Cant 4:13-14); she sings (Prov 7:17), "I have perfumed my bed with myrrh, aloes and cinnamon." The spices are earlier attested at the epithalamium of a foreign princess. In Sappho's wedding song for Hector and Andromache, "myrrh, cassia and libanos were mixed"; of the groom marrying a Tyrian princess (Ps 45:9), "myrrh, aloes and cassia are on all your garments." The true home of cassia and cinnamon was the land we have learned to call Vietnam.

In cult the women had a monopoly on two seeming contrasted opposites: ecstatic dancing with the Anatolian tambourine (Hebrew *tuppiym,* Greek *tympana*); and abandoned mourning as for Tammuz/Adonis. But Aristophanes (*Lys.* 387–89) combines *tympanismos* and *Adoniasmos* as if features of a single ceremony. Jephthah's daughter comes out with her tambourine and is mourned annually by the daughters of Israel (Judg 11:34-40); Ezek 8:14 found women sitting in the Temple and wailing for Tammuz. Both peoples in their art represent the female tambourinist.

Perhaps also jewels with their international names were early known on the fingers of fancy women, as Cynthia's beryl in Rome (Propertius 4.7.9). But in our texts they first appear in myths of a better world: jasper and emerald in the myth of Plato's *Phaedo* (110D) and in Ezekiel's myth (28:13) of the Garden of Eden (which adds sapphire). And they are even more worn by men: the Jewish high priest (Exod 28:20), Maecenas in Augustus's imagination.[6] The griffin *(gryps)* or cherub *(kerūb),* its form learned from some Near Eastern artwork,[7] has its own place in the art and literature of both lands. It watches over gold in Eden and Scythia (Herodotus 4.13) and forms a throne for kings and gods.

---

6. Macrobius *Sat.* 2.4.12.

7. A Jewish sarcophagus from the Catacomb Torlonia in Rome has a griffin taking the place of the indigenous cherub.

The Ethnic Paradigm

As Israel and Hellas agree in such relations to the surrounding human world, they also agree in the grammatical form of names by which they designate foreigners. A *masculine singular* names the eponymous founder of a people or the people itself: thus Sidon as man and city, Ascalon, Ionian (Greek *Iaon,* Heb. *Yawan*), Arab (Heb. *'arab,* Greek *Araps*), Cilician (Heb. *Ḥeylek,* Greek *Kilix*). A *masculine collective or plural* for groups of soldiers, colonists, slaves, traders: Aramaeans (Heb. *Arammiy,* Greek *Eremboi*), Pelasgians (*Pelasgoi*) and Philistines *(Pelištiy),* Achaeans *(Achaioi)* and "Hivites" *(Ḥiwwiy).* A *feminine singular* for a foreign woman or land: Sidonian (Heb. **Ṣedniyyah,* Greek *Sīdoniē*). The forms are extended for common nouns and in some special features of men's language. Anatolian peoples with Libyans are known as mercenaries to both Israel and Hellas. Prehistoric migrations brought foreign peoples to Hellas—Cadmeans and Danaans; and to Canaan—Dorians, Cretans, Pelasgians, Achaeans ("Hivites"), and Gergithes.

Omne ignotum pro magnifico (Tacitus *Agricola* 30.4). Since the God or gods are far from humankind and not often seen, rare imports from distant or unknown lands partake of the nature of divinity. Spices or aromatics unknown in Mediterranean lands are most suitable for the divine cult. Especially jewels witness a better land associated with the divine.

When two peoples are at war with each other, the underlying reality is a combat between their respective tutelary divinities. In such a matter of life and death, more clearly than elsewhere the grounding of a people in the nature of things is expressed. At the end of a war, the format of the treaty is paralleled by the ongoing relationship or "covenant" between a people and its eternal principle.

In the special roles of women, rejoicing and mourning, even though transmitted to us by male informants, we catch a glimpse of the feminine relationship (otherwise hidden from us) to the unseen world. Those polar opposites of emotion define an essential aspect of what it means to be human. In the predominantly masculine world that emotional level is only achieved through the outside assistance of the noblest tree, the vine (below)—and (in Hellas but not Israel) for the victor in the games.

Internal Organization

We progressively narrow down the realm where the birth of freedom took place. The suitable physical environment extends over much of the Mediterranean; the external human environment reduces it further to states in touch with the ancient Near Eastern empires by sea or land. Here we discuss the internal social enterprises actually developed by peoples who built a city around a defensible citadel. None of the structures quite reach the essential novelty represented by Israel and Hellas (and later Rome) that accounts for the preservation of their literature. They are in principle (to the best of our knowledge) shared by other contemporary societies: Phoenicians, Aramaeans of Damascus, the Anatolian states, Etruscans, Italic peoples. But Hebrew and Greek (with Latin) texts are by far our best evidence for them—both domestically and in the other states as well. Each appears to be a necessary condition for the joint novelty of Israel and Hellas: human nature as it is, and as it might be, recorded in a people's phonetic alphabet. Even more than features of the external human environment are they colored by the new emergence of which they become an essential part.

Social Structure of the City-State

While history or legend records a *king with divine attributes* in the origins of the city-state or polis, his powers were from the beginning limited by the necessary conditions for its survival—which in the end either entirely replaced him by a body of magistrates, or reduced him to a vestigial ceremonial status. Originally he is seen by his justice as maintaining the fertility of the land, so that it bears wheat and barley; as a consequence he is the father of heroes. His palace adjoins the temple of the High God on the citadel; and, like that God, he leads his people in war.

When improved metallurgy showed iron to be abundant, the old heroic combat of bronze-clad heroes one on one was replaced by a people's army. Its role of succoring the state in wartime could not be denied it in peace, where its muster (now without arms) became a citizens' assembly. A beautiful text (Dio Cassius 37.28, 63 B.C.E.) shows the interchangeability of the assembly and the militia in Rome: all who bore arms must attend the *comitia* in the Campus Martius; but an armed guard must hold the Janiculum, and if it broke up, the assembly was dissolved—to restore the militia. Since the assembly is the opposite face of the state under arms, there was no question of women entering it.

As the officers of the militia approached old age, class differences among them were intensified, and the aristocratic formed themselves into a council of elders or Senate. By election up from the Senate or devolution from the monarchy there appeared a small group of magistrates advising or replacing the king. Thus the continued existence of the state imposed on it the three-fold structure of magistrates, council, and assembly.

The mysterious unity of the Mediterranean world is illustrated where the magistrates are a college of two: two annually elected suffetes in Carthage and consuls in Rome, two lifelong hereditary kings in Sparta, the two complementary kings of Judah and Israel (often warring). The council of elders often "sits at the gate" and has a (sub)committee of thirty at Carthage and Sparta. The people's army has a ceremonial military force of three hundred in Israel, Sparta, Thebes, Rome, and Carthage. As political body it acquires spokesmen with sacral immunity: Israelite prophets, statesmen like Solon and the reforming Spartan kings, the tribunes of the plebs at Rome.

Subordinate classes in the city still have a quasi-civic structure in their own right: women, youth, even slaves with their Saturnalia; the Roman plebeians; resident aliens. In the fully developed city-state the woman has only the choice of housewife and harlot: the two roles are made the objects of an allegorical choice for young men (Xenophon, Prov 7:5-10).

The city-state acquires law codes. Civil codes: the great inscribed code of Cretan Gortyn runs parallel to Num 36:6, where heiresses must marry sons of their father's brother to keep property in the family. Criminal codes: Plato's proposed legislation in *Laws* 9 (also set in Crete!) has many of the same provisions as the Covenant Code of Exodus 21 in the same order, including permission to kill a thief at night (but not daytime), shared also by the Roman XII Tables.

Larger Structures

Cities or tribes joined themselves into groups of twelve, to which we give the Greek name *amphictyony:* so in Israel, Ionia, around Delphi, Etruria; perhaps also in the Latin league at Lavinium. Since the group in each case has a cult center, the obvious explanation is that each member of the league administered it for a month per year. Hebrews did not recognize any larger grouping than that of *lineage:* the tribes physically or conventionally descended from the twelve sons of Jacob/Israel. Greeks put *language* first: a Greek state recognized as part of *to Hellenikon* any people speaking Greek, and welcomed trade partners in Anatolia or Libya who started to learn it (any such kinship, of course, did not block, but rather encouraged, warfare). Hebrews and Romans recognized an extended generation or *saeculum* of all those alive at a founding event, and computed the longevity of states on that basis, "unto the tenth generation" (Deut 23:3-4); this concept seems unknown in Hellas.

The new energy of the city-state increased its wealth and population, and led to extension by conquest at home or colonization overseas. Phoenician trade resulted in one colony, Carthage, which for centuries outshone the homeland states; but its early history is nearly unrecorded. Many Greek city-states founded overseas colonies, but again they are almost lacking history except for inscriptions from Cyrene. Thus the pattern of colonization (unearthed by Weinfeld) is best recorded in the legends of the Israelite conquest and the *Aeneid*. Weinfeld sees two phases: an initial phase of trade attributed to a single patriarch (Abraham and Aeneas); a second phase of true colonization inaugurated by a priestly oracle.

Sacrifice and the Seer

The sacral life of the state is divided between an inherited sacrificial priestly cult taken for granted, and the charismatic activity of individual seers with some relation to boreal shamanism.

It is unclear how far the *sacrificial priestly cult* extended around the Mediterranean. Israel and Hellas (with Rome too) share special features: the primary act is the slaughter of a large animal that bloodies an altar; the inedible portions are offered to the High God or another as their smoke goes up to heaven; the meat provides a banquet for the participants. The shared vocabulary is very extensive. The ideal victim is a bull (Hebrew *shor,* Greek *tauros*) with its horns, perhaps gilt (Hebrew *qeren*, Latin *cornu*), sacrificed (Hebrew *zebaḥ,* Greek *sphag*) on an altar *(bamah, bōmos)*. The bull sacrifice may be accompanied by the libation of wine with *its* common name. The herd of cattle further has a common name, Hebrew *baqar* and Latin *pecora*; in an old Semitic and Indo-European theme it is the natural object of theft, Heb. *gnebat,* Greek *klepos*.

The charismatic *seer* combines seemingly disparate elements. The seer is of ambiguous sexuality, likely handicapped, hysteric. In the Mediterranean of uncertain rainfall, one of his tasks is rainmaking. Salmoneus of Elis claimed to be Zeus and threw lighted torches *(lampades)* at the sky, imitating lightning (Apollodorus 1.9.7); Rabbi Simeon b. Gamaliel juggled lighted torches at the Feast of Booths when rain was prayed for (*b. Sukkah* 53a), where the torches might as well have been *lappidiym*. (The names of "lightning bolts" are very old, Hebrew *beraqim,* Greek *phloges*.) Hebrew and Greek seers have close connections with the *bear,* hibernating and risen. The witch of En-Dor (1 Sam 28:7), like Circe, controls access to a seer still powerful in death; her practice seems Sibylline and could have been transmitted to Palestine by the Trojan *Gergithes* with their relation to the Hebrew *Girgashites*.

The Fruit of the Vine and Ecstasy

Viticulture too has a strong international vocabulary, in particular the name of wine (Hebrew *yayin,* Greek *{w}oinos,* Latin *uinum*). The great enemy of the vine is the boar (Ps 80:14; *Iliad* 9.539). (Note also the fox, Cant 2:15, "Catch us the foxes that spoil the vines"; Varro *de re rust.* 1.8.5, in Asia the vine lies on the ground, *quae saepe uulpibus et hominibus fit communis,* "which often is shared between foxes and men.") Yahweh brought a vine out of Egypt and planted it (Ps 80:9); "Oineus king of Calydon was the first to receive from Dionysus the plant of the vine" (Apollodorus 1.8.1). Since cistern water is barely drinkable, normal practice was to *mix* water with wine, and the verb was taken over from Indo-European (likely Greek) into West Semitic. The wine hall (Hebrew *lishkah,* Greek *leschē*) appears in both societies. As wine "makes glad the heart of gods and men," in both societies it is the original element opening awareness of a transcendent world.

Dragon Combat

Of all mythical themes, that of combat with a primeval dragon is most deeply rooted in both societies. Before the High God could go about the work of creation, it seems, he had to overcome the sea dragon of chaos (Ps 74:14-16). At the Pillars of the world or beyond them, his combat is assimilated to the tuna fishery; in the eastern Mediterranean at the foot of Mount Kasios he fights the monster with his toothed sickle (Heb. *ḥereb,* Greek *harpē*). Perhaps the great tsunami from the explosion of Thera is mythologized as the sea monster; only after it has been taken care of is the regular order of the environment possible.

In each of these internal social structures or enterprises the High God (or his associates) plays a key role. He validates the status of the king before new conditions disperse the king's authority to magistrates, Senate, and people's assembly. He is the object of the official sacrificial cult and the validator of the charismatic seer who (among other things) conspires with him to bring the rain. Himself (or in Hellas through his agent Dionysus) he bestows the gift of the vine whose fruit makes glad the hearts of men and gods as well. Above all, through his struggle with the oceanic and monstrous forces of disorder he makes possible the emergence of a stable environment friendly to human beings.

In the ascription of all these structures to the High God, ancient peoples explain, legitimate, and guarantee the existence of their own societies. Modern anthropology is only partly able to account for the appearance of such structures. When did there come into being a divine kingship able both to hold a society together and to permit its own replacement by dispersal of power? How does the ritual slaughter of a bull act to validate the society?

What is the relation of the sacrificial cult to the charismatic seer and rain-maker? By what genetic and historical processes does intoxication by wine come to stand for a higher level of existence? (Many non-Mediterranean peoples, such as American Indians, lack genetic resistance to alcoholism.) How was the development of civilization synchronous with the softening of the glacial and tectonic catastrophes? About all we can do is to chronicle those parallel environmental and social developments, and observe how each in its way is essential to the birth of the polis, and underlies the mysterious emergence of freedom and a sense of justice.

Freedom and Particularity

None of the structures we have summarized so far was peculiar to the new societies of Israel and Hellas. All were shared to some degree by a number of other Mediterranean societies, even though the evidence often rests on Hebrew, Greek, or Latin texts. On them as foundation a new level of society came into existence in Israel and Hellas, and later at Rome. And our records of earlier structures are lit up by the emergent novelties they held in potentiality.

We begin with the climax of old Mediterranean self-awareness in *heroic honor and shame,* where the novelty in Israel and Hellas lies less in the facts themselves than in the objectivity with which our texts present them—plus at times an implied rebuke proceeding from a new understanding. That rebuke becomes explicit in the *critique of sacrifice and priesthood.* The new understanding is the emergence of *humanism:* a celebration of weakness and grandeur in a setting of family solidarity arising from a realistic facing of death. Over against the faults of heroes and the sacrificial cult stands the central discovery of the *justice of the High God* as revealed by feminine memory figures to shepherd-prophets. From the beginning there was a realization that the new insights needed to be made permanent in a *book* available to all through precious alphabetic script. The impact of these steps was so overwhelming that, as long as the autonomous city-state continued, the new culture is infused with a common *particularity:* "We are different from the others."

Heroic Honor and Shame

Such historical or legendary works as the ancient Near East produced celebrate the deeds of kings, at peace or in their capacity as generals; the king appears in a uniformly good light because he has commissioned the works. In Israel and Hellas there appear literary works, at first more oral than written, proceeding from elsewhere than the court, and displaying the motives and actions of the leaders, historic or legendary, for better or worse—a David or an Achilles—in categories that we may summarize as honor and shame. Their motives—"help friends, harm enemies"—are precisely those that achieved international status through the vassal treaty. The father of Glaucus (*Iliad* 6.209) told him "not to shame the generation of his fathers"; "A companion of gluttons shames his father" (Prov 28:7). It is the duty of vassals to have the same friends and enemies as their liege lords.

Archilochus, a near contemporary of the Homeric poets, says, "I know how to love my friend and hate my enemy"; Odysseus tells Nausicaa that a man and woman happily married "bring many pains to their ill-wishers, and joy to their well-wishers." More subtly, the author of 2 Sam 19:6-7 has Joab criticize David for mourning his rebel son Absalom: "You have shamed the face of all your servants . . . by loving those who hate you and hating those who love you." It is left up to the hearer to determine whether David is doing better or worse by breaking convention. The tragedy of the Iliad is Achilles' exaggerated sense of being "unrewarded" (*atīmos, Iliad* 1.171) while the other Achaeans are given booty and women. Greek history in Thucydides, and tragedy throughout, build on the epic insight.

Hebrew for "love" at 2 Samuel 19 is the root *'ahab*; a near parallel occurs in the rare Homeric verb (later common) *agapaō, Odyssey* 16.17, "As a father loves his son." Perhaps the word (exceptionally, for a verb) moved between cultures precisely in the context of the vassal treaty. Later in Hellas, but more definitely than in Israel, the doctrine arises that retaliation or "doing injustice in return" is excluded (Plato *Crito* 49B). A prerequisite for this realism and critique of the motives of leaders is the sharing of power between the leaders and the infantry under arms that made up the city's fighting force.

Critique of Sacral Institutions

Hebrews and Greeks inherited a common sacrificial cult from an unknown source—perhaps one of themselves, perhaps elsewhere in the Minoan area. Quite early, thinkers and poets looked at the cult with their new realism of human motivations and rejected it—as much in puzzlement as in abhorrence. Empedocles (himself a charismatic seer who offered to teach rainmaking and raising of the dead) celebrates the chaste cult of Cyprian Aphrodite in the Golden Age: "But no altar was wet with the unmixed blood of bulls." (For, he felt, in view of the "transmigration of the soul" to animals, sacrifice of such was equivalent to murder.) This is not competition between religious professionals, since Greek sacrifice is laicized, but critique of popular cult by the *only* professional religious class. So the Prophets, "He who slaughters a bull is a man-slayer" (Isa 66:3), though it is not clear what if anything the critics would put in the place of sacrifice. Lucian spoke for freethinkers when he made the gods into flies around the sacrifice (*de sacr.* 9), parodying a theme from Gilgamesh.

Humanism and Family Solidarity

The clear look of the new societies generated a description of humanity that still today stands ahead of us and not behind us. Israel understood the potential *dominion* of humanity, Ps 8:7, "Thou hast put all things under his feet"; Gen 1:28, "And have dominion," Vg *dominamini.* The Chorus in Sophocles' *Antigone* 332–75 celebrates control over birds, beasts, and fish; Ovid *Metam.* 1.77 defines humanity as a being that could have dominion *(dominari)* over the others—Jerome remembered this. The other side of this is a new *realism* about old age and death. Human beings are creatures of a day, like grass rising in the morning, faded by evening (Ps 90:5-6); a generation of leaves (*Iliad* 6.146); creatures of a day, the dream of a shadow (Pindar *Pyth.* 8.95–96). Each people somehow inherited the image of the dark underworld with its immovable gates and chaotic torrents. Still, over against this recognition of necessity stands the naked human being, at once vulnerable and defiant.

Paradoxically, while moderns look to Hellas for a notion of immortality, and to late Israel for resurrection, the historical societies are marked by their *freedom* from the Egyptian obsession with death. Their this-worldliness is in fact temporary and unique, for it is lost again after imperial conquest. What made their efflorescence of humanism possible was a *confidence in the future,* symbolized by the state with its walled citadel. The Homeric hero goes on fighting in the presumption that he will have "eternal fame" through the words of a sacred bard in an ongoing society more or less like his own. Later, in both Israel and Hellas, men are glad to fight and die for the state out of a sense of *family solidarity:* provided the state remains, what they fail to accomplish, their sons or grandsons may. A son's duty is to maintain his father's honor: a man's life rests in his sons, the greatest misfortune is to die childless. When Horace (*Carm.* 3.2.13) says "It is sweet and proper to die for one's country," *dulce et decorum est pro patria mori,* he is expressing a genuine truth for the ancient world. Still, war both vindicates solidarity and undermines it.

Nothing is more important for a man than having sons. If a man's wife cannot bear them, he has recourse to her handmaids: thus Abraham (Gen 16:1-16) and Jacob (Gen 30:1-13); so Menelaus when Helen has only a girl (*Odyssey* 4.11–14). Obedient sons are needed to punish (family) enemies and honor friends (Sophocles *Antigone* 643–44); above all, to bury their father, as with Abraham (Gen 25:8-9) and Isaac (Gen 35:29). Croesus tells Cyrus (Herodotus 1.87.4), "In peace, sons bury their fathers; in war, fathers bury their sons." Joseph's great-grandchildren are born on his knees (Gen 50:23) and so Job 42:16. "The sons of sons are the glory of the aged" (Prov 17:6). In Aristotle's analysis of the mutual love of relatives, "parents love their children *as themselves,* for being from the parents by separation they are as it were *other selves,*" *Eth. Nic.* 8.12.3 = 1161b26–27. Leviticus 19:34 (cf. 19:18), "You shall love the stranger *as yourself,* for you were strangers." Both peoples presuppose love of self, and love of others as proceeding from self. *Eth. Nic.* 1.8.16 = 1099b3–6, "one cannot be truly happy who is . . . solitary and childless; even less if one's children are wicked . . . or were virtuous and have died." The tradition that made Absalom without sons (contrast 2 Sam 14:27) has him say, "I have no son to keep my name in remembrance" (2 Sam 18:18). That is what sons are for.

The God of Justice

Besides their insight into the actuality of human motivations, the new societies also achieved a new insight into what human motivations *should* be. You might think this a later phenomenon. But opinions can differ whether Hesiod's *Works and Days,* with its exposition of the justice of Zeus, is later or earlier than the *Iliad*; and whether Amos and the early strata of the Pentateuch are later or earlier than the analysis of David's character in the "Court Chronicle" (2 Samuel 9–20) as we have it. In any case, the discovery of justice is a *different* (though related) insight, appearing in a different stratum of the people and communicated back and forth between Israel and Hellas very likely by land.

In the ancient Near East such a king as Ammisaduga of Babylon proclaims his just acts—whether or not they were truly such. The new understanding of the High God as guarantor of justice arose (it seems likely) in a crisis of land tenure. (Levin pushes that understanding yet further back in the recognition during patriarchal Israel of rightful ownership of cattle.) The geographical factor that marked Israel and Hellas above all was the land tenure made possible by the rain from the High God; in its crisis, with the confusion of boundaries and the buying up of large estates, the new guarantee was the maintenance or restoration of original holdings. (The process came later in Rome with the buildup of latifundia in the early empire.) Farmers who doubled as upland shepherds in annual "transhumance" *see* a new state of affairs (Amos 1:1); they are shown it by feminine memory figures, the Muses (Hesiod *Theogony* 22–23) or spirits of God (Isa 11:2). And what they are shown is the concrete image of Justice, enthroned with the High God. Those uplanders communicate with others of their kind through overland transport, an extension of the ass with its sacks by which they carry their produce to the city market.

The original definition of justice, as of the American republic, has what might seem strong built-in limitations. The supreme virtue of both is their *dynamism,* by which the definition is progressively enlarged. It was self-evident to the signers of the Declaration of Independence that "all Men are created equal." Initially that was not seen as applying to Negro slaves or women; but by an inexorable logic of history both came to be included. In neither Israel or Hellas was justice initially seen as going beyond Cicero's definition, "a state of mind granting each his own," *animi affectio suum cuique tribuens* (*de fin.* 5.25, and see its expansion by Ulpian of Tyre). At first one's "own" was above all *land*; and so land owners (all or nearly all men, so that *his own* is a correct translation!) were the main or only beneficiaries of the new concept. But a development culminating in the new church came to see that the landless, aliens, women, and slaves had in principle intrinsic rights of equal value that equally could be called their own, and that in the end justice could not deny them.

Hesiod *Opera* 279, Zeus "gave justice to men [rather than animals]," agrees with Ps 98:2, Yahweh "has revealed his justice in the eyes of the nations"; and hence Rom 1:17, "the justice *(dikaiosynē)* of God is revealed in [the good news]." But we should add that while the New Testament Vulgate, followed by Catholic versions, translates the Greek as *iustitia,* Protestant versions have *righteousness* (since the KJV) and *Gerechtigkeit* (since Luther). For Paul has a special understanding of what it means for a human being to be just and how that state is reached, "we are justified by faith" (Rom 5:1).

The realistic description of the hero motivated by honor and shame, as soon as it came into being, had natural protection in the circle of the civic militia, among whom it was recited. The fact that the phonetic alphabet was available there kept the historical or legendary tale alive. The shepherd's proclamation of divine justice was more vulnerable, for it had its natural adversaries in the big landowners who exercised disproportionate power in the state. The shepherd-poet with the word of justice therefore required an extra element of legitimation and found it in a status of *sacral immunity*. In Israel the word of justice is carried by "prophets" who have fallen heir to a charismatic status in the society; in Hellas by poets who can claim a special connection with their patroness the Muse; in Rome by the tribunes of the *plebs* with a "sacrosanctity" supposedly from an old vote of the people, perhaps even before that a lost sacral status. The audience addressed by those spokesmen had enough overlap with the citizen soldiers who heard the heroic legends that eventually the two sets of texts were grouped together: Hesiod joined Homer in an epic tradition; the latter Prophets (Amos and his followers) joined the former (or historians, from Joshua to Kings) in the category of commentators on the five books of Law.

The Invention of the Book

Horace (*Carm.* 4.9.25–28) imagines that "strong men lived before Agamemnon" but unknown "because they lacked a sacred bard." Actually, heroic honor would have been something different without Achilles' expectation of "imperishable fame" (*Iliad* 9.413); for though the phrase is old Indo-European, any earlier heroes to whom it might have been applied are in fact unknown. Hebrew shifts the application to its God, "The grass withers, the flower fades, but the word of our God abides for ever" (Isa 40:8). It was the simplicity of the alphabet (along with the excellence of the texts themselves) that ensured that the texts would remain when the independent societies that generated them were overthrown: a Roman historian contrasts complex hieroglyphs with the "fixed and simple series of characters" that "expresses whatever the human mind can conceive" (Ammianus 17.4.10, though he overestimates the ideographic character of Egyptian writing). In Crete about 500 B.C.E. one Spensithios in an archaic inscription is commissioned in a new role and an old, "to write and to remember"; earlier, in Israel (2 Kgs 18:18), the scribe and the remembrancer are already different persons.

The new art moved from Canaan westward, for the names of the alphabet letters are Semitic (but neither Hebrew nor Phoenician), as is the name of the "tablet" *(deltos)*. Greeks adapted and improved it. In Israel, only a simple document could be read by one who had not previously seen it, like the baneful letter from David to Joab carried by Uriah (2 Sam 11:15), echoed in the letter carried by Bellerophon (*Iliad* 6.168–69). In Israel, any more complex work needed a double tradition, both written (as *aide-mémoire* of the unpredictable materials coming up) and oral (to supply the vowels), as Levin has shown. In both Israel and Hellas, the habit of the messenger, poet, or historian reading his document out loud was so fixed that silent "reading" was a rare curiosity (Augustine, *Conf.* 6.3).

What initially sets Israel and Hellas apart from all their neighbors is that, when they lost political independence, they retained scribal groups whose job was to preserve their people's books. The book was produced under particularity but preserved under universalism. Literacy was widespread enough among both peoples so that such groups survived war and exile. The intrinsic interest of the books was great enough to give the scribes lifetime motivation—and to persuade their sons or students to carry the tradition on. In Egypt and the cuneiform world the scripts were so cumbersome that their knowledge was lost when the courts, temples, and businesses that employed the scribes fell away. The texts (it appears) were not seen as valuable enough to generate groups committed to preserving them. (But perhaps the Achaemenid Persians held in their hands or their heads the actual texts of our Avesta.) Elsewhere in the world of alphabetic scripts—Ugarit, Phoenicia, Damascus, Anatolia— literacy (though more easily acquired) must have been still the monopoly of a royal, priestly, mercantile class.

The different size and character of the two canons of texts reflect a complementarity both of language and of script. Greek epics could be longer because the metrical hexameter was easier to memorize than the mixed style of Hebrew narrative books. But the bardic tradition was always liable to forgetfulness and improvisation. Long works surely came into being first when their writing down was already possible or actual. As time went on, the written text became more and more necessary as a corrective to oral changes or mistakes. But (in different ways in the two lands) the written text had always to be supplemented by the oral. So, down to some time in the Latin Middle Ages, the "book" was a double tradition of written text and oral performance. Its custodians were a scribal community so self-contained as to survive the fall of the independent societies that had given it birth.

Particularity

During the age of their political autonomy, Hebrews and Greeks were so overwhelmed by the power of what they had produced, seeing themselves in the mirror of their own books, as to contrast themselves with the rest of the world. Thales (Diogenes Laertius 1.33) thanks Tyche that he was born "a human being and not a beast, a man and not a woman, a Hellene and not a barbarian." The synagogue service to this day begins with thanks to the God who has not made the worshiper a *goy*, a slave, a woman; it may follow Aristotle (*Pol.* 1.1.5), who recognizes the same three classes of inferiors—barbarians, women, and slaves. (In Paul's universalism [Gal 3:28], precisely the same three groups are *affirmed*.) The Greek contrasts himself with the barbarian who speaks the wrong language, the Hebrew with the *goy* of different lineage who engages in the wrong cult.

The separateness of the new societies was concretely marked by the *city wall*, surrounding a citadel with a spring of water. Ovid (*Metam.* 1.97) imagines a Golden Age "when steep moats did not yet surround cities"; Vergil more realistically (*Geor.* 2.155–57) celebrates the walls of Italian hill towns. In an age of "fire and sword" the smoke of an inadequately defended city "rises up to the heavens" (Josh 8:20; *Iliad* 21.522–23); and the city wall was indispensable to protect the law that it enclosed. Heraclitus says "the people must fight for its law as for its wall." If the wall goes, all goes (Lam 2:8-9). Only Sparta (of all places!) points to the future, "A city is not unfortified which is crowned with men and not with bricks" (Plutarch *Lyc.* 19.4); already the new departure she represents is fully realized in the character of her men, and in that alone.

Each of the novelties we have chronicled here could only have first come into being in an autonomous state guarded by a city wall: the fighter and hero motivated by honor and shame; the advanced thinker in a society where the old sacrificial cult persists; the humanistic poet contemplating the attitudes of his fellows toward death; the shepherd-prophet seeing land tenure as guaranteed by a God of justice; the poet, writer, or scribe inventing the book to record new thoughts. The prophetic word is the agency by which latent justice and the other novelties break through into history. The new free society proclaims a better order of things striving to emerge into the time sequence, whose primary evidence is that proclamation. The participants in each of those revolutions knew that they were bringing something novel into the world, and had no choice but to contrast themselves with outsiders; hence their particularity, "We are different from the others." But the wall was destined to be pulled down; and the books, once completed and turned over to scribes or grammarians, no longer needed its protection. The "fence around the Torah" (*m. Ab.* 1.1) changed character.

Most of the novelties in the fully developed city-state here noted can be seen as humanistic. But the old preeminence of the High God comes out more strongly than ever in the affirmation of his work as sustainer and promoter of justice. Here (for the last time!) we can rationalize his role as the personified justification of land tenure—the prerogative of the only full members of the society, the landed citizen militia. When their central status disappears in the breakdown of the city and its walls, provisionally this semifinal role of the High God disappears. But when Paul renews the affirmation of a God revealing justice, it is no longer on behalf of those who have unjustly lost what once they had, but of those who deserve to be given what they never had—women, slaves, foreigners. Even this can be seen as a legitimate historical development from what preceded. But the replacement of family solidarity by the individual hopeful of a victory over death permits no such easy rationalizing.

Empire and Universalism

The autonomy of the city-state was ended in a series of conquests by imperial powers. The northern kingdom of Israel was taken by Assyria, and Jerusalem itself by the Babylonians; under the Achaemenid Persians a partial return was permitted and control relaxed. Many of the Greek states in Asia Minor fell under Persian control, and the Greek mainland itself twice repelled Persian invaders. The new power of Macedon took over the Greek mainland, Asia Minor, Syria, Egypt, and much of Persia; control continued under the successors of Alexander until Rome swept all away. About 587 B.C.E. Nebuchadrezzar broke down the walls of Jerusalem (2 Kgs 25:10); in 404 B.C.E. the Long Walls of Athens between the city and Piraeus were torn down "to the music of flutegirls" (Xenophon *Hell.* 2.2.23), perhaps by the returning exiles themselves.

Besides an end of political independence, the new imperial control imposed *sanctions* on the subject states. The symbolic themes of *self-legitimation* set up by the Persian regime were boldly adopted by subject peoples on their own behalf. But the loss of the city wall raised the possibility that the natural order itself might be torn down. The new imperial control in both lands was providentially delayed until the primary treasures enshrined in the walled citadel had been transformed into a shape adapted for survival in exile. And so particularity is transformed into a cosmopolitan *universalism:* "we are different from the others" becomes "we have a mandate to carry our novelty to all." All these changes are partially reversed in the universal church and empire—but within a new context.

The Imperial Sanctions

Imperial control consisted in sanctions applied to the goods and above all to the bodies of its subjects. The Persian *taxation* attested in late biblical Hebrew was carefully noted by the Athenians and adopted for control of their own maritime empire. By the Roman period the whole world was arranged in a universal ladder of debt. Rabbinic and Greco-Roman documents illustrate the *requisitioning* of ships and draft animals taken over from Persia by the Hellenistic kingdoms and eventually Rome; the same international name of *angaria* was applied to the *conscription* of individuals for varying periods of service, with two notable instances in the Gospels. Recalcitrant individuals are singled out for public notice by *tattooing* (perhaps also branding) and punished by savage forms of *flogging,* where Aramaic inherited both an Iranian and a Latino-Greek name for the sanction—no doubt the victims carefully distinguished their treatment by the two empires.

The ultimate sanction from the Persian period to the Roman was execution by *crucifixion* with the triple motives of vengeance, deterrence, and public humiliation. Hebrew Midrash and Roman law agree in the doctrine that "bandits" are to be strung up on the scene of their depredations. The execution of a solitary symbolic figure with a woman companion proclaims the fate of a *rebel victim:* Prometheus in Aeschylus's play and the Servant of Yahweh (Isaiah 53) each is a representative figure pegged up and attacked by birds or beasts (as in all-too-historical crucifixions); Jesus is so treated by the Romans, apt pupils of the Persians and Alexander's successors. But in a historical reversal, the rebel victim is seen as ultimately victor and the savior of his people.

Imperial Legitimation

As the fate of the rebel victim is reversed in poetry and doctrine, the symbols of imperial legitimation are boldly plundered by resistance movements for their own banner. The Persian monarch calls himself "king of kings," in part realistically as limitation of his power, for he left numerous kinglets in their place—along with satraps more powerful than most previous kings. Aeschylus (*Sup.* 524) calls Zeus "lord of lords"; so (Deut 10:17) Yahweh is "God of gods and Lord of lords," where the Mishna goes one step further and makes him "King of the kings of kings." Alexander's title of *cosmocrator* "world ruler" is taken over by rabbinic for various parties. The Iranian "ambassador" (rare Greek *askandes*) is supernaturalized in the Syriac *Hymn of the Pearl* and in Mandaean; Paul (2 Cor 5:20) speaking for himself says, "We act as ambassadors on behalf of Christ," where in the Syriac translation the same Iranian word appears. What the ambassador rescues is the supernatural *pearl* known under the same name *margarita* in all languages. All armies and militias are reorganized in the now standard pattern of bodies of a hundred and a thousand. The royal and satrapal hunting parks known to Xenophon and the Hebrew Bible as the king's *paradise* are seen as the utmost symbol of felicity, and claimed for the rebel victim executed as pretender to the status of the Great King.[8] The languages of four empires—Babylonian, Iranian, Greek, and Roman—are put to work in Jesus' sayings, defining a novel alternative to empire.

The End of the World

A corollary of confidence in the future within the autonomous city-state is the general reliance on the preservation of the natural order. The making of

8. Also the attributes of the Great King—his image, diadem, gate, sword, the obeisance due him—to some degree are taken over in the symbolism of the subject peoples.

Achilles' shield by Hephaestus (*Iliad* 18) is a demythologized creation narrative parallel to Genesis. Early on, temporary breakdown of social order is regularly expressed in the symbolism of cosmic disruption. Both peoples
envisage the likelihood of cosmic destruction by flood or earthquake. Israel,
always more vulnerable to disruption, both external and internal, is more
aware of cosmic collapse. Both peoples find the sky held up by pillars, but in
Israel they are much more liable to fall. In Amos, the predicted invasion of
Israel is seen as eclipse and flood (Amos 5:8; 8:9; 9:6). The fear is intensified
with permanent breakdown of old social order. Greek philosophy of the *ekpy-
rosis* or destruction of the earth by fire magnified the threat.[9] Vergil (*Georg.*
1.468) imagines an eclipse become "eternal night" at the murder of Caesar,
and the younger Pliny sees the event in the eruption of Vesuvius. The epics
see the fall of a tree as the fall of a hero or a city, and obscurely sense the connection between deforestation and fall of society; although official thought
shortsightedly regards timber cutting, like the tuna fishery, as victories over
chaos.

Two developments are seen by moderns as key to the "decline of the
ancient world"—an eventuality mostly beyond our scope here. Environmen-
talists like J. Donald Hughes (see n. 51, p. 168) see it as an ongoing destruction of resources—most clearly documented for the two societies as
deforestation. Marxists like de Ste. Croix see it as the equally shortsighted
destruction by an urban elite of the peasant populations needed for both agriculture and the legions. How far did the ancients see what was going on? A
genuine outsider in the late first century, John of Patmos, on that lovely
island saw both the earth and its peoples as progressively destroyed by the
folly and crime of its rulers. In Rome during the same decades rhetoric overcomes even class interest in a parallel revelation of underlying realities. Tacitus entered so far into the mind of the barbarian enemy Calgacus as to ascribe
him the deathless formulation of Roman policy, *ubi solitudinem faciunt, pacem
appellant* ("Where they make a desolation, they call it peace," *Agricola* 30.6)—
which works equally well when applied to the farmer soldiers on the land and
the land itself.

The New Universalism

In both Israel and Hellas, precisely the themes seen earlier as marking the
people's particularity are reversed as features of a universal mission. Whereas
Aristotle and the synagogue agree in seeing barbarian, slave, and woman as

---

9. Zeno (Tatian, *Oratio ad Graecos* 3.3); but he strangely sees the entire course of history
identically repeated after as before.

inferiors, Paul (Gal 3:28) affirms, "In Christ there is neither Jew nor Hellene, slave or free, male or female." Eratosthenes (Strabo 1.4.9) realistically notes that "many Hellenes are bad and many barbarians civilized." (But all along by anticipation, in both societies to fear God is to love the stranger; for the stranger might be a valuable trading partner or an old friend in disguise.)

In later texts of the Hebrew Bible, the *goyim,* once rejected, are seen in pilgrimage to Jerusalem, where (Isa 2:2) "the mountain of the house of Yahweh" is established "and all the *goyim* shall flow to it"; "all the ends of the earth shall remember and return to Yahweh" (Ps 22:28). That centripetal vision is theory, symbolically realized at the Christian Pentecost. A centrifugal reverse really happened: in the Hellenistic period, as Jewish artisans spread across the Mediterranean, the Hebrew Bible in its Greek translation was made available to Gentile "God-fearers," surely for the most part not circumcised. At Antioch of Pisidia in the synagogue Paul speaks to "Men of Israel and God-fearers" (Act 13:16). (But the very success of Paul's mission within a few centuries closed shut the door so opened to Gentiles.) In Hellas, precisely the education *(paideia)* seen by men like Isocrates as the special property of Greeks is spread throughout the world of Alexander and of Rome; the Greek names of the *pedagogue* and *school* are taken over as a common phrase into Latin and rabbinic.

Above all, the fact of Roman citizenship, steadily approaching total universalism (and effective meaninglessness) under Caracalla (212 C.E.),[10] is paralleled by a philosophical universalism. Epictetus the former slave defines man as a "citizen of the world" (Arrian 2.10.3); Cicero (*Leg.* 1.61) defines the mind exactly so, *ciuis totius mundi.* The former military panoply becomes spiritualized; the military tent *(skene)* is transformed into the *Shekhinah* or Presence of Yahweh. For when the city wall crumbles, the division between insiders and outsiders, friends and enemies, also is shaken, and the conditions are in place to envisage humanity as a universal "brotherhood." Jesus in effect sees all human beings as brothers and sisters *(adelphoi),* Mark 3:35; Matt 25:40. In fact, the word means "of the same womb" *(delphys),* originally applied to full brothers in the king's harem; but it has been conjectured that the entire human race is descended from one African Lucy.

To the extent that the new situation is seen positively, there is a reversal of the focus in which the societies see themselves. They retain, more strongly

---

10. Dio Cassius 77.9; Ulpian in the *Digest* 1.5.17, *In orbe Romano qui sunt ex constitutione imperatoris Antonini ciues Romani facti sunt*; a fragmentary papyrus (*Pap. Giessen* 40), see *OCD* 383 "constitution, Antonine."

than ever, the conviction of their own excellence over against other peoples—including, at a late date, each other! But the breakdown of the wall came to be seen as a breakdown of the barriers between themselves and other peoples. It corresponded with a modification of their excellences into a form available for export. The new imperial situation opened the possibility of making their achievement open to others. (a) In part the novelty takes a *common* form in the availability of the *book:* in its original Greek for Hellas, in the Greek Bible of the Septuagint for Israel. The Hellenization of the Near East by the successors of Alexander, along with the Hellenization of Rome by a literary culture and a diplomatic chancery, provided a reading (or rather a *hearing*) public for the Septuagint. (b) Thus the novelty shared in the growing *complementarity* of the two societies: Hellas exported a language and a culture, with religious themes but more so secular; Israel supported a revised cult and a set of convictions. From particularity they moved to universalism—not quite completely in either case.

Partial Reversal in the Universal Church
The new imperialism with all its consequences leads to a second shift whereby the old solidarity and particularity are partially re-created in the new universal family of the church under an empire with full citizenship (involving more duties than benefits). For the universalism of both Israel and Hellas by themselves was incomplete. What we must now call Jewish cult could not dispense with circumcision, and pagan semi-converts were relegated to the second category of *theosebeis,* God-fearers. The Greek language could not displace Latin in the West. The new Christian church with its entrance rite of baptism (nonthreatening except for the danger of persecution), and the complete translatability of its book, eliminated both blockages.

But the new insights that emerged with the first imperialism and the breaking down of the wall could not be eliminated. (1) Although the old solidarity of the "blood" family is replaced by the universal family of the church, a newly discovered individualism cannot thereafter be denied; and the church (less clearly so the synagogue) retains and deepens the doctrine of resurrection (popularly modified as immortality). (2) The new awareness of the fragility of the natural order likewise persists; and over against the universality of the city of God, the affirmation of an end of the world remains—but with a new promise of restoration. (3) Some degree of the old particularity remains even under the new universalism. Whenever the church comes up against a novel external paganism, it reverts to the old particularity, emphasizing its unique benefits and initially ignoring whatever the outside society might bring to it.

Thus, in general, the second shift from the individual under empire to the universal church restores the unifying structures previously lost—but with a difference.

So far the themes under universalism are secular: the High God hardly appears, and no transcendent guarantee is in effect. That is because we postpone until the next section the final result of universalism, seen predominantly as negative: a new *individualism* with special demands on the cosmos. The former role of the High God as vindicator and guardian of his people is transformed into an oversight of each individual.

The Individual and the Enigma of Death

Up until nearly the beginning of our era, in Hellas and especially Israel, family solidarity held together. That solidarity presupposes the continuation of history. If the suffering and death of the rebel victim results ultimately in the redemption of his people, that retroactively is seen as his vindication. But developments undercut that solidarity. The reality of death, always from the beginning an enigma, is intensified in three ways. (1) Initially, in both societies the threat of individual death was blunted by reliance on the continuity of the family and of the people. This reliance was already reduced when the people lost political independence; it was intolerably reduced in Israel by the actual destruction of Jerusalem, first in anticipation and then in actuality. (2) The Israelite understanding of the High God as both sustainer of the people and maker of the created order raised the possibility that the created order might end when the people and its city also could be destroyed. (3) The new individualism created a new set of hopes independent of a man's future fame, his descendants, his clan and tribe, his people; it became more and more difficult to find a way of vindicating those hopes in the face of personal death.

This new universalism puts a further demand on the guarantees traditionally associated with the High God, which, unlike all the previous guarantees, is not easily rationalized into environmental or social conditions. Several schemes of symbolism raised the possibility that death might be overcome.

Recompense of Benefits as of Injuries
Early, the conviction of the justice of the High God led to the affirmation that those who did injuries would have injury done to them: certainly through the punishment of their sons or descendants for their wrongdoings; very likely in their own lives; as the concept was spiritualized, in the conviction that the act

of wrongdoing in itself degraded the human image as much as obvious external retribution or more so. But then the converse was affirmed: that an act of rightdoing brought its inevitable recompense—perhaps not in a man's external circumstances or in those of his descendants, but internally in his own character, and somehow also in a realm where the recompense of benefit would be visible to all. Meditation on the justice of the High God, which previously could be counted on in recompensing ill for ill visibly in history, either in the current or a succeeding generation, inevitably led to the extension of recompensing good for good. The new individualism in an imperial society full of injustice led necessarily to the affirmation of a realm in which the divine justice operated as surely in the realm of rewards as that of punishments, or *more so*. And that meant a realm in which somehow death was overcome.

The Beatitude

The old form of the Beatitude leads to the same conclusion. In the old days, the blessedness of the man who does so-and-so, if not clearly visible in his own vindication during his lifetime, could be satisfactorily postponed to his descendants. With the new individualism, in a society where the self-determination of peoples had been replaced by imperial control, that route is foreclosed. It became necessary to affirm somehow a realm where the death of the individual was overcome or compensated for, in which the justice of the High God was mathematically exact. The future acquires a new grammar.

Better Lands

In both Israel and Hellas, systems of symbolism arose to make concrete that realm of vindication. In Hellas, the symbolism appears most clearly in the Islands of the Blessed, originally for military heroes, later in Plato ethicized for all (women hardly yet figure). In Israel, we see hints of a blessed better life, Ps 16:10, "For thou dost not give up my life to Sheol." Later, the mode by which the dead are raised is more and more specified. The vision of the valley of dry bones in Ezekiel (37:1-14) originally was meant in the old way for the restoration of "the whole house of Israel." But its concrete symbolism, "I will open your graves," was taken literally and individualistically when the hope of restoration of the people as a whole became more and more distant; precisely this passage is quoted in the Talmud to prove the existence of a "key of the raising of the dead." Already the transition to individuals has been made at Dan 12:2, "And many of those who sleep in the dust of the earth shall awake."

Immortality and Resurrection

Roughly speaking, we may see the two affirmations as complementary and parallel: Plato on the immortality of the soul, Judaism on the resurrection of the body. It marks the preponderance of the Greco-Latin strain in the West that in Christian funerals, whether evangelical or liberal or Catholic, immortality wins out, though inconsistent with any biblical understanding of the psychosomatic makeup of the human being. The rabbinic doctrine of the "raising of the dead" is downplayed in Judaism, perhaps so as not to seem too like Christianity. Even the massive historical fact of the Holocaust or *shoah,* which drove some Jewish theologians into a paradoxical atheism, turned world Judaism toward the old political state, "Never again!" rather than to a reaffirmation of the resurrection.

The unmeasured energy of the new Christian church arose in the first place from the conviction that Jesus had been raised from the dead; and that in union with him the believer likewise was raised from the dead, after physical death and burial indeed, but also in an anticipatory way in the midst of life. We may take the doctrine as the central place where Israel and Hellas in their full complementarity merged. The doctrine of the resurrection, wherever believed and affirmed, becomes the final guarantee of the goodness and justice of God. In contrast to previous guarantees, there is no easy way fully to rationalize it in society or psychology.

As long as the human race continues, the doctrine of the resurrection can be explained more or less in rationalistic historical terms. We may say that Jesus is one who fully, like others in part, turned over everything important about himself—above all his words and actions—into the keeping of his followers. In that sense we may say that he did indeed overcome death. And to the extent that his followers do the same, preferring the well-being of their children, students, associates, followers, to their own, they too live on in succeeding generations. In a sense, that understanding represents a reversal of the individualism of the late Hellenistic and early Roman worlds. The old solidarity of family is extended to a community that serves as one big extended family—in principle, the whole human race: "Behold my mother and brothers and sisters."

But two obstinate facts undercut that simple rationalization of the resurrection in the time-arrow of the historical process. (1) The new individualism, once grasped, cannot thereafter be denied. Precisely as men and women are liberated onto a new level of existence, each becomes precious in himself or herself, and death continues necessarily to be seen as the last enemy. (2) Further, the tenure of human beings on this earth is finite. Someday the sun (it seems) will melt off the planets before it collapses into a cinder. If humanity before then has succeeded in implanting itself around newer suns, the whole history of its birth here will be denied. Something is already lost when each species becomes extinct: the mammoths whose corpses still litter Arctic wastes, the passenger pigeon, the dodo, perhaps in some near future the tiger or elephant in the wild. And in the end the whole transmission of the "torch of life" from one to another will become as if it had never been.

So the vindication of the justice of God in the end demands the affirmation of a transcendent realm where death is definitively overcome. The historical rationalization of the early Christian experience of the resurrection is (I propose) true and necessary so far as it goes, but not sufficient. Up until this point the affirmations of the High God or gods in Israel and Hellas can be explained as symbolism of processes within the historical time line. Here no longer. Now everybody must stake out their own claim. The parallel development and final merger of Israel and Hellas lead to a point where the human race must take a leap into the dark. One may say: the fact that many human beings (most in some ages) take that leap vindicates the affirmation. But many today simply see death as the end, whether for themselves as individuals or for the human race as a whole. Bleak and comfortless as this prospect ultimately must be, it does not always necessarily lead to despair. Perhaps in some future it will, and the affirmation of the realm beyond death will become necessary for the continuation of the race. Certainly the first witnesses to what they reported as the raising of Jesus from the dead saw a breakthrough of the divine reality into history. The High God and the realm beyond death are equivalent formulations of the same hope. So we end with the sobering reflection that the successive guarantees testified to in the rise of free humanity, which initially we can rationalize within the historical process, by the logic of their own sequence lead to the affirmation of a guarantee that cannot be so rationalized. Still, believers historically have not as a rule been much interested in rationalization of their stance. The affirmations that God is good and that death has been overcome have their own internal structure, which, far from deprecating the struggle for a better present, intensifies and validates it, and which in the past has warranted many books in its own right, and will in the future warrant many more.

Select Bibliography

Astour, Michael C. *Hellenosemitica: An Ethnic and Cultural Study in West Semitic Impact on Mycenaean Greece.* 2d ed. Leiden: Brill, 1967.

Barnett, Richard D. "Ancient Oriental Influences on Archaic Greece." In *The Aegean and the Near East: Studies Presented to Hetty Goldman on the Occasion of Her Seventy-fifth Birthday,* edited by S. S. Weinberg, 212–38. Locust Valley, N.Y.: Augustin, 1956.

Bernal, Martin. *Black Athena: The Afroasiatic Roots of Classical Civilization.* 2 vols. New Brunswick: Rutgers Univ. Press, 1987–91.

Brown, John Pairman. *Israel and Hellas.* 3 vols. Beihefte zur Zeitschrift für die alttestamentliche Wissenschaft 231, 276, 299. Berlin: de Gruyter, 1995, 2000, 2001.

———. *The Lebanon and Phoenicia: Ancient Texts Illustrating Their Physical Geography and Native Industries.* Beirut: American Univ. Press, 1969.

Brown, John Pairman, and Saul Levin. "The Ethnic Paradigm as a Paradigm for Nominal Forms in Greek and Hebrew." *General Linguistics* 26 (1986) 71–105.

Burkert, Walter. *Homo Necans: The Anthropology of Ancient Greek Sacrificial Ritual and Myth.* Translated by P. Bing and W. Burkert. Berkeley: Univ. of California Press, 1983.

———. *The Orientalizing Revolution: Near Eastern Influence on Greek Culture in the Early Archaic Age.* Translated by M. E. Pinder and W. Burkert. Revealing Antiquity 5. Cambridge: Harvard Univ. Press, 1992.

Coleman, John E., and Clark A. Walz, editors. *Greeks and Barbarians: Essays on the Interactions between Greeks and Non-Greeks in Antiquity and the Consequences for Eurocentrism.* Occasional Papers of the Department of Near Eastern Studies and the Program of Jewish Studies, Cornell University 4. Bethesda, Md.: CDL, 1997.

Cook, J. M. *The Persian Empire.* New York: Schocken, 1983.

Cornell, T. J. *The Beginnings of Rome: Italy and Rome from the Bronze Age to the Punic Wars (c. 1000–264 BC)*. London: Routledge, 1995.

Drews, Robert. *The End of the Bronze Age: Changes in Warfare and the Catastrophe ca. 1200 B.C.* Princeton: Princeton Univ. Press, 1988.

Dunbabin, T. J. *The Greeks and Their Eastern Neighbors: Studies in the Relations between Greece and the Countries of the Near East in the 8th and 7th Centuries B.C.* Journal of Hellenic Studies Supplementary Papers 8. London: Society for the Promotion of Hellenic Studies, 1957. Reprinted 1979.

Edwards, Ruth B. *Kadmos, the Phoenician: A Study in Greek Legends and the Mycenaean Age.* Amsterdam: Hakkert, 1979.

Feldman, Louis H. "Homer and the Near East: The Rise of the Greek Genius." *Biblical Archaeologist* 59 (1996) 13–21.

Gordon, Cyrus H. *The Common Background of Greek and Hebrew Civilizations.* New York: Norton, 1965.

———. "Homer and Bible: The Origin and Character of the East Mediterranean Literature." *HUCA* 26 (1955) 43–108. Reprinted as a pamphlet, 1967.

Gordon, Cyrus H., and Gary A. Rendsburg. *The Bible and the Ancient Near East.* 4th ed. New York: Norton, 1997.

Hanson, K. C. "When the King Crosses the Line: Royal Deviance and Restitution in Levantine Ideologies." *Biblical Theology Bulletin* 26 (1996) 11–25.

Huebeck, Alfred, et al. *A Commentary on Homer's Odyssey.* 3 vols. Oxford: Clarendon, 1988–92.

Jeffrey, Arthur. *The Foreign Vocabulary of the Quran.* Baroda: Oriental Institute, 1938.

Just, Roger. *Women in Athenian Law and Life.* London: Routledge, 1989.

Kirk, G. S., editor. *The Iliad: A Commentary.* 6 vols. Cambridge: Cambridge Univ. Press, 1985–93.

Lambrou-Philippson, C. *Hellenorientalia: The Near Eastern Presence in the Bronze Age Aegean, ca. 3000–1100 B.C.* Göteborg: Aström, 1990.

Levin, Saul. *The Indo-European and Semitic Languages: An Exploration of Structural Similarities related to Accent, Chiefly in Greek, Sanskrit, and Hebrew.* Albany: State Univ. of New York Press, 1971.

———. *Semitic and Indo-European: The Principal Etymologies, with Observations on Afro-Asiatic.* Amsterdam Studies in the Theory and History of Linguistic Science 4/129. Amsterdam: Benjamins, 1995.

Lieberman, Saul. *Greek in Jewish Palestine: Hellenism in Jewish Palestine,* with a new introduction by Dov Zlotnick. New York: Jewish Theological Seminary of America, 1994.

Malina, Bruce J. "Mediterranean Sacrifice: Dimensions of Domestic and Political Religion." *Biblical Theology Bulletin* 26 (1996) 26–44.

Marblestone, Howard. "A 'Mediterranean Synthesis': Professor Cyrus H. Gordon's Contributions to the Classics." *Biblical Archaeologist* 59 (1996) 22–30.

Margalith, Othniel. *The Sea Peoples in the Bible.* Translated by O. Margalith and S. Margalith. Wiesbaden: Harrassowitz, 1994.

Millar, Fergus. *The Roman Near East 31 B.C.–A.D. 337.* Cambridge: Harvard Univ. Press, 1993.

Miller, J. Innes. *The Spice Trade of the Roman Empire, 29 B.C. to A.D. 641.* Oxford, Clarendon, 1969.

Mondi, Robert. "Greek Mythic Thought in the Light of the Near East." In *Approaches to Greek Myth*, edited by Lowell Edmunds, 142–98. Baltimore: Johns Hopkins Univ. Press, 1990.

Morris, Ian, and Barry B. Powell, editors. *A New Companion to Homer.* Mnemonsyne Supplements 163. Leiden: Brill, 1997.

Muhly, James D. "Homer and the Phoenicians: The Relations between Greece and the Near East in the Late Bronze and Early Iron Ages." *Berytus* 19 (1970) 19–64.

Penglase, Charles. *Greek Myths and Mesopotamia: Parallels and Influence in the Homeric Hymns and Hesiod.* London: Routledge, 1994.

Powell, Barry B. *Homer and the Origin of the Greek Alphabet.* Cambridge: Cambridge Univ. Press, 1991.

Pritchard, James B., editor. *The Ancient Near East in Pictures relating to the Old Testament.* 2d ed. Princeton: Princeton Univ. Press, 1969.

———. *Ancient Near Eastern Texts relating to the Old Testament.* 3d ed. Princeton: Princeton Univ. Press, 1969.

Schürer, Emil, Geza Vermes, Fergus Millar, and Matthew Black. *The History of the Jewish People in the Age of Jesus Christ (175 B.C.–A.D. 135).* 3 vols. in 4. Edinburgh: T. & T. Clark, 1973–87.

Stern, Menahem. *Greek and Latin Authors on Jews and Judaism.* 3 vols. Jerusalem: Israel Academy of Sciences and Humanities, 1974–84.

Toorn, Karel van der, et al., editors. *Dictionary of Deities and Demons in the Bible.* 2d ed. Leiden: Brill, 1999.

Walcot, Peter. "The Comparative Study of Ugaritic and Greek Literature." *Ugarit-Forschungen* 1 (1969) 111–18.

———. *Hesiod and the Near East.* Cardiff: Univ. of Wales Press, 1966.

Weinfeld, Moshe. "Covenant Terminology in the Ancient Near East and Its Influence on the West." *Journal of the American Oriental Society* 93 (1973) 190–99.

———. "The Loyalty Oath in the Ancient Near East." *Ugarit-Forschungen* 8 (1976) 379–414.

———. *The Promise of the Land: The Inheritance of the Land of Canaan by the Israelites.* Berkeley: Univ. of California Press, 1993.

———. *Social Justice in Ancient Israel and in the Ancient Near East.* Minneapolis: Fortress Press, 1995.

West, M. L. *The East Face of Helicon: West Asiatic Elements in Greek Poetry and Myth.* Oxford: Oxford Univ. Press, 1997.

———, ed. *Hesiod: Theogony.* Oxford: Clarendon, 1966.

———, ed. *Hesiod: Works and Days.* Oxford: Clarendon, 1978.

Williams, Margaret. *The Jews among the Greeks and Romans: A Diasporan Sourcebook.* Baltimore: Johns Hopkins Univ. Press, 1998.

Index